Essentials for
Government Contract
Negotiators

Essentials for
Government Contract
Negotiators

LeGette McIntyre

ſſſ
MANAGEMENTCONCEPTS

MANAGEMENTCONCEPTS
8230 Leesburg Pike, Suite 800
Vienna, Virginia 22182
Phone: (703) 790-9595
Fax: (703) 790-1371
www.managementconcepts.com

Printed in the United States of America

Library of Congress Cataloging-in-Publication Data

McIntyre, LeGette, 1959–
  Essentials for government contract negotiators / LeGette McIntyre.
    p. cm.
  Includes index.
  ISBN 1-56726-175-2
    1. Public contracts—United States. 2. Negotiation—United States.
  3. Government purchasing—United States. I. Title.

HD3861.U6M39 2006
352.5'3—dc22

                                     2006046194

About the Author

LeGette ("LeGs") McIntyre is President of McIntyre, Inc., a Florida-based corporation specializing in all areas of federal acquisition support and training. He has 20 years' experience as an Air Force leader and over 25 years' experience in the federal acquisition process. He has extensive experience in contract negotiations, as well as in applying acquisition principles, business process analysis, strategic planning, corporate staffing and organizational analysis capture, and market research techniques to the OMB Circular A-76 competitive sourcing process. He is known as one of the premiere acquisition instructors throughout the government and is a nationally recognized speaker on A-76. He has a BS in Business Administration from The Citadel and an MBA from the University of Missouri. He currently resides in Niceville, Florida, where he pursues his passion for sailing.

LeGs and his associates offer one-, two-, and three-day seminars based on the negotiation principles discussed in this book. For information, or to register, send an e-mail to lmcintyre@mcintyreconsulting.com or visit www.mcintyreconsulting.com.

This book is dedicated to my beautiful wife, Jill. After many years of experience I've realized, to my chagrin, she's always been a much better negotiator than I'll ever be. Thanks, Jill, for being ever-lovingly patient while I slogged through. Finally, I give thanks to Almighty God, without whom, of course, none of this would have ever been possible.

Table of Contents

Preface

I started writing this book out of frustration. Many of the courses I taught as an acquisition instructor contained blocks of instruction on "discussions" and "negotiations," with the text of these courses explaining the *process* of conducting these topics extremely well. Over time, however, I had more and more students approach me with questions. Although they were many and varied, they all boiled down to one basic question: Now that I know the *process* of negotiations, how do I actually *do* it? When I found that "Read the course material" was not an answer that scratched the itch, I realized I had to go much deeper.

Now, I have negotiated for the government for years. I've used tricks and been the victim of tricks. I've developed and used all sorts of strategies and tactics to all degrees of success and failure. I've seen the good, the bad, the ugly, and the downright illegal. I've had my victories, taken my licks, and learned my lessons. I've even negotiated for the "other side" as a contractor—in a special assignment while I was in the Air Force, as a private business owner, and later as the president of a corporation. I had done the *do* part of negotiations many times.

So, how should I answer their questions? I started thinking back on how I was trained to negotiate, way back when I first started, and my mind drew an absolute blank. I realized it wasn't because I was getting old and losing my memory; it was because I too was never trained by the government on *how* to negotiate. I was taught the process, but precious little else. Especially lacking was training on how to plan, prepare, and use strategies and tactics, and how to counter them if they are used against you. I had to learn this important stuff by actually conducting negotiations, and I'm sure the government paid dearly for some of my lessons.

I now knew that things hadn't changed much, and there was still a need to know this stuff. I also realized that most government negotiation training concentrated solely on the contract award process, but that wasn't the only time most of these folks would be negotiating. This was my "Ah-ha!" moment. I realized that there's a training gap that needs to be filled, so I began preparing a seminar on *how* to negotiate. Two or three days' worth should do it, I thought.

As I started my research for the seminar, I discovered that much material exists in the federal government that addresses the overall government negotiation *process*. Published books and training courses developed by both the government and private industry abound, with step-by-step instructions leading the individual through the steps of the negotiation process itself. However, very few (if any) of these sources actually teach the reader or student *how* to negotiate—the strategies and tactics negotiators need to know to hold their own in an actual sit-down negotiation session with a skilled counterpart. There is no formal method to teach negotiators the *art* of negotiation—and it is an art.

Think about it. The government routinely sends untrained GS 9s, 11s, 12s, and enlisted and junior officers to complicated, high-dollar negotiations with private industry pros who have *years* of experience and training both in government and industry negotiations. Who do you think has the best chance at coming out with the better deal?

I'm a taxpayer too. I want the government contracting officers and contract negotiators representing me as a taxpayer to have the absolute best training in negotiation skills available. I want them to be able to hold their ground. The good news is that you can greatly improve your practice of this art called negotiation by acquiring and practicing the right skills.

The even better news is that the information you need is already out there. Even a quick look at any major bookstore or in-flight magazine will reveal many great books and seminars that address negotiation preparation, strategies, and tactics essential for business-to-business or personal situations. Unfortunately, these products fail to address the many rules, regulations, and restrictions that make negotiating for the government truly unique and challenging. This book is intended to fill the gap. It brings both halves together to show the reader how to apply business-savvy negotiation skills in a government-unique environment.

WHO IS THIS BOOK FOR?

First, this book will benefit anyone who conducts discussions or negotiations with the private sector as a government negotiator across all federal agencies, including contracting officers, contract specialists, contract administrators, price analysts, cost analysts, legal staff, small business specialists, program personnel, program managers, project managers, contracting officer representatives, and quality assurance specialists. In fact, anyone who comes in contact with a contractor in an official capacity has the possibility of getting thrown into a negotiation situation, and should know how to deal with it.

Second, most state and local governments rely on contractors just as the federal government does. They also have a need to negotiate, and to produce fair and reasonable contracts that benefit their citizenry. This book will help those folks at the state and local levels who require negotiating skills to succeed in their jobs.

Third, this book can benefit individuals employed by contractors who negotiate. Whether you're negotiating with the federal government, with subcontractors, or with other commercial firms or suppliers, the principles, tactics, and strategies in this book will help you reach better deals that are more favorable to your firm. This may improve your bottom line. If you're a contractor, you may also want to read this book simply to know what the other side is being taught!

Finally, this book will benefit any individual who wants to apply sound negotiation strategies and tactics in their personal life. Knowing the strategies and tactics in this book will help you the next time you buy a car, a house, or find a lamp you like at a flea market. The basic concepts are, for the most part, universal.

HOW WILL THIS BOOK HELP YOU?

This book will make you a better negotiator. It is designed to leave you with a better understanding of the negotiation process, how to plan for it, how to develop strategy and tactics, how to anticipate and counter the other side's strategy and tactics, and how to conclude and document the negotiation successfully.

You'll learn some basics that pertain specifically to federal government negotiations. You'll learn the answers to questions like: Where does the authority to negotiate on behalf of the government come from? You'll learn the goals you should strive for—and are expected to adhere to—as a federal government negotiator. Do you think they differ from private industry's goals? You bet! You'll learn what private industry considers *their* goals for the negotiation process. Only when you can see both sides can you begin to compare and contrast these goals, and find that you have unique responsibilities and restrictions that may not apply to your industry counterparts.

Now some of you may think something like, "Well, I never negotiate contracts. I only administer them, analyze them, benefit from them" and so on. Or, "I'm not the contracting officer; I'm the customer, so I'll never need to know how to negotiate." Please understand, *anyone* in the government who comes in contact with a contractor in any way may actually find themselves in a negotiation situation—and they're usually unprepared for it. Even if you're administering an already awarded contract, you'll have to be prepared to negotiate, and these negotiation will be the toughest kind: sole source!

This book will expose you to some "nifty" negotiation strategies and tactics. However, nothing—not all the tricks and books in the world (this book included)—can replace the importance of properly preparing for negotiations. So we'll talk about it. I'll give you some hints on conducting market research (aka "intel") that will give you important insights into not only the company you're dealing with, but the person who will be sitting across the table from you.

This book gives an in-depth look at how to prepare a truly effective negotiation plan. If you get *this* part right, the actual negotiation event becomes easy: You simply execute your plan!

You'll understand how to choose and prepare your negotiation strategy—your overall course for the negotiation—and how to link this strategy to your plan. You'll be introduced, in great depth, to quite a few of the hundreds of tactics used in negotiations. These are often referred to as the "tricks of the trade" that a good negotiator can use to keep the upper hand.

Government negotiators will not be able to use all the tactics covered in the book. Some tactics are rather unscrupulous, and the government negotiator must be "fair and reasonable" to *both* sides. But the "other side" may not be bound by this mantra! This book covers some of these less than ethical tactics—so the government negotiator can recognize when they're being used—and I explain how to counter them.

You'll next learn how to conduct the actual negotiation event properly to achieve a true best-value result, using your planned strategies and tactics, bounded by your unique role as a government negotiator. You'll be able to answer questions such as: How do I set up for the negotiation event? How do I start the negotiation? How do I control the negotiation? How do I handle impasses? How do I conclude the negotiation? Remember, this part should be relatively simple, if you have planned well. However, there's always a chance the other side can spring something totally unexpected on you—no matter how well you have planned and anticipated. How do you handle that? We'll talk about it.

Finally, we'll discuss how you wrap up the negotiation session, making sure everyone has the same understanding of what was agreed to. It's critical to ensure that whatever you have agreed to is "nailed down" and truly represents a meeting of the minds, or you're in for trouble. Of course, nothing's finished (especially in the government) until the paperwork is done. We'll conclude with what you need to know to document the negotiation properly, so you will have not just an agreement, but an unambiguous agreement that can be implemented and interpreted fairly.

Once you understand the negotiation process better, you can practice it as an art. Better negotiation skills mean better negotiation outcomes. Better outcomes not only help your customer, the government, and the taxpayer, but also directly reflect on your personal performance record, which can lead to promotion, career enhancement, and higher self-esteem.

Becoming an artistic negotiator is a journey, not a destination. Time, training, and experience will move you along that road. I strongly encourage you to continue your professional education in this important field. Sign up for negotiation seminars. Read every negotiation book you can. Constantly be on the lookout for opportunities to practice your skills. I also strongly encourage you to seek out and latch on to someone in your organization who is experienced in negotiating and is willing to share their time and skills with you. Formal education and training, coupled with hands-on experience guided by a mentor, will be your recipe for success. Now buckle your seat belts and let's get started!

LeGette "LeGs" McIntyre
Niceville, Florida

Acknowledgments

I didn't know how hard it would be to write a business-oriented book until I sat down and actually started writing a business-oriented book. Some things I guess you just have to learn by experience. I do know that if the right people hadn't done the right things and created the right environment along the way, I'd either still be writing (probably somewhere in Chapter 2) or I would have abandoned the project altogether and moved along to more challenging things—like watching TV. I was blessed to have the perfect combination of smart, generous, and giving people placed in my path to make this book possible.

Thank goodness for good friends like John and M.J. Raymer. You realized how hard it was for me to concentrate on writing a book at home with all the day-to-day distractions and an active two-year-old running amok, and offered to let me use your beautiful, historic home in Valparaiso, Florida. While you were away during the day at work, your home became my perfect writing retreat. Pages started flying, not crawling. The incredible view of Choctawhatchee Bay from your lanai became my daily motivation. Thanks, John and M.J. Everyone should be blessed with friends like you.

Thanks to my long-time friend Stephanie Granger. Although you didn't have to, you took time from setting your own business world on fire not only to discuss ideas with me and give me encouragement, but to provide a much-needed technical review of my manuscript. You made sure the whole thing made sense. Thanks, Steph. You're wonderful.

Thanks to my teaching colleagues and friends at Management Concepts. I don't think you can find a more intelligent collection of human beings on the planet. Your willingness to give me advice and wisdom kept me going. Thanks especially to Tom DeAngelis and Bill Hamm—we make quite a team!

Thanks to the entire staff of the Wyndham City Center Hotel in Washington, DC. My teaching schedule made this my home-away-from-home for many weeks, and a good part of this book was written in various rooms at the Wyndham. You knew me by name, knew I was writing a book, and went way above what anyone could have possibly expected in extending me every courtesy. Thanks for the special care—you're all awesome!

Thanks to the publishing team at Management Concepts, especially to Myra Strauss and Jack Knowles. Your patience with a wet-behind-the-ears author was long suffering. You said the book would be harder to write and take longer than I expected. I confidently said, "Nah." Guess who was right? Thanks for your guidance and toleration.

Thanks to the authors of all the negotiating books I have read in the past. The collective skills I have picked up throughout the years from reading your works can't help but be reflected in this book. Although I have never met you, special thanks to Roger Fisher and William Ury, Ron Shapiro and Mark Jankowski, Roger Dawson, and Herb Cohen. All readers of this book would be crazy not to have copies of your works, which I have cited in Appendix A, Recommended Reading. I honor your wisdom and success.

Thanks to my students—all of you. You have allowed me to use the podium as a crucible to test ideas and have given me crucial feedback about every aspect of negotiation. You *had* to be there; I was *privileged* to be there. Thanks.

Finally, thanks to my beautiful wife, Jill. Baby, I couldn't have done this without your constant love, praise, patience, and support. You are the absolute epitome of the perfect Southern lady, and you've made me the luckiest man alive. *Shmily!*

Part One

Getting Started

Chapter 1

Overview of Federal Government Negotiations

I t's long been the policy of the federal government to satisfy its requirements for supplies and services as much as possible from the commercial marketplace. Accordingly, the government spends more than $200 billion each and every year buying the stuff it needs from contractors. Whole industries have sprung up to service the federal government as a customer. It's also federal government policy to buy these supplies and services at fair and reasonable prices, so the government relies on smart folks to negotiate business-savvy deals with private industry. Although almost everyone who comes in contact with a government contractor may find themselves in a negotiation situation, highly trained contracting officers (COs) and contract negotiators bear the brunt of this effort. That's what this book will focus on—you as the professional government negotiator.

In your position as a government negotiator, you not only represent your particular agency and office, but you represent the entire federal government and every American taxpayer. That's an awesome responsibility. So what exactly gives you this authority?

Although the government's authority to enter into contracts is loosely derived from the Constitution, your authority to negotiate on behalf of the American people ultimately comes from the U.S. Congress and the President of the United States. Congress, of course, controls the purse strings of our government and is responsible for passing laws directing how the federal government spends its money. These laws, along with precedents derived from court decisions, executive orders, and so forth, have been summed up and put into one regulation: the Federal Acquisition Regulation (FAR). You are bound *by law* to follow this regulation when you negotiate. The President is responsible for appointing the heads of each federal agency, and the FAR gives agency heads the responsibility and unlimited authority to enter into contractual relationships to support their agencies.

But think about this. The agency head for the Department of Defense is the Secretary of Defense, for example. Now, do you *really* think the Secretary of Defense has the time to negotiate personally every supply and service the Department of Defense needs on a daily basis? Of course not! This person, as soon as they are appointed by the President, immediately delegates this authority in writing down to the agency senior procurement executive. This person, in turn, further delegates down the chain in writing to the heads of the major departments in the agency. Those folks do the same, and on and on, until this authority to contract is pushed down all the way to the CO.

Now, the COs may be, in turn, supported by other team members like contract specialists and price analysts (who may have authority to negotiate), but only a CO, acting in the scope of his or her authority, can obligate—or bind—the government. The limits of authority are spelled out in writing right on the CO's warrant. The warrant is a piece of paper that must be permanently displayed.

So, that's how you, the CO, obtain the authority to negotiate and bind the government as a result of those negotiations. It's an unbroken, written chain that starts with the President. But, remember those laws? Remember the FAR? The FAR spells out *how* you are to go about your business: what you *must* do, what you *can* do, and what you *can't* do. The FAR also lays out in general terms what you must strive for in every negotiation. First and foremost, you must uphold the goals of the federal acquisition system and your responsibilities as a CO, so let's take a look at them.

GOALS OF THE GOVERNMENT NEGOTIATOR

Your first goal, quite simply, is to get your customers what they need. Negotiation isn't an end in itself. Always remember you are negotiating to satisfy your customer's needs in terms of cost, timeliness, and quality. Remember also that your *ultimate* customer is the American taxpayer. Unlike your industry counterparts, which we'll discuss later, you must also comply with and make sure that all requirements of law, executive orders, regulations, and all other applicable procedures (like clearances and approvals) are upheld. Folks, that's a tall order! For instance, there are laws supporting federal socioeconomic programs that you *must* abide by, even at the sacrifice (sometimes) of cost and timeliness.

Do you think the government expects its negotiators—its representatives—to uphold the highest ethical standards? You bet. And there are laws about that too. This is one of the disadvantages you have as a federal negotiator. Unlike your industry counterparts, you are sometimes bound to sacrifice the best deal you could negotiate, from a pure price standpoint, to support the "law of the land." The FAR also precludes you from taking advantage of a contractor who has made a mistake or grossly underpriced his offer. You can't be silent, let the mistake become binding, and then do "high fives" about how you "killed the contractor in negotiations." You are bound to be fair and reasonable to *both* sides.

The government expects its negotiators to treat contractors—your counterparts in negotiation—fairly, impartially, and equitably. Do you really think this is a prime goal when private companies negotiate with each other? But, you are held to this. And, if you think about the big picture, it makes sense. To survive as a government, we need a robust private sector on which to draw for things we need. We decrease this by being unfair, partial, and inequitable when we deal with industry. We are not in the business of putting businesses out of business!

In addition, if you treat a contractor unfairly, what are the chances of that contractor ever wanting to do business with the federal government again? Word of your unfair treatment could also spread, and soon whole sectors of contractors may pull out of doing federal business. What would that do to competition? How would that satisfy your customer? So treat your contractors fairly. It's the right thing to do—and it's the law.

Hand in hand with the concept of fairness is your requirement to negotiate in good faith. Negotiating in good faith means that you must have an honest desire to reach agreement on differences through compromise and that you are not trying to take unfair advantage of the other party. Leading a contractor on in negotiations by implying you have funds available to consummate the deal, when in fact you know you *don't*, is an example of negotiating in bad faith. In this case, at the *very* least, you have caused the contractor to expend time, energy, effort, and money to no good purpose, which is not fair to the contractor. Your ultimate goal, the result of your negotiation, should be an agreement that is fair and reasonable to *both* parties.

Now, let's contrast your goals with the goals of your counterparts in industry.

GOALS OF THE PRIVATE SECTOR NEGOTIATOR

So what do your counterparts, industry negotiators, want to get out of negotiations? Are they bound to reach an agreement that is fair and reasonable to both parties? Do you think they are under the same requirements to comply with all the laws and regulations to which you are bound? Absolutely not! Their *primary* goal, if they are a corporation, is to maximize shareholder wealth. (If they are a sole proprietorship, their goal is to maximize the owner's wealth.) They usually have certain profit objectives (or goals) given to them by management to attain for each negotiation. These goals usually, in turn, link back to the company's overall profit objectives. Sometimes these objectives are a certain dollar amount for profit; sometimes they are a percentage. As a representative of the government, you will probably *not* know these objectives.

Sometimes these negotiators may have other company goals they have been told to strive for that, on the surface, don't seem directly tied to profit objectives. An example is *strategic placement*. In other words, by winning this particular contract, the company will strategically place itself ahead of its competition for capturing future business along certain lines. They may also want the *prestige* and *exposure* that being a prime contractor on an important government contract can bring. This usually positively affects their commercial sales, and ultimately their profit. Winning a large government contract can also increase their standing among companies that are in the business of rating other companies, like Moody's or Standard and Poor's. Higher ratings, in turn, give them access to more ways to capitalize. More creditors are willing to lend them money, allow them to float bonds, underwrite stock issues, and give them breaks on interest rates.

Companies may also have a goal to capture a contract to keep up the general *volume* of their business. Contractors have overhead, right? They must continue to pay this overhead regardless of whether they have any business in-house at any given time. They need a certain level of business income to pay these overhead costs, to ride out the lean times, and possibly to prevent costly "idle" situations. I've known contractors to go into barely break-even contracts just to have enough business volume to keep paying everyone.

But don't be fooled! All these "other company goals" have an effect on the bottom line: They all will relate in some way back to the first two prime goals of every business: to maximize wealth and to meet profit goals. Don't let yourself be misled by a company negotiator that says, for example, "At the prices we're proposing, we're really losing our shirts on this deal, but we don't mind because _____." They can provide any number of other company goals to fill in the blank, and they'll make it sound convincing. But rest assured, every company is in business to make a *profit. You* may have to be a fair and reasonable negotiator to both sides, *but they don't.* I'm sure company negotiators would be more than happy with what they considered a win–win result, but they are usually just as satisfied with a win–lose result, as long as they are on the win side of the equation. Only by understanding this can you properly prepare for negotiations.

Chapter 2

Negotiation
Opportunities—
More Than You Think!

C ommonly, the average person on the street (and many government folks, too) sees government negotiations as relating to the source selection process—the way we award a
contract in competitive situations. This is a well-defined and well-
trained process with specific steps: development of evaluation factors, exchanges with offerors, request for proposal (RFP) preparation, proposal analysis, price analysis, cost analysis, competitive
range determination, and so forth. There are already many good
books, training courses, seminars, and other forms of guidance that
cover this material well. Rather, this book concentrates on how to
be successful in negotiations. We'll concentrate on learning negotiation skills that can be valuable to you not just in source selection,
not just in discussions, but in *any* negotiation situation.

THE IMPACT OF THE FEDERAL ACQUISITION
STREAMLINING ACT

The need for professional negotiation skills has increased in recent
years. When Congress passed the Federal Acquisition Streamlin-
ing Act (FASA) in 1994, it represented a sea change in the way the
government conducts its contracting business. Before then, concepts such as *best value* and *performance based* were rarely heard of,
much less used. Everything was, basically, a price shootout.

The government would dictate the requirements, step by step, to
the contractor and they would simply price the solution we dictated to them, with the best price winning. Negotiations were

relatively simple then. Because we dictated the technical approach to the competing contractors, in true read-a-step, do-a-step, get-a-banana fashion, all the proposed technical solutions looked the same—no innovative approaches were allowed. Price was pretty much the only thing left to negotiate. COs back then were more or less simply procurement clerks or technicians who followed a rigid, predictable process that churned out a contract award.

FASA changed all that. Things are a lot less formal and a lot less process driven now. What's important today is not how well you can follow some rigid procedure, but how well you can make a commonsense good business deal. And, as you'll see, moving from "lowest price wins" to "best value" and from "dictated specifications" to "performance based" has made negotiation skills more important than ever.

Best Value

Instead of awarding contracts based on the contractor who could give the best price while meeting the minimum requirements, the FAR now dictates that every contract award must be based on best value. Best value is simply picking the contractor based on the overall benefit—the best value—to the government, price *and other factors* considered.

Although it's true that sometimes price alone is still the best determinant of best value, now we can look at other things, such as past performance, and factor them into the award decision. We can look at the contractor's technical approach to solving the problem and many other nonprice factors, such as résumés of key personnel, to help pick the "right" contractor. We simply have to state what the evaluation factors are going to be when we go out with our solicitation. When the proposals come in, we can now *trade off* technical superiority against price. In other words, we can now award to other than the low-priced contractor, if the technical superiority of their solution merits it, as long as we can justify spending the extra bucks to get the extra bang.

This is great news for your customers, but it complicates your job as a CO and a negotiator. No longer is price the only thing to be negotiated. Rarely will the contractor's idea of best value—the mix of price and technical factors they submit with their proposal—be *your* idea of best value. The mix often has to be negotiated, and this can get complicated. You now are not only negotiating price, but other things such as warranty terms, level of effort, delivery dates, level of government involvement, validity and chance of success of various technical approaches, and so forth. And you have to balance all these factors ultimately against price. How can you ensure best value if you're not trained in how to negotiate to it?

Performance-based

Instead of dictating the specifications (the process to solve the problem) to contractors, we now simply state what we need in terms of outputs and invite *them* to come up with the process to solve the problem. This is performance-based contracting. As the government moved away from writing its own specifications and moved toward having the contractors propose the solutions, it unleashed the incredible innovative power of the private sector. Industry has come up with creative solutions to our problems that we never could have dreamed of on our own. After all, they're usually the experts, not us!

Again, that's great for your customers and the taxpayers, but it greatly increases the difficulty you'll face in proposal analysis and, ultimately, in negotiations. When the proposals come in, you can no longer do an apples-to-apples comparison, because all the proposed technical solutions can be vastly different, and they come with different price tags.

One company, for instance, may propose to satisfy our needs by relying heavily on manual labor, whereas another contractor's proposal may rely on automation and technology. Both proposals can meet our needs; they just have different ways of getting to the end result. Because each proposal can be substantially different, you now have to have separate negotiation plans for each contractor, tailored to the strengths and weaknesses unique to their proposal. And when you negotiate with these contractors, you have to talk about the merits of their particular technical approach in addition to negotiating price.

To make matters worse, you start off with an immediate negotiation disadvantage. *They* are the experts in their particular technical approach, not you. After all, they wrote it; you just reviewed it. They are in a superior knowledge position about the process because *they* came up with the process. And the process will drive the price. Only by possessing good negotiation skills can you overcome this inherent disadvantage and ensure you end up with a fair and reasonable deal.

NONCOMPETITIVE NEGOTIATIONS

As you know, you can have negotiations for *noncompetitive* contract awards too. Sole-source negotiations can be tough! In these cases, you don't have the power of competition to give you an advantage. This is precisely where, in my opinion, most of the standard government training is found lacking.

Here's the problem: The government has a clear preference for competitive contract awards. Because of this, the vast majority of *contracts* awarded by the government go through the competitive process. The power of competition tends to self-regulate the contractors, virtually ensuring their proposals will be fair and reasonable. If not, they get beat by the competition. Because of this heavy reliance on competition alone to determine prices to be fair and reasonable, the government has slowly gotten out of the business of teaching its folks *how* to negotiate. The thought process was, "There's no need to. Competition will take care of it." Unfortunately, not all your negotiations for contract award will be competitive, and very few of your negotiations will even be for contract award at all.

As a matter of fact, your most difficult negotiations will come with contractors *after* contract award. Not including those times when you have to negotiate a sole-source contract, here are some examples of other times you'll be negotiating sole source after contract award:

- Negotiating contract modifications, also called *supplemental agreements*

- Resolving contract disputes

- Negotiating contract claims

- Adding in-scope work to the contract or deleting work

- Negotiating government-furnished property (GFP) issues

- Negotiating billing rates or settling indirect rates

- Negotiating adjustments for award or incentive provisions

- Negotiating a contractor's proposed subcontracting plan

- Negotiating terminations for default and convenience (or for cause)

- Negotiating intellectual property rights.

I'm sure you can think of others. Folks, there are many other times during contract performance when a clause or simple common sense requires either you or the contractor *do* something if such-and-such happens. Most of these events will result in *equitable adjustments* to the contract, and *all* of these have to be negotiated. And because you've already locked in a winning contractor, these will all be sole-source negotiations. Luckily, the skill sets you need to be successful in these negotiation situations are basically the same, as is the process. This book shows you these basic skills and that process.

The basic steps are, in a nutshell:

1. Prepare for negotiations.

2. Conduct negotiations.

3. Conclude and document what you have done.

Sounds simple, doesn't it? However, these three simple steps have a lot of important substeps embedded in each, and we will cover them in the following chapters. In addition, we'll give you some useful tools you can put to work immediately to make yourself a better negotiator—both for the government and in your private life.

The next part of this book talks about what I consider to be *the most important step of all*—preparing for negotiations.

Part Two

Preparing for Negotiation

Chapter 3

Assembling Your Negotiation Team

There are eight important steps I'm convinced you need to master to prepare for a negotiation. We'll cover all these steps in detail. Being properly prepared when you walk into a negotiation is, by far, the best negotiation strategy you can have. Here are the steps for preparing to negotiate:

1. Assemble the team.

2. Gather data.

3. Identify your priorities.

4. Establish your prenegotiation objectives.

5. Research the other party.

6. Develop your negotiation plan.

7. Rehearse your plan.

8. Develop your negotiation agenda.

If you follow these steps, and give careful consideration to what you are doing in each step, your negotiations should go well. By the way, do you think a book like this on government negotiations has some bleedover into your everyday life? You bet! As you go through these steps, think about how properly executing them can help you cut a better deal next time you buy a car, or a washing machine, or a house.

First of all, please understand, properly preparing for a negotiation takes time. Each of these eight steps requires an investment in time, but the payoff is well worth it. Just remember that when you build your acquisition time lines, give yourself enough time to prepare properly.

I know this looks like a *lot* of work—and it is—but thankfully you don't have to do it alone. In fact, can you see how hard it would be to conduct the negotiation, be the technical guru, take notes, observe the other side for reactions, double-check contractor facts and figures, and think up tactical maneuvers singlehandedly all at the same time? It would be impossible! Even if you are the sole negotiator, you'll probably work extensively with your support team to help you prepare before you sit down at the negotiation table. In almost all negotiation situations, you'll be able to draw from the power of a team, both before and during negotiations. And you, the CO, are responsible for putting the team together—sizing it, choosing the team members, and training it. So, who are your potential team players and how do you pull this team together?

CHARACTERISTICS OF A NEGOTIATION TEAM

A negotiation team is truly a unique creation. First of all, it's usually created for a one-time event. It's not normally an ongoing enterprise. Once you finish the particular negotiation for which it was created, it goes away. Although there may be some bleedover of personnel, for the most part you'll have a different team for each negotiation, depending on what customer you are supporting and the technical knowledge required for whatever you are buying. The good news is this allows you to tailor team composition and team size to fit your situation. The overall scope of negotiations, expertise required, complexity, dollar value, visibility, and so forth, are some of the factors you should consider when you're creating the team. The bad news is that this constant shifting of team membership complicates your team training and coordination efforts.

Second, your team will not be a naturally cohesive unit. It will consist of people who do vastly different jobs, report to different bosses, and have dissimilar and sometimes opposing goals and agendas. Team members, especially your technical specialists, realize they will only be together as a team for a short time and then go back to their "normal" jobs. The very reason they were selected to be team members—their unique abilities, training, and skills —tends to work against team cohesiveness. This makes the negotiation team a very difficult team to lead. And you, as the CO, are the leader! Your challenge is to unite all this discord into a unified front that gets the job done, while not squashing the very uniqueness that makes this kind of team so effective. This task, in itself, may require good negotiating skills on your part. It's true that sometimes the hardest negotiations you'll ever be in are with members of your own team.

Finally, and on the good side, this fluid negotiation team structure allows you to fit the right people with the right expertise into the right position to address the peculiarities of the negotiation situation. This ability to tailor the team composition to fit the situation greatly increases your ability to achieve a best-value result that satisfies your customer in an effective and efficient manner. It also means, thank goodness, that you don't have to be the expert in everything. You won't have to spend nights boning up on technical jargon and processes. You won't have to become a property expert overnight. You won't have to research the legal ramifications of doing this or not doing that. You have smart folks on your team who specialize in these areas, which leaves you free to concentrate on the things you are trained to do best—planning for a professional negotiation that achieves an optimum business outcome that's best for everyone.

You have a number of team players to choose from, representing all kinds of different expertise. And remember, you always have the option of adding team members (in other words, bringing in particular experts) when and where the situation justifies it. Let's now look at some of the traditional members you'll pick to be on your negotiation team.

TEAM MEMBERS

A host of team members make up the negotiation team. Each plays an important role leading to a successful outcome for the government team.

The Team Leader

Every team needs a team leader, a quarterback, and the CO usually fills that role. As the CO, you need to be in complete charge of your team in preparing for the negotiation—and *everyone* needs to know it. If you don't establish firm control of your team from the outset, things can quickly get out of hand, confusion will reign, and mistakes will be made. You, the CO, are responsible for conducting the negotiations, and it's a true leadership role.

As a CO, hopefully you have been well trained to use sound business judgment to resolve problems in the taxpayer's best interests, and *you* are the one (usually the only one) trained in the intricacies of federal government procurement rules, regulations, and policies. *You're* the expert! No, you may not be the most technically competent when it comes to the actual *substance* of what you are negotiating, but you need to be an expert at pulling together the appropriate functional experts and leading them through a business process—and a negotiation is definitely a business process.

Contract Specialists

If you're lucky, you may also have a contract specialist to assist you in preparing for and conducting negotiations. These are folks from the contracting office who are fully trained in contracting practices and procedures, but they aren't warranted as official COs. In my opinion, contract specialists are the unsung heroes of the acquisition world. They do most of the grunt work, make their share of important contracting decisions, and then pass all their work to the

CO for approval. Unfortunately, the CO is usually the one who gets all the glory, and the contract specialist is simply rewarded with more work.

When I was a government CO, I was blessed to supervise some of the best contract specialists in the world. Some of these folks actually had more contracting experience than I did, and they "saved my bacon" on quite a few occasions. They can be worth their weight in gold to you, especially during the negotiation preparation stage. Some contract specialists are even trained as expert contract negotiators and can be put into negotiations as the team leader. You would be wise not only to delegate as many functions to them as possible, but to seek their advice and counsel actively during the negotiation process.

Price Analysts/Cost Analysts

In many complex negotiations, especially if you plan on negotiating a cost reimbursement-type contract, or have special, complicated incentives on fixed-price arrangements, you'll definitely want a price analyst or a cost analyst on your team. These are the folks that can *really* "do the math." In fact, that's their sole job and focus. They are trained to do things like price analysis, cost analysis, should-cost analysis, learning curve applications, overhead and indirect charge applications, profit and fee analysis, forward-pricing rate projections and adjustments, and so on.

Do you think these talents will give you a leg up in preparing for negotiations? You bet! They can help you prepare for negotiations by tearing a contractor's proposal down to its basic cost elements and analyzing them. They then can crunch the numbers to give you, in their expert opinion, what the numbers actually should be—given different situations. They can help you prepare "what-if" scenarios and help you develop the dollars-and-cents rationale behind your minimum, maximum, and target negotiation positions. They are your experts on all pricing matters.

During negotiations, their expertise can be vital in defending your position, backed up with hard, cold, mathematically verifiable facts. They can also greatly aid you in determining the cost/price impact of proposed changes that may come about as a result of the give-and-take of negotiations. Do you think you could use their expertise on your team? You bet! Unfortunately, not every agency has them, and some that do don't have enough of them. If you're unable to get price/cost analysts assigned to your team, guess who picks up their responsibilities by default? Yep. You guessed it. You, the CO.

Technical Representatives/Technical Experts

Technical representatives and technical experts usually come from your customer's organization, and they are absolutely essential for the success of your entire negotiation. They are the people who have intimate knowledge of the design and technical approach for the product or service you are negotiating for. It's *their* need that you're fulfilling, and they are the experts in knowing what can and can't satisfy that need. Their expert knowledge of the technical aspects of the requirement is just as important as your price/cost analyst's work, since design and technical approach have a huge impact on cost, risk, quality, and so forth. They are experts on such things as: the merits and chances of success of various technical approaches, the customary technical practices in the commercial marketplace, quantities and kinds of material, number and kinds of labor hours and the labor mix, special tooling, scrap and spoilage factors, and the feasibility and acceptability of proposed changes to work methods or approaches. They're the backbone of your negotiation team, the reason you're there in the first place, and the reason you have a job! Treat these folks with the respect they are due.

By the way, they can also help you, the CO, understand more about the thing or service you are negotiating for by putting the technical jargon in layman's terms. But remember, although they may have no peer when it comes to the *technical* aspects of the negotiation, they usually have little or no training in the *process* of negotiation—the business side to getting the deal done. That's your area of expertise. And that's why it's critical that the negotiation team leader be from the contracting "side of the house."

Program Managers

Sometimes you may have other representatives from your customer's organization who aren't necessarily technical experts, but have a keen, vested interest in the outcome of the negotiation. Program managers are an example, and they can be members of your negotiation team. Their job is to manage and direct the overall program that your contract supports. They are responsible for meeting performance, schedule, and cost goals and they usually have management authority over all technical and business aspects of the program. They usually have their own customers to support— the ultimate end users of the product or service for which you're negotiating—and they'll want to be included in the negotiation to represent their customers' and the program's interests.

Program managers may be (and usually are) higher in rank or grade than you, the CO. Although your job is to contractually support the program manager as your customer, always remember that *you* are in charge of the negotiations. You have specialized contractual training and knowledge the program manager doesn't, so you *must* control the show despite rank or grade differences. You'll find that most good program managers already know this and are more than happy to let you be the boss during negotiations.

Obviously, there are more potential team members—auditors, legal counsel, small business specialists, quality assurance specialists, property specialists, and so on—that you'll want to consider adding to the team if the situation warrants. These folks don't necessarily have to be permanent members of your negotiation team, but can simply be "matrixed in" for short periods as the situation dictates. Bottom line: It's your responsibility as the CO—the team leader—to assemble a team tailored to the needs of the specific negotiation situation.

A few more points before we move on to the next step. Always pick the first-string players to be on your team, not the scrubs. You may get a lot of "help" from your customer, who may volunteer members to you, but *you* ultimately must pass judgment on their qualifications (on whether they are right for the job). Remember also that your support team can (and should) be much larger than the few members you actually take into the negotiation event with you. These other team members (the ones who help you prepare for negotiations) are just as critical to your success and should be thought of as full members of the team.

Now, for any team to be successful in negotiations, it must have a few crucial attributes: good leadership (that's you), clear objectives, and *one* consolidated position. The team, as a unit, must also be able to take advantage of the wealth of information, knowledge, and expertise that's represented by all the individual members of the team. So your next step, after you select your team, is to get them together to kick off the endeavor.

BRIEFING THE TEAM

As soon as you select the members of the team, your next step is to schedule a face-to-face kickoff meeting with them. You, as the CO and leader of the team, are responsible for doing this. You'll need to schedule this meeting as soon as possible after the need to ne-gotiate is identified, and plan for the meeting to be about an hour in length. Remember, your team may consist of more people than you will actually take into the negotiation room, so don't forget to include those folks too.

Be sure to give yourself enough time before this meeting to estab-lish a written agenda—it can be informal—and to prepare for what you're going to say and what you need to cover. If time permits, try to get copies of the agenda to the team members beforehand so they'll also know the topics of discussion. You'll use this meeting to organize your team and start the training process.

After making introductions, start by clearly establishing your authority as the CO and leader of the team. This is especially important if some of the team members outrank you or are a higher grade than you. Then assign and clarify each team member's roles and responsibilities in preparing for the negotiation. This is usually a no-brainer, because these roles will logically fall along functional lines. Let them know this will probably be the first of several get-togethers you will have as you prepare for negotiations.

After roles are assigned, clearly dictate to each team member the specific duties you'll expect them to accomplish to help the team prepare for negotiations. This will become your negotiation preparation action plan, and it's crucial to keep things on track and to make sure you cover all the bases. Again, these duties will usually fall along functional lines and the areas of expertise of your team members. Make sure to attach "action dates" (which sounds better than "deadlines") to each duty you assign, and make sure you assign each duty to a specific team member. You may have the best action plan and milestone chart in the world, but if you don't assign actual people to the tasks—and make sure they understand they are responsible for getting their tasks done on time—your plan will simply crumble.

The first duties you'll assign will support the team's data-gathering effort. For example, you will most likely ask your contract specialists to do market research into other similar contracts, or have your program manager or technical representative research what's standard practice in the industry for what you're buying. You'll also ask your technical folks to develop specific questions on the *technical* aspects of whatever contractor proposal you'll be negotiating. Your job, or the job of your contract specialist, will be to research the *business terms and conditions* in the proposal, and which business terms and conditions are common to that industry. Assign your price analyst the job of crunching the numbers.

Just because you're the team leader doesn't mean you assign all the duties to everyone else. Always save some duties for yourself—like researching the contractor's financial position, competitive position, and probable negotiation strategy and tactics. Remember, unless you delegate it, you are responsible for it, in addition to ensuring that all team members meet the goals you establish. Always have someone record meeting minutes and distribute them to your team members after the meeting.

The kickoff meeting is also a great forum to educate the team on how to conduct government negotiations. Because some team members may not be familiar with their responsibilities, brief them on procurement integrity, rules on disclosing source selection–sensitive or other government information, and restrictions on disclosing a contractor's bid or proprietary proposal information. Remember, this first meeting is to set the stage for the negotiation process and to kick off the data-gathering effort. You'll need other meetings to discuss the data gathered, choose your negotiation strategy, come up with your government position and objectives, assign roles for the actual negotiations, and practice the negotiation. If you can, set the times for these meetings during the kickoff meeting.

End the kickoff meeting by stressing the importance of the negotiation to the customer (and ultimately the taxpayer) and stress preparation as being the key to success. Most of these folks are smart (or you wouldn't have them on your team) and they will have many other things on their plate vying for their attention. You have to convince them that *this effort* should be their *number one priority.*

After you adjourn the meeting, remember to provide the team members (and their managers) with a copy of the minutes as soon as possible. Make sure the minutes have appropriate markings if they contain source-selection or proprietary information.

Please understand that the key to preparing for negotiations is to gather pertinent data. As you just learned, it's a team effort. So, where do you go to get the data? What kinds of data and information do you need? There are basically two types of information you'll need to gather: information to help you establish your pre-negotiation objectives, and information about the "other side." We look at gathering data in the next chapter.

Chapter 4

Gathering Data

There is a wealth of information out there that can help you and your team prepare for the negotiation. In fact, you'll be staggered by the sheer volume and number of sources of useful information that's available. When faced with this large amount of data, it is important to remember the main reason you are gathering data: to verify that the contractor's proposed pricing, terms, and conditions are fair and reasonable and, if not, to develop and defend *your* position on what you consider fair and reasonable. Keeping this in mind will help you limit your search and prevent information overload. So, let's talk about some of the kinds of data you'll want to get, and where to get it.

Remember that the data gathering you're doing at this stage of negotiation preparation is solely to help you come up with your negotiating position, given the contractor's proposal and your customer's needs. We'll discuss in a later chapter how to gather additional data to give you important clues and insights into the folks that will be sitting across the negotiating table from you. The following are some of the most important sources of data you will need to help you establish your negotiation positions.

THE REQUIREMENTS PACKAGE

Before you start gathering data, you need to know what you're gathering data for—in other words, what you're buying. This important information is contained in the requirements package your customer has forwarded to you. The requirements package will contain all sorts of important information: the purchase request document, the government cost estimate, delivery or performance requirements, requests for waivers of competition requirements or publicizing requirements, required amounts, delivery dates, performance periods, available GFP, and so on. However, the heart of the requirements package is the requirements document. This document is your customer's description of the supplies or services he needs. You'll eventually wrap the business terms and conditions around this requirements document to create the solicitation document—another key document you need to help you prepare for negotiations. We'll talk about it later.

Don't get hung up on definitions here. Requirements documents are called by many names: statements of work (SOWs), performance requirements documents, specifications, performance work statements (PWSs), statements of need (SONs), statements of objectives (SOOs), and so forth. Your agency may prefer a particular term, or may even have a completely different name for them. Although there are some differences represented by the different names, they are all forms of requirements documents.

You and your team need to know—and I mean *really* know—the requirements document. You can't be an informed buyer if you don't have a full grasp of what you're buying and why. If you're truly being a business advisor to your customer, as the FAR requires you to be, you should have had a hand in helping your customer develop this document. If not, you need to get your hands on it as soon as possible, even if it's in draft form, and even if you get it well ahead of receiving the rest of the requirements package. Because you're not expected to be the technical expert, some of the language in the requirements document may look like Greek to you. Make sure you ask your technical experts to explain the parts of the requirements document you don't understand to you in layman's terms, so you fully understand what you're negotiating for.

THE SOLICITATION DOCUMENT

The solicitation document is what was sent to the prospective contractors inviting them to submit bids, proposals, or quotes. As mentioned earlier, the requirements document will form the heart of the solicitation document, but it's not all the solicitation document consists of. The solicitation document tells the prospective contractors not only what the government needs (the requirements document), but gives them additional guidance about how to go about fulfilling that need when they submit their proposals, what their proposals should look like, and how you are going to conduct the evaluation of their proposals after they are submitted to you. This information is also crucial to planning for the negotiation.

Chances are, you'll already be familiar with the additional information contained in the solicitation document, since you were the one who put it together, but the rest of your team may not be. Make sure all team members are educated on what the solicitation document requires contractors to do. For instance, how long did it give the contractors to respond with their proposals? Did it require any additional information from the contractors not asked for in the requirements document, like strike plans, small business subcontracting plans, or additional reporting requirements? Did it inform the contractors they would be evaluated using the lowest price/technically acceptable (LPTA) method or the tradeoff method? What factors did it state that are going to be used to evaluate the proposals, and what is their relative importance to each other? What type of submission was requested—a proposal or a quote? Are oral presentations required? Can partial awards be made, or are only all-or-none submissions going to be allowed? Is this acquisition being treated as a simplified acquisition?

These are most of the "biggies," but not necessarily all the information a solicitation will contain. The answers to all these questions will have an impact on your negotiations, and on how you must prepare for negotiations. They will dictate how the proposals will look when they are submitted, the level of competition you'll have, the importance of technical factors versus price, the extent and depth of information expected in the proposals, and so forth. Not only you, but your entire team, will have to understand the solicitation's impact on all these things to prepare and conduct the negotiation properly. One of the biggest mistakes I've seen government teams make when planning for a negotiation is to concentrate only on the requirements document and not on the entire solicitation document.

THE CONTRACTOR'S PROPOSAL

The next most important source of data in preparing for negotiations is the contractor's proposal. A common saying in negotiations is, "He who speaks first loses." Now remember that with government negotiations, you don't want any losers; you want a fair and reasonable outcome for all. However, having the contractor's proposal without giving the contractor the benefit of your cost estimate is one of the *huge* advantages you have in negotiations. You force *them* to speak first by requesting they send you their proposal, which must be priced. Simply by having that proposal, you already know the contractor's going-in (or maximum) position. A careful analysis of the proposal can yield other important facts too—like who their negotiators might be, what other business goals the contractor might be trying to attain, and so forth.

The proposal also will have that particular contractor's technical approach to addressing the needs your customer outlined in the requirements document. It's their "how-to" solution to your customer's problem. You'll have a technical team review their approach in detail, and this review, or technical evaluation, will create many of your issues and positions for the negotiation. The technical team will summarize all this in a technical evaluation report, which is your next source of important information in preparing for the negotiation.

THE TECHNICAL EVALUATION REPORT

After the contractor proposals are received, you'll have your technical experts evaluate them. This evaluation will find weaknesses, significant weaknesses, deficiencies, strengths, and so forth, in the contractor's proposed process for fulfilling the need. Your technical team will generate a technical evaluation report summarizing all their findings and comments, tailored to each contractor's unique approach. This document, addressed to you, the CO, will form the crux of your prenegotiation positions on the *technical* aspects of the negotiation. In fact, it's the most critical document you'll have to prepare for negotiating the technical merits of various proposed solutions. Make sure your technical folks write this report in language you, a nontechnical expert, can understand.

FACT-FINDING/EXCHANGES

Another important source of information may be notes or memos written by the government as a result of fact-finding or other exchanges between the government and contractors—either prior to or after receipt of their proposals. The preaward stage has several opportunities to have exchanges with contractors: communications, clarifications, competitive range determinations, and so forth. In noncompetitive negotiations, your ability to gather additional facts to help you prepare your negotiating position is even more wide open. All these exchanges are documented and can be the source of useful data to help you prepare for negotiations. In all cases, you're gaining more information about the contractor's position, and this better prepares you to negotiate when you sit down at the bargaining table.

PRICE ANALYSIS AND COST ANALYSIS

While your technical team is scrutinizing the technical aspects of the contractor's proposal, you and your other team members are taking a look at the dollars and the business terms and conditions the contractor is proposing. When the government reviews the contractor's cost proposal, it uses price analysis, and sometimes cost analysis (depending on the type of contract contemplated). Cost analysis, used mainly for cost reimbursable-type contracts, can give you a detailed analysis of the important individual elements of cost that make up the contractor's proposal. Price analysis is simply a comparison of the contractor's "bottom line" price with other contractor bottom lines to determine whether it is "fair and reasonable." Although price analysis isn't concerned with the individual elements of cost, its results can still be useful to you as a negotiator.

An additional technique that's sometimes used is a should-cost analysis, during which you examine the contractor's technical approach to determine what it should cost, given reasonable efficiency and economy, and compare it with what they're actually proposing. Because you're considering technical aspects and relating them to costs using this method, you'll usually need the help of your technical team to perform a should-cost analysis correctly.

If you're lucky, you may be able to recruit the assistance of a price analyst or a cost analyst to help you with the evaluation. If not, you become these analysts by default. In any case, just as the technical review and report helped your team develop your prenegotiation positions on technical matters, these types of reviews help you form your prenegotiation positions on price, cost, and business issues.

ACQUISITION HISTORIES

Another great source of data is the acquisition history your agency or other federal agencies have amassed as a result of buying the same or similar items in the past. Chances are, your agency has bought this kind of stuff before. If you can find those files, you'll have a head start on gathering and evaluating data such as historical prices paid, warranties, delivery times, and so forth. You can look at what was considered fair and reasonable in the past, and use it as a starting point to form your prenegotiation objectives. Of course you may have to dust them off a bit and revise the information to make it current, but at least you have a place to start.

You can find these files by searching your agency's database, by searching databases and Web sites of other agencies, by talking to other COs, or simply by asking the contractor. In fact, most contractors will have to give the government a list of previous contracts they have worked on relating to the requirement. This information allows the CO to find them responsible and to gauge their past performance history. This list is another starting place, already tailored to your contractor, for obtaining this acquisition history.

OTHER SOURCES OF DATA

There are many other government and commercially available sources of data out there for you to use. I've listed a few of these sources in Appendix B for your use as an easy reference. I hope this helps you; but remember, this list is not all inclusive—not by a long shot!

Please be aware that creating or gathering all this information, and then sorting through it can be a huge task—and one you won't want to do all by yourself. Remember: You have a team. During your team kickoff meeting, assign gathering and analyzing data to individual team members. Consider tailoring the amount and kinds of data you'll gather to the size and complexity of your particular situation. Folks, this is a judgment call you'll have to make. Don't get caught up in the "paralysis of analysis." If you try to collect *all* available information before you negotiate, you'll never negotiate. You'll spend all your time collecting data. Collect enough data to make smart decisions and press on!

Chapter 5

Establishing Prenegotiation Objectives

After you have gathered your data, the next step for you and your team is to combine what you have learned from the data with the customer's needs to establish your priorities for the negotiation. You need to develop a systematic, efficient way to start turning this information into a sound negotiation plan. Establishing priorities will help you do this; priorities will help you channel your team's efforts toward what's *really* important.

Remember, negotiation consists of give and take. So what's your customer willing to give? What's their number one priority? Number two? What are the "gotta-haves"? The "nice-to-haves"? You need to establish a pecking order of priorities for your negotiation. Knowing your priorities is essential to establishing your negotiation plan and will serve as a guide and center of focus when your plan comes face-to-face with the confusion and shifting positions a negotiation can cause.

Some of your priorities may be dictated to you. Other priorities may be constrained by things like time, available dollars, contract type, law, sheer number of issues, and the demands of your upper management and those of your customer. Your own experience (or lack thereof) as well as that of your team members may also constrain what you can focus on as priorities. However, there are usually many issues that you and your team still have a good bit of control over. All this affects what's important to you and where these issues rank in importance to each other. And this, in turn, affects how you will plan your negotiation.

FOCUS ON YOUR CUSTOMER'S NEEDS

The identification of priorities (of *your* needs) is truly a true team effort, but the folks with the biggest stake are obviously your customers. They're the ones who have the need. They're the ones who will have to live with the result of the negotiation. Because they have the biggest stake in the outcome, they should have the lead role in identifying priorities for the negotiation.

So, the first step in identifying priorities is to find out your customer's needs. Only they can tell you the importance of quality, timeliness (the schedule), cost, and risk, and what they consider to be most important, second important, and so on. You've already spent time analyzing their requirements document—and that gave you insight into their needs—but now it's time to talk to them to understand their true needs. Identifying your customer's needs should be the focus of your second meeting.

A common CO mistake is to assume your customer's priorities are the same as yours. Traditionally, COs are known to zero in like a laser beam on price and treat it as if it's the only issue, or at least the overriding issue. Hey, we're trained to do that stuff and it's always more comfortable to focus on doing what you're trained for, right? The problem, of course, is that your customer may have other priorities, and some may be more important than price.

For example, you may find that your customer isn't as concerned about price as he or she is about the maintainability of an item. Or they might be willing to pay a higher price if they can get a specific delivery date or some sort of extended warranty. As the team leader, you must make sure to allow the team to develop its own priorities, not just uphold yours.

Your job is not to establish the priorities, but to guide the team in establishing their own priorities in an efficient, effective way. Obviously, you'll want your team to focus more on the high-priority items—what's most important to your customer. You want your team to spend most of their precious time concentrating on the really big issues and not get bogged down in the muck of trivial issues. It's better to be *well* prepared for a few *big* issues than to be *somewhat* prepared for *all* possible issues.

Here's where your abilities to lead start to become important. Will your own team members disagree on priorities? You bet, and this may happen frequently. Your customer's organization is not one huge monolith; it's made up of people, each with a different take on what's important and what would be the best outcome for their organization (or sometimes for themselves). Your job as team leader is to pull them together and referee disputes.

You've got to squash the internal sniping and provide the team with a framework to enable consensual decision making. In fact, presiding over this internal give-and-take may very well be your first opportunity to practice the art of negotiation! Some of my most difficult negotiations weren't with contractors, but with members of my own team.

DETERMINE "MUST" POINTS VERSUS "GIVE" POINTS

You and your team have already analyzed and evaluated the contractor's proposal from all angles: technical, cost, price, and business terms and conditions. This analysis resulted in a list of issues (weaknesses, deficiencies, questions, and so on) that you'll need to address with the contractor during the negotiation.

Your next step is to lead the team in arranging these issues in a list from most important to least important. To do this you will use the customer priorities you helped the team establish earlier. When this exercise is done, you will have a prioritized list of issues you want to discuss during negotiations.

After the list is created and agreed to (which, by the way, is not always an amicable process), you then need to draw a line somewhere near the middle of the list. Here comes the hard part: Everyone must agree where the line goes. (Be prepared; this can really get contentious.) Label all the issues above that line "must" points. Label all those below the line "give" points.

"Must" points are those issues that *must* go your way—in other words, objectives that *must* be met or an agreement may not be reached. "Give" points, on the other hand, are issues that would be great to have, but not getting them won't derail the negotiation. You'll still negotiate for the "give" points (they are important), but they need not be insisted on in total. You're willing to *give* on them a little to reach a final agreement. "Must" points are your "gotta-haves"; they should be the concrete *needs* of the government. "Give" points are your "nice-to-haves"; they usually reflect the *wants* of your customer.

After all the issues are labeled, ask your team for a few additional "give" points and add them to the bottom of the list. Price, by the way, should always be below the line as a "give" point. It almost always changes as a result of the give-and-take of negotiation. Both sides usually incorporate some flexibility in price, and both sides expect some fluctuation. In addition, tradeoffs on other issues are usually made against price.

Now that you have your "musts" and "gives"—arrayed in priority order for all team members to see—the team will start to gel in common support of the plan that's evolving. You're slowly helping them create focus out of confusion, a plan out of the stacks of paperwork they had to wade through, and they can now see the rough sketch of a roadmap to get them where they want to go. You've also created something that's absolutely essential to every negotiation: *flexibility.* Creating this prioritized list, enhanced with those few extra "gives" you threw in, provides you with tradeoff opportunities when you get to the negotiation table.

You now have "give" points to use as bargaining chips, begrudgingly giving in on them and trading them to achieve your "must" points. This is why you should always have plenty of "give" points handy. In fact, you should have many more "give" points than "must" points.

Don't feel the least bit guilty about creating and adding "give" points to your list that you know you're going to use to trade away later. You're not the only one preparing for the negotiations. The other side is busy doing the same thing, arranging their own list of "musts" and "gives." Neither side, of course, knows the other side's "must" points and "give" points. As the dance of negotiation starts, the opportunities for both sides to trade positions will form the essence of the give-and-take of negotiation.

There are two things you must remember as you establish your "must" and "give" points. First, *you* are the team leader. If your team disagrees on how to label a particular issue ("must" or "give") and they "lock up" over the issue, you must break the deadlock. You make the decision. Second, never forget your duty as a government representative to be fair and reasonable to *both* sides. Make sure your "give" points are legitimate goals of the team (just not as important as the "must" points) and not something contrived that you absolutely don't want in the first place. Creating totally false "give" points, and arguing for them in the negotiation just to trade them off later, can be considered negotiating in bad faith.

After you have established and ranked your negotiation priorities, and then decided on your "must" and "give" points, you're now ready to finalize your prenegotiation objectives by establishing your acceptable negotiation *range* for each issue.

FINALIZE YOUR PRENEGOTIATION OBJECTIVES

FAR 15.406-1 requires the CO to establish prenegotiation objectives before any negotiation that includes pricing actions. You should tailor the scope, depth, and amount of time you spend on establishing these objectives to the complexity, importance, and dollar value of your situation. Always check your agency's supplements; your agency may have a particular way they want you to establish these objectives, and possibly even a format or a checklist they want you to use. In all cases, these objectives must be in writing.

These prenegotiation objectives are your initial negotiation position for each issue and are based on your analysis of the contractor's proposal, your customer's needs, and a review of all the other data your team has gathered. As you've seen, you come up with these objectives as a team—and that in itself may take some internal negotiation!

For each significant issue you'll be negotiating (each issue you labeled as a "must" or "give" point), you must now establish three positions: a minimum (MIN) position, a target (TGT) position, and a maximum (MAX) position. Because you're the buyer, your MIN position should be your best-case scenario (in other words, if everything worked out exactly like you want it to). Your TGT position is your estimation of the most likely result based on the give-and-take of negotiation. This position is not all you hoped for, but it's about what you expected, and you can live with it. It's usually around the midpoint between your MIN and MAX positions.

Your MAX position is the worst-case scenario. This is the point at which either your customer's true needs (not just wants) cannot be supported (delivery, quality, cost, and so on) or the point at which you, the CO, can no longer determine the price to be fair and reasonable for what you're getting. Basically, your MAX position is your point of maximum hurt, your walk-away point.

You'll need not only to identify these three positions for each issue, but to be able to defend each position with facts. If you've done your homework during the data-gathering and analysis stage, this should be a snap.

By creating these three positions, you have now defined the amount and degree of your flexibility on each issue. You have, in essence, created an acceptable *range* to allow concessions and movement during negotiations. The FAR calls this *bargaining*, and it's an essential part of true negotiations.

Now, I know what you're thinking. There are some issues that are simple "gotta-haves." True, there may be some issues you have little or no flexibility on at all. In that case, why not *build* in some flexibility? Remember your "must" and "give" points? Why not tie some of your "give" points to one of those inflexible "must" points? This packaging together of "must' and "give" points into a single negotiable issue will give you greater flexibility and a better chance to end the negotiation with everyone seeing it as a win–win situation. (We'll talk about this in-depth later when we discuss the tactic of coupling.)

Remember, the other side doesn't know what your "must" and "give" points are, and they will have no clue you have packaged two of them together. They'll just see the package deal as a single issue. Never get so bogged down on individual issues that you lose sight of the big picture. You now have a better chance of getting your inflexible "must" point because you gave something in return.

While you and your team are going through the process of establishing your MIN, TGT, and MAX positions for your issues, guess what the other side will be doing? Yep. Exactly the same thing. So when the negotiation starts, each side will have established MIN, TGT, and MAX positions for each issue, but neither side will know the other side's positions. Hopefully, somewhere between *your* MIN and *their* MAX, your goals will intersect.

It's precisely here—where your range of flexibility intersects with theirs—that the possibility for the give-and-take of negotiations occurs, and the possibility of an agreement exists. This is called *the zone of potential agreement.* Rarely will your ranges and the contractor's ranges not intersect between these MIN and MAX positions. The essence of negotiations, then, is to try to find out the positions of the other side while not revealing to them what *your* positions are. Both sides are doing this at the same time, and that's negotiating!

When you ask most average folks to define the term *negotiation,* they'll define it in terms of an *event*—when two sides sit across the table from each other. They'll say it starts at a certain hour on a certain day and ends when an agreement is reached. We know better! We know negotiation is a *process*, not an event, and the majority of it takes place before the actual sit-down meeting. The meeting, what most people think of as negotiation, is simply the culmination of a long process.

During this meeting (the actual negotiation event), both sides go to great lengths to conceal their true positions, interests, needs, and priorities. In fact, a trained negotiator will make it extremely hard for you to discover things such as their deadlines, costs, positions, and so forth, during the actual negotiation event. Your best chance of getting as much of this crucial information as you can about the other side is *before* you're sitting across the table from them.

Remember, information builds knowledge, knowledge builds power, and power helps you succeed in negotiations. The next chapter shows you how to build your knowledge about the other side beforehand—how to research the other party.

Chapter 6

Researching the
Other Party

In Chapter 4 we discussed gathering data to help you understand the requirement you'll be negotiating and your customer's needs, as well to help you develop your own negotiating positions. The data you gathered through market research focused mainly on the acquisition itself, not on the folks who will be sitting on the other side of the table.

In this chapter, we shift gears and look at how to collect data and other information that can give you clues about what to expect from the other side during the negotiation event. To prepare for the negotiation properly, you want to get as much general information as possible on the company you'll be dealing with. You'll also want to know as much as possible about the individuals who will be sitting across the table from you. This chapter shows you where and how to gather this important information.

RESEARCHING THE COMPANY

Do a little research into the company's past negotiation history. Look for the following: Do they have a reputation of driving a hard bargain? Do they have a habit of using certain negotiation strategies and tactics in the past? How effective were they? How concerned are they about their reputation in the marketplace? About their reputation of being perceived as fair?

What are the company's goals—both long term and short term? What do they pride themselves on? What are their published core values and vision? Can you find insight into the company's unstated goals? Sometimes goals on paper are just that; the company may have other, unstated priorities that influence how they will act.

Where do they stand in the marketplace compared with their competitors? Are they a new company? An old company? Are they considered a market leader in their industry? Follower? Innovator? Are they trying to expand into a new market? Is this their first government contract? If not, what percentage of their business is with the government? Are they small or large? Are they a subsidiary of a larger company? What are their limitations and market pressures? The answers to all these questions will give you important clues to how they are going to behave in the negotiation and how you should craft your approach to dealing with them.

Also do some basic homework on the company's cost structure. I'm not talking here about the specific acquisition you have in front of you to negotiate, but on the company in general. What's their standard profit margin? How do they price their goods or services? Are they profitable? Are they considered the "low-cost bubba" or the "high-priced icon?" Are their business or profit margins expanding or contracting? Are they starved for cash or desperate for business? What's their debt ratio? Are there takeover rumors? Are they unionized? What kind of relationship do they have with their employees? What do their employees think of working for them?

Finally, see if you can discover any (what I call) standard company tendencies. These are things like standard terms and conditions that they habitually adhere to or ask for. What's their discount policy? What kinds of warranties do they offer? How do they usually try to limit their liability or risk? What do you know about their overall risk tolerance? Do they walk away from deals they perceive are too risky? Do they have a reputation for trying to "buy in" on contracts?

Obviously, there is much more research you can do on a company, and you'll see soon how readily available most of this information is. What I hope you understand is how useful this company research can be to you during negotiations.

RESEARCHING THE COMPANY'S NEGOTIATORS

If you can, you also want to gather as much "intel" as possible on the *person* who's representing the contractor in the negotiation. True, it's useful to research all the personalities on the opposite team, but you are safe concentrating on the team leader—your counterpart across the table—because he or she will set the tone for their entire team. Remember, negotiating is a process, culminating in the actual sit-down meeting. Don't wait until then to get information about the company's negotiator. Start as early as possible. Of course, if the negotiation session is the first time you meet the negotiator, some things can't be discovered until then. But you should start your research as soon as you know who you'll be negotiating with. You need to "go to school" on them.

How do you find out who's to be your counterpart? All you need to do is ask the contractor! You could even consider asking in your solicitation to have them identify this person when they submit their proposals. Or you could ask when you send the contractor a copy of your draft agenda for them to review (we'll talk about draft agendas later). The earlier you start this personal research, the better. One caution, however: The contractor may switch negotiators on you. Hey, they know this game too! If they do, well, that's sometimes how negotiations go. Whoever they submit, especially if they *do* make a switch, make sure that person has the authority to negotiate and bind the company. When we talk about the ambiguous authority tactic later, you'll see why this is important.

Once you've nailed down who your counterpart is going to be, check out that person's history in previous negotiations. If you haven't had previous dealings with him or her, contact someone who has (like another CO). Remember, you don't have to limit yourself to COs you know or who are within your own office. You can search agency-wide or even outside your agency. How will you know who to call? Just check the contractor's proposal. Chances

are, you have requested and received past performance information from the contractor. This information will tell you what contracts they have had in the past and will identify the points of contact for these contracts. Call these folks and talk to them about the
contractor.

What's this person's job title in the company? Does he or she even
work for the company as an employee? Or are they a hired gun, a
professional negotiator brought in on a fee or contingent basis?
How many government negotiations has this person been in? What
agencies were the contracts for? Are they new to the company? Are
they new to government negotiations? What's the historical range
they usually hit between going-in position and the final negotiated
price of the contract?

Is he or she a well-known negotiator? Well respected? Do they
have a reputation for being trustworthy? Are they known for ethical or unethical behavior in the past? Do they have a reputation
of making concessions or driving a hard bargain? When do they
habitually make most of their concessions—up front, during, or
right at the end of negotiations? Were they pleasant to negotiate
with or a pain? Are they known as a "people person" or a loner?
Are they sloppy or well organized? Are they a technical subject
matter expert in the function they're negotiating or simply a business expert or "number cruncher"? What's their reputation in the
company? In the industry? Are they egotistical? Prone to make
snap judgments? What can you find out about their personal values and background?

What kind of negotiation style and tactics is this person known to
use? Do they change their style and tactics, or are they predictable? Are they perceived as using "negotiation tricks"? If so, which
tricks do they like to use? Are they known to be a talker or a good
listener? (It's important to notice how some people seem to dominate conversations and talk about themselves. You can turn this
into a *great* advantage at the negotiation table.) Do they like to take
risks or are they cautious and risk-averse?

Probe for this person's personal strengths and weaknesses (I sometimes call these *hot buttons*) that are peculiar only to him or her. What are their true underlying motives? Are they predictable? Do they have a family? What are their hobbies? What other outside interests do they have? Are they a member of any professional associations or clubs? Are they seen as a "fast-burner" on their way up? Or a "has-been" on their way down? Do they have a desire to be liked and to please people? What outside pressures are pushing in on them personally? Professionally? What's their personal stake in the negotiations? Could a promotion be tied to how well they negotiate or how much they can get out of the negotiation? Could they face the possibility of demotion or disgrace if they are perceived to do badly during the negotiation? What are their time pressures and deadlines for this deal?

As you gather this information on your counterpart and start assessing it, try to put yourself in their shoes. How do you think *they* see the situation? How do you think they see or perceive you? This exercise (of putting yourself in his or her shoes) will help you assimilate the pieces of information you have collected or observed into a general picture of that negotiator as a real, live *person*. With this picture in mind, you can better predict how that person will act and react in the negotiation room. And that, folks, will help you prepare your own strategy, tactics, and countertactics.

Two last points on researching the other side. First, be very careful about the information you get from other government COs who have been in negotiations with that person or that company. You can't always take what they say at face value. These COs may have unknowingly been the victims of effective tactics used by the other side. For example, you may ask another CO about a company negotiator and be told something like, "Oh yes! She was great! You'll have no problem dealing with her. She's very pleasant to deal with." The reality may be that this CO fell victim to any number of negotiation tactics a professional negotiator can use, which are designed to make that CO feel just that way! Hopefully, after reading this book, that person will never be you. We're going to go over many of these tactics: how to recognize them and how to counter them.

Second, you may ask, "Hey, is it ethical for a government negotiator to collect this kind of data, especially since some of it can be extremely personal in nature?" Or, "Ethics notwithstanding, is it worth my time and effort to collect this stuff at all?" In my opinion, the answer to both questions is a resounding yes! In a negotiation, information is power, and the most informed side becomes the most prepared. The side that's most prepared for the negotiation usually comes out on top. Don't feel bad about researching the other side. If you're up against a professional negotiator, I guarantee they're already busy collecting this same information—as much of it as they can—on both your agency and *you*. Later in this book, when we discuss some of the tactics that you can use or that *can be used against you*, you'll agree with me that it is well worth your time to learn everything you can about the other party prior to negotiations.

Here's an example. Have you ever had a contractor call you out of the blue, and say something like, "Hey, I just happened to be in town, and I thought it would be nice if I came by and met you in person so I could connect a face to a name," or something similar? I'm sure you thought it was an extremely customer-oriented, friendly gesture. What a nice person! You probably responded with something like, "Sure! Come on up to my office and we'll get acquainted!" And that's just what the professional negotiator was betting on.

He or she may truly want to be friendly, but their ultimate goal is to get into your office, your own private space. Give a professional negotiator five minutes in your office and they can find out more about you than *you* even know about you! As they engage you in friendly banter, their eyes will dart around your office and they'll pick up important clues about you as a person—clues that will help them in future negotiations with you. Your office tells volumes about you. Are you a neat person or are you a slob? Are you married? Do you have children (pictures on the wall or on your desk)? What are your hobbies? How devoted to them are you? What sports do you like? What teams are you a fan of? What do you like to read? Are you in an office or a cubicle? How big is your office compared with others? Do you seem particularly proud of receiving recognition (plaques on the wall)? Do you have items with competitors' logos on them, such as mouse pads, pens, coffee cups, and so forth?

From that quick study of your office, the professional negotiator will have picked up volumes of useful information about you—information he or she will attempt to exploit the next time they negotiate with you. How tidy you keep your office, for instance, can be an indicator of the type of person you are and how you will act in a negotiation. If you have an extensive "I love me" wall full of plaques and awards, they will deduce that you crave recognition and will slant their next negotiation tactics accordingly. Pictures on the wall of spouses, children, or sports will give them future topics of conversation to use to bond with you and win your confidence, as do diplomas, books, and magazines. The size and location of your office will tell them where you are in the "pecking order" of your organization. They'll know whether you're someone to be reckoned with or whether you are a "worker bee" required to get approvals "from above."

I'm not saying not to meet with contractors if they drop in. I just don't suggest you take them back into the inner recesses of your building or into your own personal office space. Meet them in your conference room or some other neutral ground. Don't let them "go to school" on you!

INFORMATION SOURCES

Now you know it's important to do research on the other party—both the company and the negotiator. But where do you go to get that kind of information? Do you have to break into the company after hours and snoop around? Actually, that could land you in jail and complicate the negotiation a bit. No, you don't have to become a corporate spy to gather the information you need to research the other party. We've already talked about getting information on the other negotiator by talking to folks who have dealt with him or her before. Now let's look at some information sources for researching the other side's company in general.

Getting information about the other side is not as daunting as it first seems. There are plenty of sources out there that are easily available that you can tap into. I've never found amount and availability of sources of information to be a problem, especially with the Internet just a click away. In fact, you probably have a lot of what you'll need already lying around as a result of your previous market research efforts for the acquisition.

In Chapter 4, we looked at ways to gather data to help you identify and set your negotiation positions and priorities. Many of these same sources you've already tapped can now give you a "double bang" by revealing general clues about the other side. The contractor's proposal, for instance, usually contains useful management summaries that give a glimpse into the company's overall motives, values, and objectives.

As the negotiation process continues, you'll also have many chances for any of a number of prenegotiation exchanges with the contractor (clarifications, communications, fact-finding, and so on) to obtain certain proposal-specific information. All these exchanges are opportunities to expand the usefulness of the exchange well beyond just the information you're seeking. You can use these exchanges to research the company and the negotiator: attitude, how they react to certain approaches, how forthcoming they are, how willing to please they are, and so forth.

We've talked about how you should get information from other COs who have done business or negotiated with the contractor before. You may also want to expand this source base by talking to government customers, technical personnel, and even auditors who have had some experience dealing with that company. Often, their assessment of a company and their people is "dead on." Certain professions and technical fields develop bonds between their practitioners that can transcend company and even company/government boundaries. Because of these ties, these other government folks may know a lot more about the real situation than their COs do!

One of your best sources of information about the company is straight from the contractor you'll be dealing with. Any company in business usually has publicly available catalogs, brochures, news releases, and the like, that contain a wealth of useful information. But the *best* way to get information on the company or the negotiator is one we often overlook: Simply ask them! We tend to shy away from asking questions, especially ones we don't think will be answered or will offend someone. If that's you, you've got to get over it. We'll discuss tips on *how* to ask questions later.

Government databases, such as the Central Contractor Registration (www.ccr.gov), and past performance databases from various government agencies, such as the Past Performance Information Retrieval System (PPIRS; www.ppirs.gov), can yield important information. Although PPIRS is quite robust, and more and more agencies are signing on to participate in it over time, we don't yet have one truly centralized government past performance database. So if your agency does not yet use PPIRS, you'll have to check your agency's particular system.

Also, be sure to check other agency systems that aren't in PPIRS yet for information on the contractor you'll be dealing with. You will be amazed at the useful information you can pull from just these past performance databases alone.

There are a host of private sources out there that compile information on companies that can be useful to you. Most of them are on the Web. You'll want to check out industry and trade association Web sites for the particular goods or services you're negotiating for. Other private database sources include Dun and Bradstreet (www.dnb.com) and the Thomas Register (www.thomasregister.com).

Finally, another fantastic source of information, particularly on a company, is the Internet. Just punch the company name into a search engine like Google and you'll be amazed at the information that will pop up. Many times you can get similar results searching on the name of the negotiator you'll be dealing with. Also be sure to do a search of the topic (the goods or services) you'll be negotiating for. This search should bring up useful Web sites, like professional organizations.

INFO-GATHERING TIPS

Quite frankly, I don't think government negotiators, as a whole, do a good job researching the other side before negotiations—and it's not from the lack of accessible information. The most common reason I hear from government negotiators for this lack of in-depth research on the other side prior to negotiations is *time*. A common observation goes something like, "Yes, I know I should devote more research into this negotiation, and in an ideal world I would, *but I just don't have enough time.*" There always seems to be a short time fuse on what you're asked to negotiate, and then there's all the other work you have.

Sound familiar? I'm sure I'm guilty of using these same excuses for not doing in-depth research when I was a government negotiator. And they're not just excuses; there's some truth behind the time constraints you face today as a government negotiator. But do you see how important it is to gather this information and do this research so that you can achieve a best-value solution for your customer and the taxpayer?

You know you should do the research; you know it will result in you doing a better negotiation job, but you have these nasty time constraints. What to do? You've got to learn to use your limited time wisely and learn to develop shortcuts that get to the essential information you need quickly and efficiently. Here are a few suggestions to accomplish this.

First, just as you do for negotiations, treat researching the other side as a *process*, not an event. Break it into bite-size chunks. If you set aside, for example, a particular day to cram it all in and "get that block checked," you'll get bored, frustrated, and you'll miss a lot of important information. If you plan just one day, or hour, to get that information, your information-gathering antenna most likely will shut down after this time and you'll miss the stuff that pushes its way to you automatically or by accident.

So, pace yourself. Cut the research into manageable chunks and stretch it out. In addition, be aware that some of the information you need could find its way to you without you seeking it. Always be in information-receive mode.

Second, don't kill yourself trying to find this information. Remember to tailor your research effort to the situation. Your time, energy, and effort have a real dollar cost, not only to you personally, but to your agency and the taxpayer. So don't spend an inordinate amount of time doing elaborate research for small-dollar, non-complex negotiations.

Tailor the amount and complexity of your research effort to the dollar value and complexity of what you are doing. You can also cut down on effort if you already have experience with the company or their negotiator, or know a trusted source who does. You're an important asset, so try to manage your vital time wisely.

Third, don't be afraid to ask questions directly to the contractor! You're using the power of basic human nature here. Most human beings have a natural tendency to help people they see as less informed—or weaker, or less knowledgeable, or even less intelligent than they are. They can't help it; it makes them feel superior, or at least good inside.

One way to create this perception (of being less informed) is to admit you don't have all the answers. Use this weakness as a strength by phrasing questions such as, "I don't understand your market. What kind of competition do you have? Please help me." Admitting you don't know all the answers humanizes you. You're no longer "the bureaucratic, all-knowing government." It makes people more receptive to you.

When you ask questions, make sure never to phrase them so that you get a simple yes or no answer. Encourage elaboration. Ask open-ended questions.

When you ask for help, you're also tapping into our natural human tendency to talk about ourselves and what's important to us. Even if you don't get a direct answer when you ask a question, you gain information. You now know they won't answer that question for some reason, and you can note the negotiator's reaction to being asked for more information. You can also use questions to confirm information you already know and to gauge whether someone will be truthful with you.

By the way, once you ask a question, *be quiet*. The vast majority of us aren't great listeners, but it's a habit you need to develop if you want to be a successful negotiator. Resist the urge to elaborate or butt in after you've asked a question. You can't learn anything from talking, only from listening. By *listening*, you pick up a lot more information than just the little tidbit of information you asked for.

Unintentional slips, verbal intonations, or a certain emphasis could send a message quite different from the words being spoken. Train yourself not only to hear what is being said, but to hear what isn't being said. Regardless of whether you realize it, your negotiation has already started when you start asking questions and researching the other party.

We've assembled our team, gathered market research data about our customer's requirement, established our prenegotiation objectives, and researched the other party's company and lead negotiator. Chapter 7 will take us into the next step: developing the negotiation plan.

Chapter 7

Developing the Negotiation Plan

Your negotiation plan is *how* you are going to go about achieving your prenegotiation objectives—your blueprint for the actual negotiation event. When written down, it's the document that pulls together all the things we've discussed so far into a logical process that can be implemented. The quality of your negotiation plan is always directly related to how successful you'll be during negotiations. Of course, you, as the government lead negotiator, are responsible (with the help of your team) for developing the plan, so how do you do it and what does it include?

Many government agencies have their own excellent template negotiation plans for you to use. There are also quite a few good plan templates created by authors and available to you through books or the Internet. Although these plans vary in details, most good ones will, at a minimum, cover the following areas:

- Objective statement

- Background information

- Team members

- Negotiation objectives

- Major issues

- Negotiation strategy

- Schedule and logistics considerations.

OBJECTIVE STATEMENT

The plan should start off by describing the *overall objective* of the negotiation. Why are you taking all this time? What end are you seeking? Just as an organization needs a clear, concise vision statement, the negotiation plan needs a similar objective statement to add focus to the plan, to provide a rally point for the team, and to provide a road map for the negotiation.

FAR Part 15 tells us that the primary objective of negotiations is to obtain the *best value* for the government, price and other factors considered, based on the requirement and the evaluation factors set forth in the solicitation. You'll want to be a bit more specific when you formulate your negotiation plan objective statement, homing in on your particular requirement. But don't get carried away; this should be a summary, at a high level, of your overall negotiation objective.

The objective statement is where you should discuss broad goals like overall dollar objectives, preferred contract type, contract financing terms, GFP, and other preferred business terms and conditions. Please remember your objective is to get best value at a fair and reasonable price to *both* parties. Your objective is not to try to "hammer" the contractor in negotiations so you can brag about how much you got them down or how clever a negotiator you are.

BACKGROUND INFORMATION

Next, your plan will include some brief background information related to the proposed acquisition, the contractor, and the overall negotiating environment or situation. Most of this information will come from work you have already done: the acquisition plan, the solicitation documents, your market research, forming your prenegotiation objectives, and your research into the other party.

The background information should make the rest of the negotiation plan (why you are doing what you are doing and why you are doing it a certain way) make sense. Talk about the general market environment. Discuss the level and amount of competition. Here's where I'd also put things like who the negotiators will be for the contractor, their job titles, the contractor's previous history with you, and the like. Again, you don't have to write a book here. A good, brief summary will do.

TEAM MEMBERS

Next, the plan should indicate the names, positions, and roles and responsibilities of the members of your negotiation team. Remember, your team may include people who will not actually be with you during the negotiation meeting. What we're talking about here is the people who will actually be in the room with you. Here's where you determine who will be your technical experts for issues, your "technocrats," your "good cop" and "bad cop," your "sweeper," and the like. These will be your actors to carry out your strategy and tactics. We'll talk about assigning negotiating roles later in the book.

One team member that *must* be included in this plan, and is often overlooked, is the meeting minutes keeper or note taker. Do you think it's a good idea to have detailed notes taken as discussions progress and agreements are reached, changed, renegotiated, modified, and finally reached again? Do you think you, or any other member of your negotiation team, can carry out their assigned roles and take official, detailed notes of the whole negotiation at the same time—and do a good job at both? Folks, don't do this to your people or yourself! Think ahead and have someone not involved in the negotiations there to take notes.

Many people ask me if it's OK to bring a tape recorder and tape the negotiation session. You can do this if you get written permission from everyone who will be in the room. Check the particulars with your legal folks, but I don't recommend it. Knowing you're being taped has, in my opinion, a certain intimidating effect on people, even if it's on a subconscious level. I believe it inhibits the free flow of information and can mask verbal clues that can be important to you during negotiations. In my opinion, it's more of a detriment than a plus.

By the way, every good plan has backups. I suggest you include possible alternate team members in your plan to cover contingencies such as absences. I also use this section of the plan to state that all team members have been properly briefed on procurement integrity, limits on exchanges, limits on authority, nondisclosure of proprietary and source selection information, and ethics.

NEGOTIATION OBJECTIVES

Next, the plan will include your specific negotiation objectives for each issue. Here you'll lay out your prenegotiation positions (MIN, MAX, and TGT) in priority order, issue by issue. For example, issue 1 will be your *most* important issue and you will discuss it completely before moving to issue 2, and so forth. Remember to include both your "must" and "give" points. Obviously, your "give" points will be last on the list. Now, this doesn't mean you have to discuss the issues in this order during the negotiation. The strategy you pick—and we'll discuss this later—will set the discussion priority.

Remember that MIN, MAX, and TGT are your government positions on each issue. You'll also want to include the contractor's anticipated positions on these issues. Most of this information will come from your assessment of the contractor's proposal and your research into the contractor's likely strategy based on their interests. It's a guess, but if you've done your homework, it can be a very educated guess.

Then lay out the results of the government's technical evaluation of the contractor's proposal for that issue. You can take them right out of the technical evaluation report or simply reference the report. These are your strengths, deficiencies, weaknesses, and so forth. Personally, I briefly summarize these in my plan and then refer the reader to the technical evaluation report for more detailed information.

Next you'll want to write down your assessment of each side's relative bargaining power for that issue. Examples of bargaining power are things like level of competition, expertise and knowledge, time constraints, quality and skills of the negotiators, risks, and so forth. This helps you get a grip on just how strong you are on each issue.

You've got, if you planned correctly, several "give" points on the bottom of your list that you can use as potential tradeoffs. I suggest going a step further and identifying, *for each issue*, potential items within the issue that can be traded off. Obviously, the most common one subject to tradeoff is price. This is why you have MIN and MAX stances in the first place. You expect, and the other side will expect, some leeway on price. But also look at other things as potential tradeoffs, like delivery dates, FOB points, warranties, financing, as well as technical considerations.

Naturally flowing from things you've identified as potential tradeoffs for each issue are some preplanned counteroffers in this section for each issue. Now, you already have three objectives (MIN, MAX, and TGT) for these issues, but I'm not talking about them. You never want to go straight to your TGT, for example, if the other side initially rejects your going-in position. These planned counters should be small tradeoffs you have already considered and discussed with your team that do not take away from your overall position, and usually should be comfortably under your TGT. For instance, providing financing or receiving some technical benefit for a gizmo may not be all that important to you (your "give" points), but it may be very important to the other side. Having the ability to "give up" these things may allow you to receive concessions in return in areas *you* care more about.

As stated earlier, every issue has a MIN, MAX, and TGT position. Every issue probably has "must" and "give" points. When you think of all the possible combinations and possible counters for them, you may start to feel overwhelmed. To keep your sanity and make your plan simple and executable, don't even try to come up with all the possible permutations of possible counteroffers. It's simply too difficult and the course of negotiations will be too unpredictable and dynamic to make this level of detailed planning of much use anyway. So keep your preplanned counters simple and keep them issue-specific, at least for your written negotiation plan.

The last item you should address in the negotiation objectives portion of your plan is which team member to assign to lead the discussion on each issue. Although you are the team leader and should initiate discussion on each issue to keep control of the pace and order of the negotiation, you won't be an expert on all the issues. You'll have to turn the technical issues over to your technical experts to discuss. For most of the business issues, you'll be the expert and will lead the discussion, but feel free to delegate technical issues to your technical folks and management issues to the program manager, for example. Make sure to assign these roles in writing and make sure that everyone understands which issues they are expected to take the lead on. After opening the issue, you will then call on that team member to take over. Just remember to keep overall control of the discussions so things don't get out of control. We'll talk about some techniques to do this when we talk about conducting negotiations later in the book.

MAJOR ISSUES

Let's see where we are. In developing our negotiation plan, we have written our objective statement, included our background information, listed our team members and their roles, and formulated our negotiation objectives for each issue we plan to discuss. The next section of the plan—major issues—will contain important factors that affect the entire negotiation, not just any one specific issue.

Because you have prepared the plan essentially issue by issue up to this point, this section of the plan should identify those things that *cut across boundaries*. Examples could be major terms and conditions proposed by the contractor that are different from what the government requested in the solicitation. Another example could be when the government has encouraged the contractor to propose alternative ways of solving a particular problem (like lease vs. purchase). How these are resolved could affect the entire negotiation and are not issue-specific.

In this section, also discuss any unique aspects of your requirement, such as quality assurance requirements or higher level quality control requirements. I frequently include avoidance points in this section too. *Avoidance points* are things you don't want anyone on your team to mention. You don't want the subject to come up because you already know you are weak in that position, or you know it is a "must" point for the government that could be a potential deal-breaker. Put major points of disagreement between the government and the contractor in this section, including how far apart the two sides are on the issue.

I always use the major issues section to link my negotiation plan to the source selection plan. Your source selection plan is done prior to releasing the solicitation in competitive acquisitions. Each agency has certain dollar levels that will trigger writing one of these plans. This plan lists things such as your evaluation factors for award, how important they were, and how you were going to trade off price to achieve superior results on the non-price factors that were important to you. Obviously, these price and non-price factors can shift dramatically as a result of negotiations, so you want to make sure the direction of the movement is consistent with your source selection plan.

After discussions, you will ask the contractor to submit a revised final proposal, based on what went on in discussions, and the give-and-take on issues that resulted accordingly. You then have to conduct a completely new technical and business review and analysis of that revised proposal. Linking your negotiation plan to your source selection plan will keep your team on track and make this second round of reviews easier.

NEGOTIATION STRATEGY

The next step is to develop your negotiating strategy. Formulating your strategy simply builds on all you've done up to this point. Strategy is the vehicle that you will use to achieve your negotiation objectives. It is your overall plan to address the issues, conduct the negotiations, and control the negotiation process. To choose an effective strategy and then use tactics to achieve it, you have to have a clear understanding about your strengths as opposed to the strengths of the other side. No strategy can be correctly chosen or successfully carried out without understanding this concept of *bargaining power*.

Assess Bargaining Power

Before you can properly choose an overall strategy for the negotiation, you must know where you stand in comparison with who you'll be dealing with. Which side has the most power (the most negotiation leverage) going in to the negotiation? Your answer to this question will guide you toward a negotiation strategy. Here's a list of the major categories of bargaining power that can affect negotiations:

- The power of legitimacy

- The power of competition

- The power of time

- The power of expertise

- The power of risk tolerance

- The power of precedent

- The power of options.

Some authors have suggested more categories, but these are the main ones you will have to consider in government negotiations.

The first is the *power of legitimacy*. Which side is perceived to be more legitimate? Here, you'll have most of the power simply because you represent the government. What could be more legitimate than that? This simple fact gives you an immense advantage in negotiations: You're on the side that made the rules. If contractors want to play, they *must* play your way and by your rules. The FAR is the rule book, and you represent that rule book.

Legitimacy can also be established by official titles and positions. For instance, "Contracting Officer for the United States of America" can be very intimidating to contractors first doing business with the government. I once dealt with a new contractor who actually thought I had deputized arrest power and could throw him in jail on the spot if he did something I considered wrong. To him, contracting officer meant contracting *officer*, as in police officer. Now *that's* bargaining power! By the way folks, don't overuse or abuse your legitimate power in situations like that. Remember: fair and reasonable to *both* parties!

Legitimate power in the form of titles and positions can work against you too. If you were a new negotiator, don't you think you'd be a *little* intimidated if your counterpart is president, CEO, or senior fellow, or has some series of important-looking letters after his or her name? But don't be overawed by titles and other trappings of legitimate corporate power; they can be deceiving.

When I started my first consulting partnership, we had a very impressive address in a major corporate high-rise building in a major city. We had a secretary to answer our calls and let only the important ones through. Everyone who dealt with us got the impression we were a multimillion dollar company because we had all the trappings.

Actually, we didn't have any office space in that impressive building. We simply paid a small fee for a "virtual office," complete with an answering service that "played secretary" for us. Of course, this service did the same for many other small businesses with virtual offices in that building. Our company was identified simply by a light on a console, so the secretary would use the correct business name when he or she answered. But, hey, our business cards were impressive, and people thought we must be really busy and important if we had to have a secretary screen our calls.

Everything is not always as it seems, and power is effective only if the other side *perceives* it as power.

Another form of legitimate power—and this one is uncannily effective—is the power of the printed word. Most people tend to believe anything they see in writing, especially standard forms or signs, even if they would question the information if they just heard about it. For some reason, we are conditioned to assume printed words have authority, or legitimacy.

Here's an example I read about that illustrates this point. Back in the 1980s, illegal drug smuggling by car up Interstate 95 out of Florida was reaching epidemic proportions. To stem the tide, Florida state troopers put to use the unquestioned legitimacy of the written word. They posted a sign along I-95 that said: PREPARE TO STOP. RANDOM DRUG SEARCH. ROADBLOCK 2 MILES AHEAD. Now, there really was no roadblock two miles ahead. Stopping cars for random drug searches was illegal in Florida at that time.

What was also illegal, however, was making a U-turn across the median of the interstate. Cars running drugs would see the sign, panic, and make an illegal U-turn. Craftily posted patrol cars would then pull over the cars for the illegal turn and subsequently "find" the drugs. Hundreds of drug runners were caught this way before the courts made Florida stop the practice.

Here's another example I heard of during my Air Force days. I can't vouch for its veracity, but it does illustrate the point. Have you ever seen, at airports, those trucks with the big FOLLOW ME signs on the back? They're used to escort arriving planes to their proper parking places. An Air Force officer had instructed an airman to take the base's FOLLOW ME truck into the local town for some minor maintenance. The airman didn't take the FOLLOW ME sign off the back of the truck. As the airman drove through town toward the garage, he picked up a string of cars that dutifully stayed right with him through every turn he made. When he arrived at the garage, he had a string of cars behind him lined up like ducks. One driver actually got out of his car and asked, "Hey, what are we supposed to do now?"

The lesson here is: *Use your legitimate power.* Put things in writing. Look at the mind-boggling number and variety of standard government forms you can whip out. Use your title, but don't be intimidated by the contractor's titles or written "standard procedures."

Another power you'll have to assess is the *power of competition.* If you have other offerors competing for the contract, the power of competition is on your side. If you have little competition or are in a sole-source situation, the other side has more power. The government, of course, has enshrined this power of competition into its acquisition policies and procedures. Simply following the already established rules gives you significant power when you strive for "full and open competition."

Time is another power that can work either for or against you. Who is up against the shorter deadline? The contractor may be under intense pressure to capture a certain amount of business by a certain date. They may have other important projects to which they need to divert their top negotiation team members by a certain time or lose that business.

You, of course, may be under time pressures too, which gives the *other* side bargaining power. What's your customer's delivery date requirement? How critical is it? Are you getting pressure from "on high" to get something contracted quickly for some reason or another? And an all too common pressure: When do your funds expire?

If one side feels the other side has more technical knowledge, experience (both technical and in negotiating), or superior information, that other side now has considerable *expert power.* Who knows the business better? Your technical experts or theirs?

The side that can afford to take more risk accrues *risk tolerance power.* Now, there are a lot of ways to mitigate risks to both sides—contract type, price and cost ceilings, and so forth—but neither side can totally eliminate contract risk. Your willingness to accept risk and uncertainty versus the contractor's risk tolerance will affect the balance of power.

You have already done most of the work to assess *precedent power*. Unless conditions have changed dramatically, a contractor will be hard pressed to justify huge price increases not in line with previous contract award amounts. They have established a pattern, a precedent. Remember, though, you have too, by agreeing to those contracts.

Finally, there is power in having *options*. If the government has an alternative source or method for the contractor's product or service, or if they can do it in-house, you have power. If the contractor doesn't *really* need the government's business (for example, they have a robust commercial market to which they can turn), then *they* have power. In their book *Getting to Yes* (Penguin Books, 1981), Roger Fisher and William Ury used the term *BATNA* ("best alternative to a negotiated agreement") to describe these options. We'll discuss BATNAs and how they are useful next.

Bottom line: You'll choose your negotiation strategy based on your assessment of the power you have versus the power the contractor has (in other words, relative power). You'll then adjust it if necessary to take into account the contractor's likely strategy and your BATNA. So, what's a BATNA anyway and why do you need one?

Establish Your BATNA

Simply put, your BATNA is your walk-away point. It's your next best alternative if you cannot reach an acceptable agreement during negotiations. To develop your BATNA, simply ask yourself: At what point is it no longer worthwhile to continue negotiating? Your BATNA is usually somewhere near your bottom line, but it doesn't have to necessarily *be* your bottom line.

In competitive negotiations, your BATNA could simply be to go with another offeror's proposal. Or it could be to cancel the solicitation and resolicit with changes or modifications to your requirement. In noncompetitive negotiations, your BATNA could be to do the work in-house. To establish your BATNA, you simply list all your choices short of reaching an agreement with the contractor and pick the best one. Now you have a BATNA.

If you think about it, a BATNA is really a measure of how much power one side has over the other—*relative power*. This power, as we have seen, is created through alternatives, or options. If you have more choices than I do, your BATNA will be stronger than mine.

The contractors will also have alternatives, so, if they're smart, they will come into the negotiation with a BATNA too. Examples of a contractor's BATNA could be the point at which their money, time, and effort could yield a better return elsewhere, rather than agreeing to your negotiated price. They may have commercial customers they can substitute for you. Remember, part of researching the other party we went over earlier dealt with trying to figure out the contractor's alternatives—identifying *their* BATNA.

During the give-and-take of negotiations, information is shared that might not have been available or easily gathered during your negotiation preparation. Any time additional information is presented, it may affect each side's BATNA. You may learn, for instance, that the contractor has fewer options than you thought they had. Conversely, you may learn that an alternative source for the goods or services you are seeking has dried up. So keep in mind that BATNAs are dynamic; you may have to shift yours during negotiations.

How do BATNAs help you? What purpose do they serve? Well, first of all, your BATNA serves as a standard against which to measure any proposed agreement. It prevents you from accepting an agreement with unfavorable terms. The very process of negotiations, especially the time and effort you have put in, may make you *too* committed to reaching *some* kind of agreement, even if it's not favorable. Having a BATNA protects you against this trend. Remember, every award you make must, according to the FAR, be fair and reasonable. Having a BATNA helps prevent you from making an award that is not fair and reasonable.

Comparing the other side's proposed solution with your BATNA can also give you clues on what to counter with to improve the terms of agreement. Finally, going into a negotiation already knowing what you will do if you fail to reach agreement can make you a more confident negotiator. You have less fear of the unknown, and you can settle down and concentrate on getting what's right for your customer and the taxpayers.

Only now—now that you've assessed the relative power of both sides, considered the contractor's likely strategy, and developed your BATNA—are you ready to choose a strategy. After you choose a strategy, the choice of tactics to support that strategy falls out pretty simply. The choice of strategy is simple. You've already done most of the work. All you need to do is to choose the one that's right for the situation.

Choose a Strategy

In my opinion, there are four basic strategies from which you can choose:

1. WIN–LOSE strategy

2. Loss prevention strategy (also known as *defensive strategy*)

3. WIN–WIN strategy

4. WIN–win strategy (that's big win–little win)

Again, many authors and negotiation experts have come up with many different permutations of these over the years, but they pretty much all boil down to these four.

WIN–LOSE Strategy

This classic strategy sets you up to win at the expense of the other side. Now, notice we don't talk about LOSE–LOSE as a possible strategy. Unfortunately, that's one of the probable *outcomes* of a negotiation, but we aren't going to discuss it as a strategy you should choose to pursue. It indicates that both parties essentially "lose" potential gains by compromising. Nobody walks away satisfied.

WIN–LOSE, also known (depending on the author) as the *offensive strategy*, the *distributive strategy, positional bargaining, zero-sum*, or the *traditional strategy*, has gotten a lot of bad press over the years since the book *Getting to Yes* came out. Actually, in certain cases, the WIN–LOSE strategy might be the best strategy to pick to give you a practical and efficient agreement. It really *does* have its uses and place as a strategy to consider. It has been slammed in books by authors equating it to a very negative approach to negotiating. However, if you consider that most people perceive negotiation as being an exercise of getting the most gain for the least expense, it fairly defines WIN–LOSE.

If, after your assessment of relative power, you feel you have the preponderance of power, WIN–LOSE might be appropriate as a strategy. It allows you to make maximum use of your power edge in crafting an agreement that meets most, or all, of your "must" points, and even many of your "give" points—at close to your minimum objective for price. As long as you can find the price fair and reasonable to both sides, you're free to use WIN–LOSE as a strategy. This is particularly true if you perceive the contractor's going-in position to be unreasonable. In this case, you *want* them to lose on that point!

The WIN–LOSE strategy is also highly effective if your analysis reveals that the negotiation objectives of the parties are pretty much *mutually exclusive*. You are able to realize your negotiation objectives, but almost entirely at the other party's expense. Despite all the press WIN–WIN has gotten during the past few years, you'll find WIN–LOSE is still pretty prevalent in government negotiations, especially when you are in a competitive situation. You want to pay less; the contractor wants to charge more. Your objectives and the contractor's, in a competitive environment, tend to be more mutually exclusive simply by virtue of the government source selection process. You can't make major changes in your objectives to address deeper interests (more about that when we talk about WIN–WIN), because you then have to give all offerors a chance to propose on the revised requirements to keep a level competitive playing field.

With the WIN–LOSE *approach*, both sides will assess strengths and weaknesses, and will set objectives for each negotiation point. They'll have a firm "going-in" position, and a limit beyond which they won't go. Both parties usually open with extreme positions, knowing that, through the give-and-take of negotiations, an agreement will likely be reached relatively close to their desired outcome. The negotiation, then, is about the tactics used by each party to maximize power to attain their goals. Reaching an agreement usually comes down to whether the negotiation range of both parties overlaps somewhere. That's the zone of potential agreement.

In WIN–LOSE, you will do your best to learn the other side's true objective, or position, while at the same time doing your best to conceal your own. You'll use the information flow during the negotiation, both to you and from you, to strengthen your own BATNA while trying to weaken theirs.

So, WIN–LOSE can be used when you have most of the bargaining power, objectives are mutually exclusive, the contractor is being unreasonable, and the short-term results of the negotiation are more important than a long-term relationship with that particular contractor.

Loss Prevention Strategy

Loss prevention is a defensive strategy you'll use only if you perceive the other side has the predominant balance of power. You may find yourself, for instance, in a sole-source environment and you *must* have what the contractor is offering. In this case, the balance of power is definitely in favor of the other side and your objectives, as opposed to *their* objectives, will usually be at odds. If you find yourself in this position, try the following *strategic points.*

First, arrange your issues in the order of *least to greatest* importance to you. You can also arrange them by your perception of ease of agreement. The things you think will be easy to agree to should come first. Both of these strategies get the other side used to saying "yes." The more "yeses" you have, the least likely (hopefully) it will be for the other side to want to break the synergy with a "no." The more "yeses" you can get the other side to say, the more tension is eased. Something about saying the word *yes* out loud works on the mind. Even if you are simply getting the other side to agree to their own position by saying yes, something magical starts to happen. The more "yeses" you get them to say, the softer they become. Simply getting them to agree to your draft agenda for negotiations can be your first yes. You're already starting to condition them to say yes!

Next, try to create options. Don't immediately sacrifice your goals; try to expand them or explore other ways to get to them. Use "what if" when you present your suggestions. This is know as a *trial balloon* and we'll talk more about it when we discuss strategies in depth. If you don't think you can win on one point, bring in several points that may set up both of you as winners. But be careful! Because of the nature of government acquisition, this may be hard to do without breaking competition rules. You might want to run the strategy by your legal counsel. In any case, your goal is to keep the other side negotiating. This may shift the power of time (as we discussed earlier) more to your side. It also allows you to use the tactic of time investment effectively, which is something we'll talk about in a little bit.

Finally, don't forget your BATNA. We've talked about how to create one and what it can do for you, so use it if you have to! Remember, your BATNA protects you from making an agreement you should reject. It's the standard you have created and against which you will measure *any* agreement. When you use the loss prevention strategy, you sometimes may have to walk away. As a matter of fact, in government contracting, you must *never* agree to a price or arrangement that you, as a CO, cannot find fair and reasonable.

You want to also consider the *other side's* BATNA. If they are in such a strong negotiation position, why are they negotiating at all? Maybe you are not in as bad a position as you think. They could have been overly optimistic when they weighed their own alternatives for reaching an agreement. So try to learn as much as possible about their alternatives. If you think their BATNA is overly optimistic or too simplistic, use any additional information you pick up to lower their BATNA expectations and strengthen yours.

So, the *approach* you should use when you're in a weak bargaining position should maximize the strengths you *do* have and should attempt to lower, in the other side's eyes, the desirability of the alternatives they are relying on as *their* BATNA. Remember these additional loss prevention approaches:

1. Never act weak, unless it's a part of your tactics (we'll discuss this later).

2. Consult outside experts. They may come up with a creative solution you haven't thought of.

3. Consider adding to your team. Bring in new strengths and talent.

4. Use your weakness as a strength; learn to say "help me." With this approach you will tap in to a natural tendency for humans to want, even subconsciously, to help people they consider worse off than they are. It makes them feel good, and in their act of kindness, pity (call it what you will), they usually will help you out more than they really planned. Spouses use this approach on each other all the time!

Lastly, use the tools that are uniquely available to you as a government negotiator to limit your liability and risk, and to encourage the possibility of competition. Here's some examples:

- *Require cost or pricing data, or information other than cost or pricing data.* On certain contracts, cost or pricing data are required (sometimes even certified cost or pricing data). Most contracts and modifications, however, are exempt from you asking for cost or pricing data. However, you can always ask for information other than cost or pricing data if you need it to determine a price to be fair and reasonable. This can force the contractor to show you what cards they're playing! See FAR Part 15 for more information on this.

- *Select the appropriate contract type.* You have more than 20 different contract types and variations from which to choose, and you can mix and match them to create an almost endless array of contract types. Each contract type defines a unique risk-sharing relationship between both parties. For example, you'll want to push for a cost reimbursement-type contract if the work can't be defined clearly.

- In sole-source situations, remind the other party you have to complete a *justification for other than full and open competition.* Make sure they know that part of that justification is a section that discusses the steps you will take to foster competition in the future. Sometimes just mentioning this will change attitudes.

- Remind the other side you must prepare *a past performance report* at the end of the contract. Make sure they understand the contents of this report are subjective and can include things such as "willingness to cooperate."

- Inform the other side that you cannot, under law, ever award a contract at prices or terms you do not consider to be *fair and reasonable.* And who determines fair and reasonable? You do!

WIN–WIN Strategy
This is the negotiation strategy that's gotten all the press during the last few years. And it just sounds good. WIN–WIN. Everybody wins! But not so fast …

As mentioned earlier, in 1981, a 200-page paperback book written by Fisher and Ury—*Getting to Yes*—quickly became a national bestseller. It immediately had a *huge* impact on how negotiations were conducted in the commercial marketplace and, if I remember correctly, made the crossover to affect government negotiations around the 1987–1988 time frame. All of you, if you don't already, need to own a copy of that book.

In *Getting to Yes*, the authors pointed out that the predominant style of negotiating (they called it the *confrontational method* or *positional bargaining*) was not the best way for either party to get what they wanted. Their book recommended replacing positional bargaining with a new method of negotiation they called *principled negotiation* or *negotiating on the merits*. If done correctly, they argued, principled negotiation could result in *both* sides getting what they wanted—a true WIN–WIN situation. Hence, we had the birth of the WIN–WIN, or problem-solving, strategy.

In classic WIN–WIN, you focus on interests, not on positions. Both sides work *together* to satisfy each other's needs. You also use open communication to share your needs with each other. Instead of splitting up the "pie" (the thing you're negotiating for) between the sides, resulting in no one side getting all they want, you collaborate to make the pie bigger, so everybody can get all they want.

The example the authors use is one I'm sure most of you have heard: Two children are quarreling over an orange. Using the old art of positional bargaining, they decided to divide the orange in half (splitting the "pie"). But who gets to cut? Finally they come up with this solution: The one who does *not* cut gets to pick the first half. Pretty smart, huh? Well, the orange is halved. The first child takes his half and immediately eats the fruit and throws the peel away. The second child takes his half, throws away the fruit and uses the peel for a recipe. As Fisher and Ury say: "Too many negotiators end up with half an orange for each side instead of the whole fruit for one and the whole peel for the other" (Penguin Press, 1981, p. 57). Had the children collaborated, they could have expanded the pie instead of splitting it, and both sides would have been better off.

So, in WIN–WIN, *power* is not that big of a player because you don't try to use it against each other. Instead, both parties realize that they have *shared objectives*, not mutually exclusive positions. The strategic points that naturally follow are:

- A focus on mutual interests, not mutually exclusive and conflicting positions

- Effective listening to determine the *interests* behind the positions

- Working together, not against each other, to come up with creative solutions.

But—and this is crucial—for the WIN–WIN strategy to work, *both* parties need to agree to use it. Both parties have to play by the WIN–WIN rules. Here's a tip. If you are all sunshine and lollipops about WIN–WIN and the other side is pumping WIN–WIN right back at you, but secretly planning a WIN–LOSE strategy, you're going to get *hammered* in negotiations. So, for WIN–WIN to work, both sides have to trust each other. You've got to focus on interests, not positions. And you've got to be committed to seek out creative solutions actively that are best for both sides.

Now, although I hear government negotiators talking about WIN–WIN all the time, please realize Fisher and Ury didn't write *Getting to Yes* for a *government* audience. There are serious obstacles to putting the WIN–WIN strategy to use in the government contracting arena.

First, there's the history of government/industry relations. It used to be *horrible*. We had a very adversarial relationship with our contractor base. That's the reason we came up with things like cost accounting standards, cost or pricing data, and all those certification requirements. They didn't like us and we didn't trust them. It's gotten a whole lot better now, but some hard cases on both sides will always remain wary of WIN–WIN because of history.

Next, contractors are trained on WIN–LOSE gamesmanship. They're taught all the "tricks of the trade" to maximize that shareholder wealth we talked about earlier. To make matters worse, the *government* side lacks truly effective training on WIN–WIN. Have any of you received any training on this before you had to negotiate? Probably not. Government training, when it exists, is still heavy on positions and positional bargaining, not what Fisher and Ury would call *principled negotiation.*

Another obstacle to WIN–WIN is sometimes your own bureaucracy and upper management. You may want to try a WIN–WIN approach, but your upper management (who were around in the dinosaur days when we had an adversarial relationship with our contractor base) may veto that approach. "You can never trust those cheating, nasty, blankety-blank contractors!" You've probably heard something like that or close to it.

Finally, federal law itself often precludes truly innovative WIN–WIN solutions like the ones outlined it *Getting to Yes.* Without going into any great detail, there are laws, applicable only to government acquisitions, that effectively restrict long-term investment, restrict multiple-contract deals, and restrict innovative cash flow solutions such as contract financing and advance payment. These are all-important tools that allow the negotiation flexibility that WIN–WIN requires. So, WIN–WIN is an ideal, but in reality it's a rarity in its pure form in government contract negotiations.

WIN–Win Strategy
A variant of the WIN–WIN strategy was brought up by Ron Shapiro and Mark Jankowski in their book *The Power of Nice* (Wiley & Sons, 2001). By the way, don't let the title fool you; this is another must-have book for serious negotiators. In fact, here's a quote from their book that they call "the myth of WIN–WIN":

> Negotiation experts (and amateurs) have been preaching WIN–WIN for some time. The trouble is, it's unrealistic. The expression WIN–WIN has become more of a pop cliché than

a negotiating philosophy. It's either a winner's rationalization for lopsided triumph, a loser's excuse for surrender, or both sides' phrase for when everybody is equally unhappy. There's no such thing as both parties winning identically, that is, both getting all of what they want. One party is bound to get more and one less, even if both sides are content with the outcome. The latter is possible. Both parties can be satisfied, but both cannot win to the same degree. (p. 45)

Folks, does this make sense, even at the expense of throwing some cold water on the WIN–WIN negotiation philosophy? What Shapiro and Jankowski are talking about is another form of negotiation strategy. It's called WIN–win (big win for you, little win for them; or, simply, big win–little win). With this strategy, either side may have the predominant position of *power*. Relative power is a player, but it is not the overriding factor. The same goes for *interests*. They may overlap, intertwine, or be totally mutually exclusive.

With WIN–win, we achieve all or most of our goals while letting the other side achieve *some* of their goals. Now, all the same *strategic points* of WIN–LOSE can be used, but you also take action to satisfy the other party's interests. You probe the other side's position to determine what the other side really wants. Once you figure it out, you satisfy your interests *well* and their interests *acceptably*. Because you have allowed their side to achieve interests that are important to them, they walk away feeling as if they have won! Now do you see why it is so dangerous to attempt WIN–WIN if the other side is secretly planning WIN–win or WIN–LOSE?

The WIN–win negotiation *approach* includes the following:

1. Never make the first offer. It's a negotiating axiom that the person who puts the first number on the table loses. The other side, if they're smart, will immediately use the tactic of bracketing your number. We'll discuss bracketing when we get to tactics.

2. Never accept their first offer. We'll teach you how when we describe the vise tactic a little later.

3. Ferret out their true interests, and satisfy them, but not at the expense of *your* goals.

So, to recap, there are four basic negotiation strategies: WIN–LOSE, loss prevention, WIN–WIN, and WIN–win. Now in reality, most negotiations are a complex combination of these four strategies, and yours has to be able to change quickly to adapt to new situations or information. Because of this, you have to know how to apply all four strategies equally well.

Let's take a quick look at where we are. In developing the negotiation plan, we've covered the four types of strategies you can use and when to use which one. In a little while, we'll go over some *tactics* to back up your strategies, but first let's finish our negotiation plan by talking about *schedule and logistics considerations*.

SCHEDULE AND LOGISTICS CONSIDERATIONS

In this last section of your negotiation plan, you'll draw up your anticipated schedule of events leading up to and ending in the completed negotiation, with anticipated times for major milestones along the way. You'll also address logistics issues—those little details that can create or frustrate a smooth negotiation event.

More than likely, your agency's FAR Supplement will require you to get some kind of higher level approval of your prenegotiation objectives and your negotiation plan, so prepare for it and build that time into your schedule. The approval process may be done orally or in writing. You need to make sure your management understands and approves of your objectives, issues, selection of team members, roles, schedules, and planned concessions. Some of your agencies already have templates they want you to use for this approval process to make sure you cover all the bases they want you to cover.

Folks, use this approval process to catch errors and to get a feel for how much negotiation room, or leeway, you have been given by your upper management. This, in turn, will strengthen your confidence at the negotiation table—and confidence is a key ingredient to a successful outcome. During my career, I've heard some COs grumble at the thought that someone else has to review their work—"micromanage them," they say—especially if the action to be negotiated is within their warrant level. Please don't take this attitude.

When you're preparing for negotiations, you want to use every extra set of eyes and every additional brain possible to make sure you're truly ready, haven't missed anything, and are thinking clearly. Even the experts mess up. And the other side is doing the same thing. Most likely they've already subjected their negotiation plan to several reviews, including what's called a *red team review* of disinterested third parties. They're going to be *ready*. You should be happy to accept any additional help you can to get ready too.

As far as the location of the negotiation site, you will usually have home court advantage because you are the government and the buyer. Don't let the other side talk you into conducting the negotiation at their place or even a neutral location unless it absolutely can't be helped. *You want home court advantage.* With home court advantage, you'll be more comfortable and confident. You also are surrounded by your trappings of power as a government negotiator (remember, legitimate power). You have better control over time, quicker access to information, and, more important, you have control over your physical surroundings. We'll talk more about what an advantage that can be when we discuss tactics.

Make sure to line up your supporting cast prior to the meeting. I'm not talking here about your negotiating team. You want to have people available to take minutes, make copies, facilitate lunch, do quickly needed research or confirm data, and keep the room clean. Try not to delegate any of these functions to one of your negotiation team members. They'll be too busy to be distracted by these things. Plan ahead.

By the way, you *always* want to be the side that takes the official minutes. That won't usually be an issue because you are the government team and are expected to take the official minutes, but don't let the other side talk you into letting them "be nice" and take that "burden" away from you. Simple word choice or word placement or tiny word omissions can totally alter what you thought the agreement meant. You want to keep the "power of the pen."

Now, as far as the physical site, remember you usually will be the host, so *act* like a host. Make sure:

- The room is large enough.

- Lighting is adequate.

- There are enough chairs and they are comfortable.

- Table space is adequate.

- Audio/visual equipment is set up and working if it is needed.

- A second room is available for private caucuses.

- There is easy access to phones, computer lines, and so forth.

- Paper, pencils, and pens are available for each attendee, and extras are available.

- Essentials like coffee, snacks, restrooms, and so on, are available.

- Water, ice, and drinking glasses are available in the room.

- A large wall clock is available and can be seen by everyone in the room.

- Parking spaces and passes, if required, are prearranged for the other side's team members.

- Escorts are available for negotiations in secure or classified areas, and are available for the other side during breaks. Preferably, escorts should *not* be members of your own negotiation team. (You'll see why this is important later when we talk about the caucus tactic, the walk-in-the-woods tactic, and the concept of dividing and conquering.)

Who knows? Your graciousness may be rewarded by an unexpected concession from a contractor who feels obligated to reciprocate in some way. Don't laugh; it happens! We'll talk more about setting the stage for the negotiation later. After you've made all these arrangements, make sure they're reflected in your negotiation plan and all your team members have a copy so everybody knows what's going on.

Obviously, you won't send the other side a copy of your negotiation plan. You'll tell them what they need to know—and only what they need to know—when you send them a copy of your draft agenda, which we'll talk about a little later.

We've now finished our negotiation plan (whew!), except for identifying the preplanned tactics (which we'll discuss later). After you rehearse the plan and develop your agenda, which we'll talk about in the next chapter, you'll be ready—*finally*—to negotiate.

Chapter 8

Rehearsing the Negotiation Plan and Developing the Agenda

D on't "blow off" rehearsing your negotiation plan with your team members. You've spent a lot of time and brain power preparing for the negotiation, and the last thing you want is for sloppy execution to turn all this into wasted time and effort. The crucial step of rehearsing your negotiation plan is habitually ignored by even experienced COs, and it can cripple a negotiation.

Think about it. Your team is probably ad hoc (consisting of people from many different functional areas of your organization who have been put together as team for this negotiation only) and they simply aren't used to working together. Heck, you don't even know at this point if they *can* work together! The only way to get them accustomed to each other is to rehearse the plan.

Rehearsal will also give confidence to all the team members, uncover trouble spots, get folks used to following your directions and lead, and get everyone used to pulling together. I suggest you develop some sort of checklist, or rehearsal plan, that covers, as a minimum:

- Reviewing the negotiation plan and negotiation strategy

- Making sure everyone understands the roles of each team member

- Assigning homework to team members

- Conducting a mock negotiation session

- Reviewing government negotiation "do's" and "don'ts."

REVIEW THE NEGOTIATION PLAN AND NEGOTIATION STRATEGY

Sit your team down and review the negotiation plan and negotiation strategy with them. They may have had some input, but it is *you* that is ultimately responsible for bringing it to fruition. And higher level reviews may have changed certain aspects of the original plan. During the negotiation meeting, you don't want to be the only person on your team who understands the plan. Can you imagine a football team winning if only the quarterback knew the game plan and strategy?

Make sure all your team members know your general plan. What's going to be your opening statement? What tactic are you going to lead off with? What are your "give" points? What are your "must" points? In what priority are you planning to introduce them? What are your avoidance points and why are you avoiding them? And so on.

Give your team members a quick education on the type of strategy you have chosen (WIN–LOSE, loss prevention, WIN–WIN, WIN–win) and why you chose that particular strategy. You might even want to use tools you've picked up in this book to explain some of the approaches you'll use to implement the strategy.

Discuss your assessment of the relative power of each party and how you feel that should impact the negotiations. Let your team know what to expect from the other side, given their negotiation history. All this information will give them a better "feel" for the negotiation environment you're trying to create, so they can contribute to it, not pull against it.

MAKE SURE EVERYONE UNDERSTANDS THE ROLES OF EACH TEAM MEMBER

Everyone on your team should have already been assigned roles in preparing for the negotiation, as we've already discussed. You also will assign each member of your team roles to play during the negotiation. Because assigning these roles is part of the tactics of negotiation, we'll save this discussion for a little later. Right now, just know that your negotiation plan rehearsal gives you one last chance to make sure all your team members understand the roles you have assigned to them and how you expect them to play their roles.

Go one step further. Make sure everyone understands not only their particular roles, but everyone else's roles too.

ASSIGN HOMEWORK TO YOUR TEAM MEMBERS

You want all your team members to be totally prepared, as you are, for the negotiation, so you may have to assign them some homework. They need to have an in-depth understanding of your negotiation plan, the solicitation, the proposals, the source selection criteria, the other side's habits, and the general situation surrounding the negotiation. They're going to have to do some reading, usually on their own time, to be effective team members.

This can be a hard sell for government employees. You can "sell" this more easily if you let them know, right up front at the first kickoff meeting, that there will be homework reading required. Make sure their supervisors know too, so you can ensure their buy-in for the time their folks will have to put in and how important this is to a successful negotiation. I suggest even making it a part of your written agenda in your very first kickoff meeting—that way, nobody can say they were unaware of the requirement.

CONDUCT A MOCK NEGOTIATION SESSION

Sometimes you may want to conduct a mock negotiation session as part of your rehearsal. Truthfully, I have rarely seen this, and then only for complex, high-dollar negotiations. With the realities of federal contracting today, you just don't have time to do it all. However, if you do decide to enact some kind of mock negotiation session, make sure you assign someone to play *devil's advocate*— someone on your team, or an outsider, who pretends to be the contractor. His or her job is to poke holes in your plan, disrupt the flow of your mock session, throw in objections, introduce problems, and generally be disagreeable.

It's much better to grapple with these problems and how to work through them in front of a friendly audience instead of at the actual negotiation table. If you can afford the extra time, a mock session can not only be productive, it can be fun!

REVIEW GOVERNMENT NEGOTIATION "DO'S" AND "DON'TS"

During one of your negotiation preparation meetings, or when you assemble your team to rehearse for the first time, review the government "do's" and "don'ts" as they relate to negotiations. *You* know there are some things you simply cannot do as a government negotiator. *They* don't! They're not contracting folks. They need to know basic things like the following: You can't *lie* to the other side, even if you're using it as a tactic. It's okay on a cop show if you're trying to get a confession, but it's not okay for any federal official, even during negotiations.

The FAR calls the complete list of negotiation don'ts *limits on exchanges*, and you can find them in FAR 15.306(e). The FAR says any government person involved in negotiations can't engage in conduct that:

• Favors one offeror over another

- Reveals an offeror's technical solution or any information that would compromise that offeror's intellectual property to another offeror

- Reveals an offeror's price to *anyone* without their permission

- Reveals the names of individuals providing reference information about an offeror's past performance

- Knowingly furnishes source selection information in violation of the FAR and the law.

You're probably already very familiar with these things, but the rest of your team most likely isn't trained in contracting. Tell your team what they need to know to keep them out of trouble and to allow the negotiation to continue without a hitch. This is also a great time to rebrief the team on procurement integrity, ethics, and how to handle source selection information. Some COs I know make it a point to bring in lawyers to help them with this part. I think that's a great idea.

By accomplishing all these steps when you rehearse your plan, you're actually doing more than simply rehearsing your plan. You're giving your team practice in working together as a team before they actually have to do it in front of the other side. You're making sure your team will pull together, know what they're talking about, and know what *not* to do and say. If you impart this knowledge to your team in an agreeable way, it will also go a long way in helping establish your credibility as the expert in the *process* of negotiating, which will solidify in their minds that you are the leader of the negotiating team—and that is crucial to success.

DEVELOP A NEGOTIATION AGENDA

After you've finished your negotiation preparations and rehearsed the plan, your next step is to develop an agenda for the actual negotiation session. The agenda is a critical tool to get the negotiations started right, and to assert control over the pace and the process. The agenda will also be how you let the other side know critical things like location, time, access requirements, and the like, without giving them your entire negotiation plan.

Here's a crucial point: *Never* let the other side take control of setting or running the agenda. Remember, you want to keep the "power of the written word" as an important negotiation advantage. In fact, sending out your draft agenda for contractor comment may be your first preplanned tactic. If the contractor agrees to it, you have already started them in the habit of saying yes to you. If they disagree or provide comments or suggestions, they have just divulged additional information about their position you didn't have previously.

You can now use this additional information to your advantage to detect possible shifts of power. As a result, you may discover hidden agendas, or even have enough information to revise your BATNA or your opinion of theirs. Remember that information—*any* additional information—increases your negotiating power.

In your agenda, you'll first want to provide general information such as time, location, breaks, duration, points of contact, seating capacity, and so forth. Next, you select and list the negotiation issues you wish to discuss, in the priority that supports your strategy. Remember, contractor feedback about the items and issues you've said you want to discuss and their order of priority can give you valuable insight into *their* strategy, interests, priorities, and negotiation approach.

Don't leave the rest of your team members out of the process. Before you send the draft agenda to the contractor for review and comment, make sure your own team reviews it and makes suggestions.

You then should send it to the contractor in "draft" form, labeling it as a "proposed agenda." Make sure to give them enough time to respond. As you have already guessed, this draft agenda accomplishes more than just finalizing the order of events in the negotiation. You can use it as a fishing expedition!

When you send out your draft agenda, you'll also want to have the other side answer a few "procedural" questions. Have them tell you who their lead negotiator will be and what authority he or she has to finalize any agreements or changes you come up with during the negotiation session. This is important information, since you want to make sure their lead negotiator does indeed have authority to bind their company. This ensures that your negotiation session is truly conclusive, and prevents the other side from using a negotiation tactic called *ambiguous authority* against you, which we'll talk about later.

You also want to find out the title of their lead negotiator. I used to love negotiations when I found out the lead negotiator for the contractor was one of their marketing reps. Bad mistake! Think about it. What's the job of a marketing rep? To make promises to potential customers to capture more business. That's what they're trained to do, and usually their performance reports and bonuses are tied to how much business they can bring in. Their job is to make the other side happy. This puts them in a bad situation if they are also tapped to negotiate the final terms and conditions of a deal. They, in essence, have a built-in conflict of interest, don't they? Do you think they'll be hardball negotiators? Give me a negotiation with a marketing rep any day. If you find this to be the case, your negotiation power has just increased tremendously.

You'll also want to have the other side tell you how many people they plan on bringing to the negotiation, who these folks will be, and what expertise they represent. The main reason will be to make sure you have enough chairs, refreshments, and so forth, to accommodate them. Another reason is to make sure your team matches their expertise person for person. If one of their negotiation team members is a lawyer, for example, you might want to consider adding a lawyer of your own to your negotiation team. Knowing how many folks the other side is bringing also sets you up to use the tactic of *strength in numbers*, which we'll talk about later.

When you get your draft agenda back from the other side, with or without additional comments from them, you now can finalize the agenda. Remember the comments that come back on your draft agenda can give you additional insights into the other side, so look for these things first. If the other side has provided comments or suggestions, it doesn't necessarily mean you have to *change* your agenda; that's totally your call. Remember, *you* control the process!

Update your agenda based on the comments you have received (or not) and change it from "draft" to "final." Make sure to provide a copy to everyone who will attend the negotiation session on your side, a copy to key members of your supporting cast who may not actually participate in the negotiation (such as program folks), a copy to the contractor, and a copy to your boss.

Now you're ready to negotiate. You've assembled and briefed your team, done your data gathering, established your priorities and your prenegotiation objectives, and researched the other side. You've developed your negotiation plan, taking into account your assessment of power, and you've established a BATNA. You've picked a negotiation strategy and you've rehearsed it. Finally, you've developed an agenda to use as a road map for the negotiation session.

But before you sit down to negotiate, you need to be aware of certain negotiation tactics—some legitimate, some shady—that you can use or that may be used against you. That's the subject of the next part of this book.

Part Three

Negotiation Tactics

Chapter 9

Introduction to Tactics

In the next two parts of this book, we'll go over some of the most common tactics used in negotiations. We won't come close to covering *all* the tactics out there—there are literally hundreds of tactics and permutations of tactics—but these are the most common. Part Four contains common tactics you can use as a government negotiator. Of course, they can also be used against you. Part Five goes over some tactics that are considered anything from a little shady to downright unethical. These are the tactics you can't use as a government negotiator, but still can be used by the other side against you.

Remember, you have a special trust by virtue of being a government negotiator. You represent the federal government in your actions, and this can put you in a difficult negotiation position when it comes to tactics. You must be fair and reasonable to all parties—including the other side—which precludes you from using shady, misleading, unfair, or unethical tactics. But because the other side is not under the same requirement that you're under to be fair and reasonable to all parties, these tactics can definitely be used *against* you, and I bet some of them have been. Accordingly, even though you won't be able to use the tactics in Part Five, and may even be hesitant to use some of the tactics in Part Four, you at least need to *understand* them. In this way, you can recognize them for what they are if they're used against you, and use countermoves to negate their effect.

Obviously, it does no good to be able to recognize a tactic when it's being used against you, but not know how to do anything about it. So after discussing each tactic, we'll also discuss some of the most common countertactics (I call them simply *counters*) you can use to make the attempted tactic's effect null and void. We'll do this for every tactic in this book—both those you can use and those you can't. Knowing how to counter tactics used against you is just as important as knowing how to use the tactics yourself.

Most of the tactics we'll discuss have been around since the dawn of time. Ever since Eve negotiated sharing that apple with Adam, tactics have been used in negotiations. Tactics have been used to start wars and end wars. Tactics have been used instinctively by every child ever born when "negotiating" with parents—usually very successfully! Of course, these tactics have evolved and have been refined throughout the years, but the basics have always been with us.

Please understand that not all tactics are bad and manipulative, and it's okay for you to use most of them as a government negotiator. The use of tactics has gotten a bad rap from all the stories you've heard about the used car salesman and the shifty government contractor. You're probably tempted to think, "Well, *I'm* above playing any cheesy, sleazy games or tricks. After all, I want to be seen as credible and fair. In fact, I'm bound by regulation to be fair to the other side. I'll just give them, right up front, what I think a fair deal is. They will respect me for that. I don't need to learn or study any of these gimmicky tactics and tricks!" Honestly, have you ever had thoughts like that?

Actually, you *should* know, study, and use tactics as a government negotiator. Why? Well one reason is that the FAR says so! Would you agree with me that whenever you bargain, you're essentially using tactics? Look up FAR 15.3. It tells you that when you conduct contracting by negotiations, you'll hold "discussions" with all offerors remaining in the competitive range. It goes on to say that discussions may include bargaining. What the FAR doesn't tell you is *how* to bargain. Hopefully, that's what you'll get by reading this book. Your job as a government negotiator is to reach a fair and reasonable conclusion for the taxpayers. Negotiation tactics help you achieve this goal.

Another reason you need to know tactics is because, as we've discussed, they can be used *against* you. Remember, contractors aren't under the same restrictions you are when it comes to playing fair in negotiations. They're free to use all the strategies and tactics they want. In fact, most of them are highly trained in how to use these tactics effectively. If you don't *know* the tactics, how can you *recognize* when they are being used against you? If you recognize them for what they are, you can apply the appropriate counters to prevent getting hammered in negotiations. Knowledge is power, so we're going to spend quite a bit of time going over some of the most commonly used negotiation tactics and how to counter them.

My primary purpose in showing you these tactics is to make you a better government negotiator. After all, you are responsible for spending my tax money, and I have a personal vested interest in you doing your job effectively. But, because these tactics are universal, knowledge of these tactics and how to counter them can also help you in any personal negotiation situation you'll run into in your daily life. Reading and studying this book will directly help you the next time you buy a house, a car, or a major appliance. It can even help you negotiate aspects of a personal relationship.

I'm extremely interested in how effective this book is in making you a better negotiator, and I'd love to hear from you. Drop me an e-mail message if you find any of these tactics useful to you, or anything in this book worthwhile for that matter. Also, let me know of any difficulties you have in implementing these tactics. I'd love to hear from you!

Chapter 10

Assigning Negotiation Roles

W e talked about assigning roles to the members of your negotiation team earlier, and now is a good time to define those roles further. There are five traditional roles team members can assume for a negotiation: team leader, good cop, bad cop, technocrat, and sweeper. Each of these roles must be well defined and practiced, and assigned long before the negotiation begins. Some people, by virtue of their nature, naturally make good picks to play certain roles. Obviously, experience in carrying out these roles is highly desirable.

As a government negotiator, it's perfectly okay to assign these roles, or any roles you wish, to your team members. Of course, not assigning roles is okay too, but I guarantee it will cause your team to be less effective during the negotiation.

Many negotiation experts agree the ideal negotiation team should consist of three to five people. Obviously, if you have five roles to assign to team members, more than one role may be assigned to one person. This can be easily done, because some of the roles mesh well together with no problem. If you're the only negotiator, obviously you'll have to assume at least the key responsibilities of all the roles.

Even if you don't care to assign roles, you still should be familiar with them, because the other side will probably assign roles to their team members. As you'll see, these roles can be the setup and launch pad for a number of tactics. Consequently, you want to attempt to identify the roles the other side's team members have been assigned either before or very early during the negotiation, and know what type of behavior you can expect from their roles.

This prepares you to deal with the standard tactics you can now expect to come from the role players. Once you understand the responsibilities assigned to each role, the role players are usually not hard to peg. Let's look at the roles and their associated responsibilities.

THE TEAM LEADER

Throughout this book, I'm assuming that you, the reader, are in this role. The team leader is just that—the leader of the negotiating team. For your side, the vast majority of the time the team leader is the CO. For the other side, it's usually someone of equivalent status in the organization, like a contract manager, although companies sometimes use program managers and even marketing managers or attorneys as team leaders. The team leader should be the person with the most negotiating experience, not necessarily the most senior person on the team.

Among other duties, the team leader opens the negotiation, sets the tone, manages the team, controls all communication by members of the team, calls caucuses, decides tough calls or breaks deadlocks within the team, sets and directs all other actions by members of the team, and summarizes and concludes the negotiation. He or she controls the agenda and the negotiation process. The team leader is responsible for the results of the negotiation.

It's extremely important to have a strong negotiation team leader. The team usually is made up of people from very diverse backgrounds and disciplines (technical, financial, legal, and so on), and getting these people to work together can be a huge challenge. Some of the most difficult negotiations a team leader can face aren't from the other side, but from members of his or her own team.

It's also important that the other side sees your team leader as strong and resolute. If they perceive the leader is weak and not in total control of his own team, they could use this to their advantage to try to get an edge during the negotiation. They could even make an attempt to hijack control of the negotiation process itself. Although strong and resolute, the team leader also needs to be seen by the other side as fair and open to diverse ideas.

You don't want a team leader to be an absolute hard-liner. Your team leader, if at all possible, needs to be a seasoned negotiator.

The team leader may assume any of the other roles, the most important probably being the responsibilities of the sweeper. Obviously, assuming the roles of both good cop and bad cop at the same time would be highly tricky, unless you can convince the other side you have a split personality. If you're short-handed, usually the team leader will step in to the role of good cop with their ambiguous authority (Chapter 19) serving as bad cop.

THE GOOD COP

The ideal person to fill the role of good cop is someone who is naturally likable. You know the type—always positive, supportive, sympathetic, attentive, and *concerned*. Someone with a good-natured, extroverted personality makes an excellent good cop, but that person should also be a good listener. A "good" good cop naturally draws people to them because of their contagious, outgoing personality.

The good cop's job is to exude sympathy and understanding for the other side's position and views. When the other side talks, he or she will nod a lot, agree with "uh-huhs," lean forward in rapt attention, and generally endear themselves to the members of the other side's team. He or she is someone the other side can identify with. They create a bond between themselves and the team members of the other side. The other side sees the good cop as at least *one* person on your team who sees things their way and is someone they can trust.

The good cop doesn't do this all at once, but slowly builds this image as the negotiation progresses. He or she may even vocalize objections to their own team's position on some issues, or seem to backtrack on hard-line stances taken by their team. They're just, well, good!

Of course, it's all a well-calculated tactic. The good cop is simply playing a role, with the specific intent being to garner trust and rapport from the other side. Pretty soon, the other side feels relaxed and comfortable around them. They're lulled into a false sense of security. Soon they don't mind sharing tidbits of information with this sympathetic person that they wouldn't dare share with anyone else on your team. This, alone, can give your side critical information that can affect the negotiations significantly. More important, the acting the good cop has done has set him or her up ideally to perform their most crucial task—being a foil to the bad cop. We'll talk about the good cop/bad cop tactic in Chapter 16.

Because the good cop complements and plays off the role of the bad cop, both their roles must be planned and rehearsed well in advance of the negotiation. If you're short-handed, the roles and responsibilities of good cop can be assumed by either the team leader or the sweeper.

THE BAD COP

The counterpart to the good cop, the bad cop's role is to play someone who's nasty to deal with. He or she is negative, constantly arguing, and always opposed to everything the other side says. They're confrontational and intimidating. You're probably thinking of several people you know who fit this bill right now! Many government teams use a technical or program person, maybe even the program manager, to play the role of bad cop. The other side usually picks an accountant or lawyer to play the role.

Although it's true that some people are just naturally disagreeable and argumentative, the bad cop is usually just playing a role. Their job is to riddle the other side's positions with objections and undermine their progress. They're also in an excellent position to throw contentious issues or extreme positions on the table without jeopardizing the apparent objectivity and fairness of the other members of their team or that of their teammates. They can use delaying tactics, emotional tactics (see Chapter 28), and the walk-out tactic (Chapter 29). They can take the blame for the strategic calling of breaks or caucuses (Chapter 17). The other side never knows when the bad cop is going to blow up next. They create tension and keep the other side in constant doubt about the resolution of issues and the result of the entire negotiation. They keep the other side off balance.

The bad cop's most important role, of course, is setting up the good cop to be effective. We explain how in detail in Chapter 16. Bottom line: The negative conduct of the bad cop enables your good cop to become endearing to the other side. Your good cop plays the role of opposing or trying to moderate the conduct of your bad cop, and this tends to gravitate the other side to your good cop. They're now more willing to share information with or make concessions directly to your good cop, who "understands where they're coming from."

The bad cop role must be planned and well rehearsed with the good cop beforehand to be effective. A preplanned good cop/bad cop playoff is the only time your team should show dissension in front of the other side, so it must be well thought out in advance. If you're short-handed, the technocrat can double as the bad cop. Don't assign the bad cop role to the sweeper.

In my opinion it's never a good idea to have your team leader also play the bad cop. The team leader needs to be perceived by the other side as fair and reasonable. Someone outside the negotiating room can also play the bad cop, like your ambiguous authority (this is very common).

THE TECHNOCRAT

Have you ever been in a negotiation with someone who can't seem to sit down and talk to you using general terms? He or she is constantly referring to studies, books, surveys, and analyses; constantly throwing numbers out; and they challenge the technical correctness of almost everything you say, even if the difference is miniscule. This role is what I call the *technocrat*, although I've also heard it called the *confuser* or the *hard-liner.*

The technocrat's role is to confuse the other side constantly by continuously interjecting facts, figures, or data that may or may not be pertinent to the issue being discussed. He or she complicates matters, throws things off track, and gives the other side additional points to address, defend, or explain. They come into the room heavily laden with files, folders, and printouts. They spread this material all around themselves and refer to it constantly during negotiations. They work their calculator and repeatedly ask to see and verify the other side's facts and figures. They're not as nasty or ill mannered as the bad cop, but they usually takes a hard line and challenges facts, figures, and assumptions the other side presents. They exude an aura of intelligence and are often deferred to by other team members, even the team leader.

This allows the person playing the role of technocrat to drag out the negotiations by using the time investment tactic (Chapter 11). The technocrat additionally can set your team leader up perfectly to use confusion as a tactic (Chapter 28). They also don't let the other side relax, because they're constantly being forced by the technocrat to double-check or validate their numbers, or justify their position.

The technocrat can even challenge his own team member's facts, figures, and assumptions, which will allow your team to retreat from positions that appear to be too generous. Of course, he does this only after the other side has tipped their hand about the concession they're willing to give your side to match your generosity—and only after it is planned in advance.

Assign the technocrat role to someone who's naturally analytical, good with numbers, or good at playing like they're good with numbers. If you need to double up, the technocrat's role can be assumed by your bad cop or, in a pinch, your team leader.

THE SWEEPER

The sweeper is nice like the good cop, but not as extroverted. He or she is pleasant, they smile a lot, and they seat themselves at the end of the negotiating table. When negotiations start, they maintain their pleasant aura, listen attentively, scribble notes, and exhibit good, open body language. However, they do not get involved directly in the give-and-take. Their main job is to listen and observe.

At crucial moments the sweeper speaks up to summarize the many different points of view and issues into one consolidated picture. He or she may then suggest a way forward from that point. They keep the negotiation free from bogging down on small issues or from straying too far off the subject. They keep everything on track and in focus. Common phrases for a sweeper to use are: "So what I hear you saying is …." and "Let me see if I can put this all together …." and "I hear what your side is saying. I hear what our side is saying. How about we consider doing …." In essence, the sweeper "sweeps" up all the crumbs and bits of what's going on and assembles them in one cognitive pile.

Another important duty of the sweeper is to observe and absorb. He or she is strategically seated at the end of the negotiating table for a reason. From that position, they can look lengthwise down the table at the other side's team members. They can see reactions the other side has to positions your team brings forth that are hidden from the rest of your team. They're better able to pick up on subtle gestures the other side's team members make, such as a quick kick in the leg under the table or a restraining hand quickly placed on the knee of a speaker.

During a caucus or break, the sweeper then reports these things to the team, and this can be extremely valuable information. For instance, the restraining hand on the knee of the speaker could be their team leader nonverbally saying, "Whoa! Slow down! You're telling them too much too soon!" The swift kick to the leg could mean, "Shut up, stupid! You weren't supposed to tell them that!"

All this gives you more insight into the other side's position. By observing the other side's reactions to what your team is doing, the sweeper can give important feedback on how your team's strategy and tactics are working, who on their side is unconvinced and who's wavering, and whether their body language agrees with their words.

The ideal candidate for the important role of sweeper is someone with a good personality, but a somewhat reserved disposition. He or she needs to be a good organizer, because they will pull different pieces of a puzzle into an understandable pile. They need to be good at seeing the big picture. They also need to be good at succinctly communicating that big picture. Lastly, they need to be extremely observant by nature.

If you're short-handed, sweeper duties can be picked up by your good cop or the team leader. If you're not planning to use the sweep tactic (Chapter 32), your technocrat may assume sweeper responsibilities.

Part Four

Tactics You Can Use

Chapter 11

Time Tactics

Time can be either a friend or a foe. Two tactics related to time that you need to understand are time pressure and time investment.

THE TIME PRESSURE TACTIC

If you remember, we already talked a little bit about time pressure when we discussed the need for you to assess your bargaining power relative to the other side. If one side is under time pressure to come to an agreement quickly, it gives the other side tremendous negotiating power. If you are on the side that has the time advantage, you can now use time as a very effective pressure tactic.

In every negotiation, both sides will have a deadline—a point in time when they have to reach agreement, or they *think* they have to reach agreement. The secret to using time pressure as a tactic is to find out the other side's deadline, but not let them figure out *your* deadline. Why is this important? Because most significant concessions in any negotiation will come very close to the deadline. This happens for two reasons.

First, people faced with a deadline usually tend to procrastinate. For example, remember that term paper you had to write in school? Although you might have had months and months to work on it, when did you *really* get cracking on it? If you were like me, it was in the eleventh hour.

Second, people tend to become a lot more flexible when confronted with time pressure. When I finally got around to completing my school term paper, do you think it was the very best product I could have produced? No! I became *very* flexible when it came to quality; I didn't even go back and correct grammatical errors and misspellings! I was simply happy at that point to submit it—submit *anything*—by the deadline to avoid "failure." Negotiators under the pressure of time act in the same way: They will make many more concessions than they ever dreamed they would back in the unhurried days of negotiation planning.

Considering what we've just discussed, if you know my deadline and I don't know yours, who has the advantage in the negotiation? Let me give you a couple of examples of the use of time as a pressure tactic.

Contractors know how to use time pressure as a tactic against the government very successfully. Some contractors will use every excuse they can think of to get a negotiation session with the government postponed until a Friday—preferably the Friday before a three-day federal holiday. They know there's nothing more prized by federal employees than their time off! Government employees consider this sacred and untouchable. They know the government negotiators will be under tremendous time pressure to reach a deal (even if it's not the best deal they could have held out for) so the negotiations won't drag on into a Saturday and ruin their weekend plans.

To tighten the screws, they will subtly drop hints during negotiations that *they* are quite willing to work all weekend if that's what it will take to strike a deal. They'll pretend they take it for granted the government team feels the same way. This usually secretly *horrifies* the government team as they see their weekend plans slipping away. It strengthens their resolve to make sure they conclude negotiations on Friday, even if it's not the best deal they could have gotten. And usually it isn't. Folks, this is a very effective tactic!

Another excellent example of using time as a pressure tactic was described by Herb Cohen in his book *You Can Negotiate Anything* (Bantam Books, 1982). As a young, inexperienced negotiator, he was sent by his company to Tokyo to negotiate an important deal with a Japanese company. To his surprise, he was met at the airport by two representatives of the Japanese company who fawned over him and escorted him to a stretch limo they had waiting for him. As they were leaving the airport they asked him if he was concerned about getting back to his plane on time after negotiations were concluded. They then offered to schedule the limo to transport him back to the airport. He thought to himself, "How considerate! They're treating me like a really important person." So he handed them his return flight ticket so they could schedule the limo for him. Bad mistake! Now they knew his deadline and he didn't know theirs.

They spent the next few days wining and dining him, and showing him all the wonderful sights of Tokyo. Whenever he'd ask about the start of negotiations, they'd say "Plenty of time! Plenty of time!" Negotiations started in earnest during the last two days of his trip, punctuated by golf and a farewell dinner. On the last day, just as they were getting to the heart of the negotiations, the limo pulled up to take him to the airport. The deal was negotiated in the back of the limo as it sped toward the airport. Who do you think got the better end of *that* deal?

Can you think of some common things that can cause time pressures for you as a negotiator that can be used against you if the other side knows about them? How about these: Are funds are expiring on your project and you need to award the contract before the money disappears? Does a customer absolutely *have* to have what the contractor is offering by a certain date? What if key members of your team won't be available after a certain date? Or maybe your own supervisor has given you a deadline and told you not to come back without a deal. These are all realities you might have to deal with, but under *no* circumstances should you let the other side know about them. Act like you have all the time in the world to reach an agreement. That will throw the pressure back on them; they have a deadline too.

Make a habit of always using time pressure as a tactic. Even if you can't find out the other side's deadline, remember, they *do* have one. Their bosses probably have given them marching orders to come back with a deal by a certain time. Maybe they need to win this contract by a certain date to solve a cash flow problem or to make a quarterly earnings report look better for their stockholders. Maybe they have another important negotiation coming up that they want their negotiators free to take on. You can effectively use the tactic of time pressure in every negotiation by simply holding your major issues until late in the negotiation. Be patient. Don't fire all your guns at once. Let time pressure work for you, not against you.

Counters to the Time Pressure Tactic

So, if you feel the other side is using the time pressure tactic against you, how do you counter it? Well, like all the tactics we're going to discuss, the best counter is simply to recognize it for what it is—a tactic. This puts you back in control and negates the emotional effect they hope their tactic will have on you. Let them know, politely, that you won't be pressured by time or by them. Let them know you recognize they're using a tactic. Getting caught using a tactic could also embarrass the other side so much that they throw you a free concession!

Another effective counter is to tie up all the preliminary negotiation details, including time allotted for negotiations, up front. You should have already done this when you created your negotiation agenda. Then, as negotiations progress and agreements are reached on issues, tie up the details of the agreements as you go. That reduces the room the other side has to drag out negotiations to apply pressure. Never let the other side convince you that, because you are in general agreement, you can work out the details later. Work them out *now* and tie them up by placing them *in writing* as you agree to them.

Finally, use your BATNA as a safety valve against time pressure. Never be forced to go lower than your BATNA because of time pressure. This is why you have a BATNA: to protect you from getting caught up in the negotiation so much you come away with a bad deal. Never be afraid to pull the plug if you reach your BATNA.

THE TIME INVESTMENT TACTIC

Closely related to the time pressure tactic is the tactic of *time investment*. This tactic works because of two principles. First, the longer you can keep the other side negotiating, the more likely they will be to move toward your point of view. I really don't know exactly *why* this works, but I know it does. Slowly, over time, their opinions change and their initial positions soften.

The most drastic example of this I can think of is something called the Stockholm syndrome (sometimes called the Helsinki syndrome). Researchers looking into the emotional state of hostages taken by terrorists stumbled on a remarkable and almost unbelievable fact. The more time the terrorists held them hostage, the more sympathetic the hostages became toward their captors. There were some reports of hostages even helping the terrorists fight off the very forces sent in to free them. Now, I'm not trying to paint the other side in a negotiation as terrorists, or you as hostages, but I think you get my point.

Second, the more personal time, energy, and effort a negotiator puts into the process, the more anxious they become to reach a deal. They don't want all their time and effort to go to waste. They have an investment of time in you and they want something to show for it—even if it isn't everything they initially wanted. Let me give you an example from everyday life.

Let's say you need to buy an expensive suit. When you walk into the suit section of the department store, what immediately happens? A helpful, friendly salesperson appears as if by magic, bubbling all over with enthusiasm to help you. Why? Because they work on commission and they see you as a sale. Practice using the tactic of time investment. Wear that salesperson out. Try on every suit in the joint. Try on every combination possible of coat, shirt, and pants. Then ask to try on a different size in all the combinations you just tried on. Then do it again with another size.

After a couple of hours of this, what do you think that salesperson is thinking? They're probably ready to pay *you* to make up your mind. You've already wasted a couple of hours of their time and prevented them from making easier sales from less troublesome customers. So when you *finally* decide on the suit you want (and you probably knew which one you wanted all along), are they going to haggle much if you offer them less than the sticker price? The last thing they'll want to do is lose this sale in which they have invested so much time. So they'll probably agree to reasonable price reductions rather than risk the possibility of either losing the sale or having you wear them out and tie them up for another hour.

Time is money to a contractor, so the tactic of time investment usually works well on them. Their negotiators are valuable assets to the company and they are expensive. Just like the coat salesperson, they need to move on to the next deal. And just like the coat salesperson, the more time they have invested in the negotiation, the more motivated they are to not come back empty-handed. Power has now shifted to you.

Counters to the Time Investment Tactic

Using the time investment tactic the way I described it in the suit salesperson example also works on car salespeople. There is one difference, however. Car salespeople are usually trained to recognize the tactic and counter it. What do they do? The same thing you should do if you recognize the other side using the tactic of time investment on you: Completely disregard your "sunk" time. Don't let it affect you. You'll probably already have time invested before you recognize the tactic and you just have to write it off.

In his book *Secrets of Power Negotiating* (Career Press, 2001), author Roger Dawson puts it this way:

> A Power negotiator knows that you should disregard any time or money that you have invested in a project up to any given point. Time and money is gone whether you strike a deal or not. Always look at the terms of a negotiation as they exist at that moment and think, "Disregarding all the time and money

we've poured into this deal up to now, should we go ahead?"
Never be reluctant to pull the plug if it doesn't make sense any
more. It's much cheaper to write off your investment than it is
to plow ahead with a deal that isn't right for you just because
you have so much invested in it. (p. 177)

In other words, remember your BATNA and don't be afraid to use
it.

So feel free to use both time pressure and time investment as tactics, but also learn how to recognize and counter these tactics when
they are used against you.

Chapter 12

Questions/Trial Balloons

The next tactics we'll discuss are super easy to use, but awesome in their effectiveness. They're called *questions* and *trial balloons*. Questions are designed specifically to receive answers, which increase information. We'll talk about them first. A trial balloon is constructed simply by putting "what if" in front of a suggestion to the other side. We'll talk about how to use this tactic too.

QUESTIONS

Remember, in any negotiation, knowledge is power. Any increase in knowledge about the other side increases your power relative to them. Use questions to probe for answers, which increase your information about the other side. Remember that during negotiation preparation you used questions to find out as much information about the other side and their negotiators as possible. Now, during the sit-down negotiation session, you'll want to continue to use questions to dig for more information about the other side's position, interests, needs, hidden agendas, and so forth.

Most negotiators, especially the majority of COs I have come in contact with, don't ask *nearly* enough questions of the other side in a negotiation. This is a combination of human nature and negotiation inexperience. It's human nature not to want to appear dumb or uninformed to the other side. But in negotiations, *acting dumb is smart*. If it's human nature not to want to appear dumb, it's also human nature for people to want to help out folks they see as less intelligent or less informed than they are. It makes them feel important.

So, like we've mentioned before, ask questions that make the other side feel superior, such as, "Gee, I'm not sure I fully grasp all the intricacies in your proposal. Would you mind explaining them to me again?" Or, "I know the dollars you are proposing are backed up with sound facts, but for some reason I'm just not getting it. Can you explain to me how you came up with these figures?" Notice you are asking for their help in both these examples. Get in the habit of asking that one question: "Can you help me …?" That's almost guaranteed to trigger the human need for the other side to feel smart and superior, and they'll give you information they otherwise wouldn't have! You also should use questions to test the credibility of "facts" the other side is asserting.

Get good at asking questions that start with "how," "what," "what else," "which," and "why." Here are some examples: "*How* did you come up with those figures?" They now have to defend their position with additional facts, and, remember, any additional information shifts power. "*What* would you do if you were in my shoes and someone gave you that choice?" This has the added benefit of bringing them around to your side, even if it's just a little bit. "What is really important to you?" After they finish telling you, you should always follow up with: "*What else* is important?" They see you as caring for their position and are likely to be more open when sharing information with you. Then ask them, "*Which* of these things is *more* important to you?" This gives you insight into their "must" and "give" positions. Test their credibility by asking: "*Why* do you think that position is fair?" That puts them on the defensive to justify their position.

Notice all these "question starters" have one thing in common: They are all open-ended. Open-ended questions are questions that can't be answered by a simple yes, no, or some other finite fact. They require elaboration. Elaboration requires more information, and that's what you're trying to get. If you ask close-ended questions, you run the risk of getting a simple answer and nothing more.

For example, if you ask them, "Don't you think your price is a little too high?" they may answer with a simple no. That gives you a little information, but not much. If you ask, "When will you be able to deliver?" they can answer with one date. Rather than asking these close-ended questions, ask something like: "*How* did you come up with that price and *why* do you think it's fair?" And, "*How* about delivery?"

Any time you can insert an open-ended question into the negotiation it's a good idea to do it. When the other side makes a statement, follow it up with a question. If they ask a question, answer it with a question of your own. For example, if they say "Your required delivery date is unrealistic," use the parroting technique and simply regurgitate their own statement back at them in the form of a question. In this case, you would say, "You feel our delivery date is unrealistic?" The way they answer that question could give you key insight into where they're coming from. Notice this time I didn't ask *why* they felt the delivery date was bad (which sometimes throws up warning flags); I merely restated their assertion in the form of a question using the word *feel.*

This simple word is an important addition to your vocabulary. If they say something like, "Our standard company policy is to never offer extended warranties," respond with, "And how do you feel about that policy?" Sometimes this can help determine whether there is any give in their position.

Oh, by the way, whenever you ask a question, be quiet and wait for their answer. If they don't immediately respond to your question, avoid the temptation to elaborate. Face it: Most of us aren't good listeners. We want to talk, expound, and strut our stuff. If you do, you're negating the effect of pulling information from the other side by asking the question! To make matters worse, now more information is flowing from *your* side instead of the other way around. Silence is golden, and it's also a crucial skill you have to work at developing to be a successful negotiator. We'll talk more about using silence as a negotiation tactic in a bit.

One other point. The other side's reluctance or even refusal to answer a question can, in itself, give you a little more information about their position. So get in the habit of asking questions. No matter what the response, you can't lose.

Before we go over some counters to the tactic of using questions, let's talk about trial balloons, because the counters to both tactics are basically the same.

TRIAL BALLOONS

You use the tactic of constructing a *trial balloon* by putting "what if" in front of a statement. Trial balloons have a magical way of relaxing the other side and making them feel freer to discuss issues, even those that they may consider "off the table."

For example, suppose the other side has strict marching orders not to agree to anything shorter than a 30-day delivery time. They've been drilled by their bosses not to give an inch on this issue. You're aware of this and you need a faster delivery. If you hit them with statements like, "I think you need to show some flexibility on delivery date" or "We think you should deliver earlier" or "Your delivery time is unacceptable," what kind of response do you think you'll get? That's right! They're going to dig their heels in and go into a defensive crouch! You've just challenged them. They have a commitment to uphold.

So use the trial balloon. Ask, "*What if* we had an earlier delivery date?" Notice two things. First, I said *we* instead of *you*. That makes it *our* problem instead of *theirs*. More important, notice what the "what if" accomplished. It takes the pressure off the other side. It's just a "what if." You aren't asking them to commit. You're not directly challenging them. With the pressure off, they're a lot more likely to open up. After all, what trouble can they get into; it's just a "what if"!

You'd be amazed at the extra information you can get using a trial balloon. Now you're likely to find out exactly why they're committed to a 30-day time frame and whether they have any flexibility on the issue.

You may even influence them to see some sort of solution their bosses didn't see when they were issued their marching orders. If that's true, they may well go back to their management for a re-thinking of the position. To be even more effective, try coupling your trial balloon with one of your "give" points. For instance, *"What if* we had an earlier delivery date *if* we relaxed our inspection criteria?" Now you've given them something to take back or think about. Heck, they didn't need to know that rigidity of inspection criteria isn't that important to you!

So use both open-ended questions and trial balloons to gather information and allow the other side to see other possibilities and solutions. But what do you do if you sense the other side is doing this to *you?*

COUNTERS TO QUESTIONS/TRIAL BALLOON TACTICS

If the other side is as smart as you, they're also going to know that information is power and that asking questions increases information. If so, you may find yourself bombarded with open-ended questions and trial balloons from *their* negotiators. Now, questions are a normal part of every negotiation, so the other side doesn't always have sinister intentions by questioning you. But if you think they're digging by questioning and "trial ballooning" you to death, try these counters.

First, trump them. You do this by simply answering their question with a question of your own. After they finish asking their question or throwing their trial balloon, say "Can you restate that?" or "Would you be offended if I told you I didn't understand?" or "Let me see if I've got this right …. Is that correct?" All these responses beg an answer, which will throw them out of the question mode.

If that doesn't work, try silence. Simply don't answer their question! Silence can get uncomfortable, as we'll talk about next. And the other side might start elaborating on their question or trial balloon to fill that silence you've created. Voila! Information is once again flowing from them to you, and that's what you want.

Now I've been in negotiations with experienced negotiators that know all this—and sometimes it can get downright funny. They ask a question. You respond with a question, such as "Can you restate that?" They then respond with a question like, "What part do you want me to restate?" And so on and so on. I've seen questions go four or five deep before someone breaks down and makes a statement. Each side vies to force the other side to do this first. And who said negotiating isn't any fun?

Chapter 13

The Silence Tactic

We've already covered using silence after asking questions or trial balloons, and using silence to counter these tactics. Now I want to talk about it a little more and explain exactly *why* silence is so effective a negotiation tactic.

USING SILENCE AS A TACTIC

Have you ever been in an elevator with people you don't know? It can be real quiet, can't it? You stare at the lights as they change, fidget, pretend to check your cell phone. The silence is uncomfortable, isn't it? You almost *will* the elevator to go faster. It's a fact that most people are uncomfortable with silence and, because of this, they tend to want to break the silence by saying something. Usually they'll tell you more than they expected to.

So use silence as a tactic in negotiations. After you make a point, be silent. More important, after the *other side* makes a point or asks a question, be silent and wait. I promise you, you'll be amazed at what transpires next. If you don't immediately answer, the other side is likely to continue to talk and elaborate. And when they do, they'll either modify their position and give you more concessions, or at least give you more information than you had before. It's human nature.

Of course, human nature applies to you as well. You'll have to fight the temptation to jump in with your own two cents worth, especially if what they're saying is wrong or doesn't agree with you. Good negotiators are better listeners than talkers, but it takes practice and patience. Wait them out in silence and see how many times they modify their own positions without you having to say a word!

Salesmen are taught many techniques on how to close the deal. One they learn on day one is the "silent close." It's probably been used against you some time in your life. After going back and forth, say, with a car salesman, they sigh, write a number down on a piece of paper, push it over to you and say something like, "This is the absolute best I can do." Then they become silent as the Sphinx. As a general rule, the next person to talk loses, and that's usually you!

Great negotiators will let you ramble on as much as possible after you start talking, even after you accept the deal. Folks, they're not being courteous. They're not awestruck at the logic of your argument or your brilliance. They're using the silence tactic on you.

So what do you do to counter this if you feel the other side is using silence as a tactic?

COUNTERS TO THE SILENCE TACTIC

I'll be honest. I can't think of too many good counters to the tactic of silence. You can always elect to "fight fire with fire" and give them the silent treatment as well. Simply refuse to be the first one to talk. Of course, this could set up some pretty funny situations, especially if both of you realize you're using the same tactic on each other. If you simply feel you can't stand it any longer and you absolutely *must* break the silence, you're safest by saying something like, "Excuse me, I have to take a break." Leave the room for awhile. When you reconvene, you've increased the probability the other side will break the silence first.

Another counter is one I've already recommended as an effective counter to every tactic. Simply let the other side know you recognize they're using the silence tactic on you. You might say something like, "Hey, you're really great at using the silence tactic. See, you got me to talk first. But since I'm talking, let me ask you, what do you *really* think of this proposal?" And then be quiet. See what you've done here? You've countered *their* silence tactic with your own use of the *question* tactic coupled with your *own* silence tactic right back at them!

In the sport of wrestling, they call this a *reversal* and you get two points. At the very least, it will relieve the tension, and maybe give both sides a good laugh break.

Another counter I've heard can be successful is not to answer with words. For example, if that car salesman pushes that piece of paper to you and clams up, get your *own* piece of paper out, write something on it, and push it back to him! In this case, you may write "Why?" or "Too high" or "Extras?" If you've made the proposal and are getting the silent treatment, you might write "Decision?" or "Do you understand?" All these beg a response, don't they? And all encourage the other side to be the first to break the silence.

Just remember, the more information you have, the more power shifts to you in negotiations. And you can't increase your amount of information by talking, only by being silent and listening.

Chapter 14

The Vise Tactic

Now I want to show you a very effective tactic I learned by reading a book. *In Secrets of Power Negotiating* (Career Press, 2001), author Roger Dawson introduces something called the vise tactic. Now that's not v-i-c-e, as in bad habits, but v-i-s-e, as in vise grip. And I think he named it appropriately, if he's the one who coined the term, because it is very effective in *squeezing* out concessions from the other side without you having to reciprocate with a concession. The vise tactic is simply using one little phrase: *You'll have to do better than this.* I know, it sounds simple, but learn to use that phrase.

I don't care how good their proposal or counterproposal sounds to you. It could be a lot more than you expected. Still use the vise tactic. Whatever the offer, respond automatically by saying, "You'll have to do better than this." You will be amazed how often the other side will respond by throwing you extra concessions you weren't expecting. One more important point. Once you say, "You'll have to do better than this," be quiet! Immediately follow up the vise tactic with the tactic of silence. These two tactics, combined in this way, are another version of the *silent close.*

Hopefully by now you've realized you can use combinations of tactics like this to increase their effect. For example, the vise tactic can be used very effectively against you as a government negotiator when combined with the tactic of *ambiguous authority*, which we'll talk about in a little bit. For a quick peek under the curtain, you may hear the other side say something like, "Gee, I really think you'll have to do better than this. I don't think I can get my director to agree to this low price." You'll soon see that the other side is combining the vise tactic with the tactic of ambiguous authority.

Dawson also discusses another way to make the vise tactic more effective. He suggests flinching visibly in reaction to the other side's proposal as you use the vise tactic. Cock your head, pull back your shoulders, and draw some air in through your teeth. Then say, that's right, "You'll have to do better than this." A flinch shows resistance and puts the other side on notice they may be pushing too far. In fact, if you don't flinch, it may embolden the other side to get tougher.

To illustrate just how effective the vise tactic can be, I'll borrow an example from Dawson's book on how former Secretary of State Henry Kissinger used it. Dr. Kissinger asked a senior staff member to prepare a report on the political situation in Southeast Asia. The staffer, wanting to impress his boss, worked diligently and produced what he thought was a masterful report and sent it in to Dr. Kissinger. It came back with a note attached that simply said—you guessed it—"You'll have to do better than this. H.K."

The staffer was crestfallen, but pitched back in, revising the report, making it more detailed, and including more charts. Satisfied, he sent the new and improved report back to his boss. It came back again with, "You'll have to do better than this. H.K." That was the last straw. The staffer put his folks to work around the clock and revised the report to what approached perfection. In fact, he was so convinced it could get no better, he scheduled a meeting with Dr. Kissinger to present it in person.

When he walked in, he said, "Dr. Kissinger, you've sent this back to me twice. My entire staff has dedicated the last two weeks to this report. Please don't send it back again. It's not going to get any better than this. This is the best I can do." Without hesitating, Dr. Kissinger simply picked it up and said, "Well, in that case, now I'll read it." So do you see how using the vise tactic can win concessions from the other side without having to give something up in return? Remember the phrase: "You'll have to do better than this!"

COUNTERS TO THE VISE TACTIC

So how do you counter the vise tactic if you see it being used against you? It's simple. Just respond, "Exactly how much better than this do I have to do?" Tag. You're it!

Chapter 15

The Order of Issues Tactic

Remember way back when we talked about planning the negotiation? I suggested that you arrange your issues in a certain order to support your strategy. You then send out your draft agenda with the issues ranked the way you want them to be. The other side's response to how you ordered the issues can give you clues as to what is most important to them. So simply ordering your issues in a certain way in your draft agenda can be an effective *probe* to gain more information about the other side. Let's now talk a little more about how the order of issues should be used by you as an essential part of your negotiation strategy.

If your analysis of relative power shows you to be in the driver's seat, you'll probably pick big win–little win as a strategy. (You might possibly pick WIN–LOSE, but remember that you have to be fair and reasonable to both parties.) To support this strategy, you'll want to arrange your issues in the order of greatest importance to *you*. This sets the tone of the negotiations early, essentially saying to the other side, "Give me this and I'll see what I can do about some of your concerns later." You then can be magnanimous and flexible on some issues that are farther down your wish list.

If you are in a position of less power than the other side, say you're in a sole-source negotiation, you have two ways to go when ordering your issues to minimize your weak position (remember, you have probably chosen the loss prevention strategy). You can choose either to arrange your issues in order of *least to most important* or arrange them in order of *ease of agreement*, putting the easiest to agree to first.

The other side probably knows they are in a superior bargaining position, and they're ready to say no to your demands and drive a hard bargain from the outset of negotiations. When you arrange your issues in order of least importance to you, you give them that chance. Let them say no to those first issues. This benefits you in two ways. First, these issues weren't high on your "must-have" list anyway. In fact, they were your least important issues, so it doesn't hurt that badly if you don't get them. Second, this now gives the other side a false sense of security by reinforcing what they already believe. They expected to do great in this negotiation and see? They are getting all the issues their way from the get-go!

After victory on several issues, however, even the toughest negotiators will feel some urge to reciprocate. By addressing the issues of greatest importance to you later, you increase the chance that the other side will finally be willing to see things your way. They may even have convinced themselves they have already "won" the negotiation, so the "later points" won't matter that much to them. Remember, only *you* know what your priorities are.

Alternatively, you can arrange your issues in order of ease of agreement. If you've done your homework, you should have an idea regarding what is important to the other side. You should already have a good idea about which issues will be tough to agree to and which issues will be a breeze. Put the easy ones first. Remember what this does? It gets the other side in the habit of saying that magic word—*yes*.

The more someone says yes, the more unwilling (even subconsciously) he or she becomes to say no. Arranging issues in order of ease of agreement conditions the other side to say yes and increases the chance they will continue to do so when you get down to your most important issues.

COUNTERS TO THE ORDER OF ISSUES TACTIC

How do you counter the order of issues tactic if it's used against you? Well, usually you won't have to counter it at all. You represent the government, and the government sets the agenda for negotiations, including the order of the issues to negotiate. So this is a tactic that can be used almost exclusively by the government team.

This doesn't mean contractors won't try to take over the agenda-setting process to force their issues on you in the order *they* want. Just stand firm and remain in control of the agenda and you'll never have to worry about countering the order of issues tactic. The other side will never have a chance to use it!

Chapter 16

The Good Cop/ Bad Cop Tactic

Most people who have never, ever negotiated before and know nothing about negotiations tactics have at least heard of this one. Good cop/bad cop is one of the most commonly used tactics in the book. It was exploited in ancient times, and it's being used by someone, somewhere right now. Some people say it's been so over-used it has become passé. But people wouldn't still be using it if it wasn't effective, would they? The fact is, it's still one of the best ways to apply pressure to the other side without risking the negative effects of a direct confrontation.

You're probably familiar with the good cop/bad cop tactic from watching TV police shows. Hollywood, for one, has done this one to death, haven't they? In fact, this is where the tactic gets its name!

You know what I'm talking about: The police bring in a suspect for questioning and stick him in that tiny room with only a table, a chair, and a two-way mirror. Sometimes they let the suspect sweat alone in that room for a bit—sometimes not. Eventually, though, two detectives (they're always partners on TV) come into the room and start the tactic. The first detective already looks like he's mad at the world, and proceeds to take out his frustrations and hostility on the suspect.

"You know, I hate petty thugs and punks like you! In fact, my mother was beaten up and robbed by trash like you last year! You're going *down*, and *I'm* gonna take you there! I hope you *fry!* You better talk and talk *fast!*" He continues to threaten the suspect with all kinds of things unless he cooperates. The bad cop gets angrier and angrier, sometimes even getting nose-to-nose with his victim. I know you've seen this on TV.

Remember what the second detective is doing while this tirade is going on? Sitting back, being quiet, and looking mortified that his partner is acting so badly. Suddenly, the first detective—the bad cop—is mysteriously called out of the room for some reason or another. Sometimes they get so mad they storm out on their own, which leaves the suspect alone in the room with the good cop.

This detective is the nicest person in the world. He apologizes to the suspect for his partner's behavior and does everything possible to make the suspect feel at ease.

"Hey, I'm really sorry about the way Sam just acted. He's usually not like this. It's just that he's been under a lot of stress lately. I know you're not at all as bad as he's saying; he's just taking his anger out on you. Tell you what. I've got a lot of pull with my partner and I know how to handle him. Trust me. If we can just give him something, *anything*, some little piece of information when he gets back, I know he'll calm down and be more reasonable. How about something small I can use, like, where did you hide the gun?"

You see what's happened here? Both detectives are playing well-rehearsed roles. In fact, you need *two* players to use the good cop/bad cop tactic, and it's something that doesn't just happen spontaneously. These two detectives have probably rehearsed this scenario many times. In fact, they may even switch roles from time to time. Like all tactics, this one needs to be rehearsed by the players to be effective. It's so overused the other side is likely to see it as a tactic if the performance isn't polished.

If the detective playing the good cop plays the role right, pretty soon the suspect starts to feel that the detective is on his side—it's the both of them against the bad cop! This makes the suspect feel free to share a lot more information with the good cop than he probably planned. The good cop curries favor by being sympathetic and understanding. He usually works at creating goodwill by starting with small things first, then slowly building up to bigger things. The good cop, for example, may have started by offering the suspect a cigarette or a Coca-Cola. The good cop slowly builds trust, enabled by the bad cop's performance.

This is the essence of the tactic. I just showed you the classic way it's used, but that's not the only way to use it. For example, the bad cop doesn't necessarily have to go first, and they don't always have to leave the room before the good cop starts his routine. In this variation, the bad cop can be used to put a brake on the negotiation whenever it's in the team's interest. The good cop is then set up to appear to waiver or backtrack on points the bad cop has made in order to build trust. There are, of course, quite a number of ways this can be played.

The good cop/bad cop tactic can also be made more effective when used in combination with other tactics. You can combine it with the time pressure tactic we've already discussed. It could then go something like this:

"Well, if it were up to me, I'd really like to agree to your terms, Mr. Contractor. I personally think they're reasonable. But my supervisor was pretty upset at your price. In fact, she's already looking for other options right now, like government performance. If I can't bring her back something she thinks is a more reasonable price, she'll likely scrap contracting this project altogether."

If the combined tactic works, the contractor might ask you what you think your boss will accept. Bingo! Who's in control now? The tactic may work so well that the contractor will actually expect you to negotiate for them with your own boss!

Some other tactics that are great when combined with god cop/ bad cop are ambiguous authority, walk in the woods, emotion, and walkout. We'll cover all these tactics later. Please remember that your role as a government negotiator precludes you from openly lying to the contractor or using any other unscrupulous methods to gain concessions. But remember: The other side is usually under no such constraint and is free to use these tactics on you. So how do you counter the good cop/bad cop tactic?

COUNTERS TO THE GOOD COP/BAD COP TACTIC

Since this is perhaps the most commonly recognized tactic, your best counter is to let the other side know you see it for what it is—a tactic. "Oh, I get it! You're playing good cop/bad cop on me! Let me guess. . . .Who's the good cop?" Or, "I know your accountant is here to play bad cop, but let's stop with the games. I really want to get down to solving this problem in a mutually beneficial way."

Because this tactic is so well-worn, it usually embarrasses the heck out of the team that is caught using it. In fact, they are sometimes so embarrassed at getting caught they'll give you a concession without asking for anything in return! Call their game for what it is and, in a nice way, let them know you won't be had.

Another counter is to create a bad cop of your own. If they bring in a lawyer, accountant, or the like to play bad cop, stop the negotiation as soon as you recognize it. Tell the other side something like, "Well, since your lawyer feels that way, I really think we should adjourn until I can get our lawyer here in the negotiation to represent us." Then bring in your own bad cop lawyer. Make sure you brief them first, so they know what's going on. But you probably won't have to train them. Lawyers are great at playing bad cop.

A third counter is to reverse their playing of good cop/bad cop right back at them. For their tactic to work, their good and bad cops will have to disagree or at least take different approaches in front of you. Wait until they start their routine and then say something like, "Whoa! Looks to me like your own team might have some differences of opinion on this. Maybe you weren't as prepared for this negotiation as I thought. Tell you what. I'll let you take a break to see if you can bring your team to some kind of agreement on this issue." Who's on the defensive now? Has power shifted? You bet!

This last counter almost forces the other side to take a break, if for nothing more than to save face. For some strange reason, we usually call breaks in negotiations *caucuses*. Actually, a caucus is technically a little different from a break. A caucus is used by a team to consult together about their position in private. Use of the caucus can also be turned into an effective negotiation tactic. We'll look at this tactic next.

Chapter 17

The Caucus Tactic

Calling a time-out or a caucus in negotiations is done for any number of reasons. You may have preplanned breaks already included in your agenda, someone may honestly have to go to the bathroom, or you may simply be tired and need a break. Sometimes one side or the other may need time to huddle and contemplate some new piece of information or gather some additional data.

Caucuses in negotiations are expected. You can, however, turn these caucuses into an effective negotiation tactic. You can either use the caucus tactic by itself or combine it with other negotiation tactics.

A caucus, for instance, can be used as a *strategic break*. Let's say the other side is on a roll. They're laying out their position, presenting you with rapid-fire facts that are becoming harder and harder to counter. As they lay out their position, as they are building to the crescendo of their point, all of a sudden you say, "Hold it! My team needs a moment to think about some things," and you take your team out of the room. What have you just done? You've totally broken their momentum. You have thrown their whole game plan out of sync. You saw power shifting to their side and you simply called a time-out.

I'm sure you've seen this tactic used in sports. There are two seconds to go in the football game, the score is tied, and the New England Patriots just got into field goal range. What does the coach of the Carolina Panthers do? He calls a time-out to "ice" the field goal kicker. Momentum is broken; rhythm is disrupted. If the tactic works, the kicker gets a few extra minutes to think about not *making* the field goal, but *missing* it.

Caucuses can also be used to *keep control of your own team*. You already know how important it is to keep control of the team if you are the team leader, but sometimes things do get out of hand. One of your teammates will say too much, disclose facts you're not yet ready to disclose, start getting angry and out of control, or (worse yet) start disagreeing with other team members in front of the other side. At that point, call a caucus. Get your team out of the room, give them a lecture, and take back control of your team. Remember, one of the worst things you can do in a negotiation is to disagree among yourselves in front of the other side.

Caucuses can also be used effectively to *keep control of the pace of negotiations.* You want the other side not only to know, but to *feel* you are in charge. If things start going too fast for your game plan, slow the process down by calling a caucus. If you are presented with facts you weren't expecting or a premature offer that changes your whole strategy, call a caucus. Get back in control.

Caucuses are extremely effective as a tactic immediately *after you receive an offer or counteroffer* from the other side. That's when your team is most vulnerable. Good negotiators know to make an offer and then be silent. Why? They know that scrutinizing the other side's reaction to the offer can give them important insights into the other side's position. They've hit a gold mine if, for example, a member of your team starts spouting out counteroffers or expressing views on the merits or concerns of the offer. Usually, these comments are not coordinated with the rest of your team and can damage your position.

Don't give your teammates the room to blow it. Immediately after the other side presents their offer or position, call a caucus. This allows your team to think through the offer calmly and privately. When you reenter the room, you'll have a consolidated team response to the offer without disrupting your game plan.

COUNTERS TO THE CAUCUS TACTIC

Simply being the government team sets you up automatically to counter the caucus tactic if you feel it's being used against you. *You* control the negotiation game rules, remember? You set the agenda. You call the breaks. Now the other side may ask for a break or a caucus, but *you* have the power to say, "No, let's continue until we get this issue sorted out."

This is a huge advantage in negotiations. Be careful that the other side doesn't take this advantage away from you (and if they're good, they'll probably try). I've been in many negotiations when the other side has slowly but deliberately started trying to hijack the negotiation process. Don't let this happen to you. Stay in control of the process, including when breaks occur and how long they're going to be.

I've even read of a situation when *withholding* a break was used as an effective negotiation tool. North Korea had finally agreed to negotiations over ending the Korean War. Although the location was a neutral one, we agreed to let the North Koreans "host" the talks as an incentive to get them to the bargaining table. Oops! That left them in control of setting the agenda and controlling the game rules, including calling breaks.

Well, the North Koreans had a *spread* ready for the American delegation when they arrived. Central to this breakfast feast was their native North Korean hot tea. The Americans were also impressed to find the North Koreans had thoughtfully provided gallons of good American coffee as well, knowing we love the stuff. They even had waiters whose sole job was to make sure the Americans' cups were never empty. The American delegation was impressed and pleased.

Had they been a little more observant, however, the Americans would have realized their counterparts on the North Korean side weren't ingesting a single drop of any liquid. What does both coffee and tea contain? Caffeine. What is caffeine? A natural diuretic! What effect does a diuretic have? It gives the drinker an increasing and finally urgent need to relieve himself.

The negotiations were pressing on. One hour, two hours. No breaks called by the "hosts" yet. Pretty soon the American delegates were seen to squirm uncomfortably in their seats. The North

Koreans remained placid and calm. About this time, the leader of the American delegation realized what was going on. The North Koreans were actually using the "power of the bladder" as an effective negotiating tactic. And it was working. After a couple of hours of drinking coffee and tea with no breaks, do you think the American team members could truly concentrate on the weighty issues of war and peace, or did they have other more pressing concerns distracting them?

The Americans had a dilemma, however. In North Korean culture, saving face is everything. The Americans knew if they asked for a break *first*, they would lose face, and thus power, in the negotiation. So there was a literal bladder standoff. Unfortunately, the North Koreans were prepared for this bladder war and the Americans were not. The Americans finally flinched and asked for a break.

The negotiations then continued and an agreement was finally reached that ended the Korean War. Was it the best deal we could have gotten? Even today, the 38th Parallel is the most heavily fortified place on earth.

Chapter 18

The Nibble Tactic

Have you ever had a situation in your personal life when you thought you had a deal worked out and locked in, only to have the other side ask for something extra "thrown in" at the last minute? If you have, chances are you've been "nibbled on." Simply put, the tactic of nibbling is to ask for a little more even after you've agreed to everything. The nibbler attempts to gain a few extra concessions by little infringements on the terms the other side already thinks are agreed to.

I bet most of you have been nibbled on or done a little nibbling yourselves (maybe without even knowing it) in your personal negotiation situations. You're sitting in that little glass cubicle at the car dealership after spending all day finally coming to terms with the salesperson on price. You don't particularly like the deal, but you're tired of fighting. Thankfully, you're now at the end. You're ready to sign, take ownership, and drive that new car home. Right before you sign on the dotted line, the salesperson pulls back the papers from you, wrinkles his brow and says, "You do want an extended warranty with this car, don't you?" Or, if he's cagy enough to know not to ask questions requiring a yes or no answer he'll ask, "Do you want the 5-, 10-, or 20-year extended warranty?" Oops. You've just been nibbled on.

Let's put the shoe on the other foot. The salesman, after spending hours of his time with you trying to sell you a car, finally has you committed to a price. He triumphantly pushes the papers to you for you to sign. You pick them up, look at them, wrinkle your brow, and say, "And what type of floor mats are you going to throw in for free? And you know how important underbody rust proofing is in this part of the country, don't you?" Yep. You've nibbled!

These two examples illustrate three important things that make nibbling a successful tactic. First, nibbling is only effective if it's used later in the negotiations, usually right at the end. This taps into the power of the time investment tactic we've already discussed. In fact, the success of the nibble tactic is directly proportional to the amount of time the other side has invested in the deal. The salesperson has just invested hours of their commissioned time on you at the expense of closing other deals. Do you think he or she is going to let you walk for the price of a couple of floor mats and get zero for all their efforts? Probably not. You've just increased the likelihood of getting those extras.

Second, nibble tactics have to be preplanned. You've got to hold something back purposely to use as a nibble later. Never ask for everything up front; you'll have nothing left to nibble with. The "give" points you developed when you were planning your negotiation strategy are always ripe issues to throw in as nibbles. You're happy if you get them, but you won't be crushed if the other side successfully counters your nibble.

Lastly, the nibble is effective because it ties into people's innate tendency to want to reinforce decisions they have already made. They have already gotten used to saying that magic word *yes* as you have come to agreement on all other aspects of the deal. In their mind, they've already bought the stuff. They're emotionally involved in the deal and the last thing they want is to back out of something they already have set their mind on. In fact, they want it so bad they don't mind caving a little here and there to keep the deal intact and not have to reopen negotiations. That's how nibbling can be effective in getting concessions late in the game that otherwise would not have been possible, or would have taken much more give-and-take negotiations.

If you're old enough to remember the *Columbo* TV detective shows, you've seen nibbling at its best. In fact, look at how many tactics Columbo could use in a single encounter. Peter Falk, playing the rumpled-looking police detective Columbo, would appear uninvited at the home or business of the powerful, high-society, and very busy suspect (tactic of surprise, tactic of time pressure). He would first spend much time admiring their office, home, and clothes, and throwing countless compliments their way (tactic of flattery). He then would start apologizing for the rumpled way he looked and for his lack of refinement (tactic of acting dumb is smart). Sometimes he would even get into comparing the way the suspect lived with the simple way he and his wife lived (all these tactics combined result in the tactic of time investment).

Columbo's act was, of course, intentional. It was meant to make the suspect feel immensely superior to this poor, blundering, confused slob of a policeman. Once he felt superior, he would feel less threatened. He would let his guard down. After all, how could this sloppy, blabbering idiot ever get the best of him? He can't even stay focused on the reason he came!

The suspect would finally impatiently ask Columbo to come to the point of his visit (tactic of getting the other side to try to close first). Columbo would respond, "Well, sir, now that you mention it, there is something that's been bothering me ...." Columbo would then ask a few questions relating to the case (tactic of preplanned, open-ended questioning), usually prefacing the questions with lavish doses of "I don't understand" or "Now, I'm not the expert, but ...." (help-me tactic, dumb-is-smart tactic). His questions, and the way he asked them, would draw terse, off-the-cuff, and unguarded responses from the impatient and flustered suspect (probe tactic, which is gaining information without reciprocating).

After he sensed the suspect was getting angry at the questions and by his continued presence, Columbo—with perfect timing—would apologize, thank the suspect for his time, turn around, and walk away. The camera would always zoom in for a second on the suspect visibly relaxing as Columbo walked away. The camera would then pan to the back of Columbo's disheveled head. Just as Columbo would reach the door, he would turn around, hold his unlit cigar up, and say his most famous line. "Ahhh (slapping his forehead in an absent-minded way). Almost forgot. There's just one more thing that's been bothering me ...." (Finally, the nibble!)

The suspect had been elated to see Columbo walking out the door, finally rid of the nuisance that was eating up his precious time and in general being a thorn in the side. Just when the suspect's guard was down and he began to relax, Columbo would hit him with his trademark line as he was turning to walk back into the room. The suspect would usually say "What is it *now?*" in an extremely exasperated voice. Columbo would then ask the key question he had saved for last. The suspect, thinking the grill session was through, usually responded to this nibble by saying way more than he had planned to say, giving just the key information Columbo was fishing for all along. Columbo ends up solving the case; bad guy goes to jail.

Can you use the nibble tactic as a government negotiator? Sure. Here's just one example. Say you're negotiating with a company to buy computer equipment for your office. During your negotiation planning you identified an extended warranty as one of your "give" points, but it was high on your list of "nice to haves." You've also done your research on the other side. They rarely agree to anything other than their standard commercial warranty. Extended warranties, if they come at all, come with a hefty price tag.

Invest time in the negotiations, giving and taking, and finally come to what they think is a meeting of the minds. Right before you shake hands, nibble: "Because the government is one of your biggest customers, I'm assuming we're on your most favored customer list. How many months over your standard commercial warranty have we just bought?"

Although you can use the nibble tactic, most of the time it will be the other side that tries to nibble on you. How can you stop their nibbling?

COUNTERS TO THE NIBBLE TACTIC

Nibbling is a fairly common tactic and is highly effective if you don't know how to counter it. You are at your most vulnerable when you think negotiations are done. The nibble plays on the time you've invested in the negotiation, so use the counters you've already learned to the time investment tactic. Remember what they are? The three counters to the time investment tactic are the following: disregard "sunk" time, know your BATNA (when to walk away), and tie up all details of the negotiation up front or as you reach agreement on each issue.

Here's another counter, and you already know this one too. When they hit you with the nibble, visibly flinch. Remember, we learned the flinch when we talked about the vise tactic. Flinching shows them your disappointment at the last-minute change to the terms, and signals to the other side that the nibble may cost them something.

After you flinch, take your team out on a caucus. Come back in with a written statement of what *they'll* have to give up to get their nibble. In other words, demand a reciprocal concession. Don't let them nibble for free. Show them, in writing, what their "extra" will cost them. Say something like, "Now that you mention it, there are a few things I'm not quite satisfied about either. I didn't want to show bad faith by trying to reopen the negotiations after I've reached a good-faith deal with you, but now that you've chosen to reopen, I believe they're fair game." We'll talk about this more when we get to the tradeoff tactic.

Finally, you can use the ambiguous authority tactic to counter their nibble. Simply say something like, "You know, this is something new. I don't think I have the authority to approve this extra. I didn't know this would come up, so I haven't briefed my boss that this would be part of the deal. I'll have to check with my boss and get back to you."

This last counter works well. It works so well, in fact, that it's a tactic in its own right. It's called the ambiguous authority tactic, and we'll talk about it in the next chapter.

Chapter 19

The Ambiguous Authority Tactic

Imagine that you're in that same small glass cubicle at the car dealership. You've slogged it out with the salesperson all day and finally think you have a deal. He nibbles with the extended warranty, but you're good. You see through the tactic and successfully counter it. Smugly, you say "Now, at the price and terms we have agreed on, do we have a deal or not?" The salesperson wrinkles his brow, frowns, shakes his head slowly, and says those magic words, "I'll have to talk to my sales manager."

Folks, have you figured out by now that there usually *is* no sales manager? The salesperson will then get up and disappear. In reality, they're not going to talk to anyone. They're taking a break, smoking a cigarette, having a soda, joking with the staff. They purposely left you in that sparse glass cubicle to stew and sweat a little bit. And what do you do? You start second-guessing your last offer. You start thinking maybe you were a little too greedy, maybe you tried to strike too hard a bargain.

At this point you start negotiating against yourself. And you're scared to death what this mysterious sales manager may do to the deal you thought was so close to being accepted. When the salesperson comes back, power has shifted, hasn't it? You have just been the victim of the ambiguous authority tactic.

You use the ambiguous authority tactic during negotiations any time you are the chief negotiator, but you don't possess ultimate authority to finalize the deal. Remember, though, you're a government negotiator. You can't deliberately lie about your authority or anyone else's authority. But you don't have to! Even if you are a CO with unlimited authority to obligate the government, you usually have some approval process to go through before signing the contract. You may have instructions to consult with your boss, the program manager, finance, some sort of review committee, or some other person or office before you finalize the deal. These people or committees will be the ambiguous authorities to which you will defer if you elect to use this tactic.

It's good practice never to go into any negotiation with unlimited authority to close the deal, even if everyone has given you preapproval to do so. Always have someone you must go back to for approval. If that's impossible and you *do* have ultimate authority, never let the other side know it. Once they find out you are the sole decision maker, you are at a severe disadvantage. They now know you are the only obstacle in the way of the terms and conditions they want. They only have one person to convince.

In his book *You Can Negotiate Anything* (Bantam Books, 1982), author Herb Cohen says the worst person you can negotiate for is yourself. A person representing himself has no higher authority to defer to, to use as a foil when things get sticky, or to help keep things in perspective. A negotiator with unlimited authority can too easily let emotions or simple ego get in the way of common sense.

The worst person to negotiate for a company (aside from the marketing people) is the owner of the company. He's too close to the business; he has too much riding on the outcome, both business-wise and emotionally. I've known business owners who have negotiated disastrous contracts for their companies because they put the emotional and egotistical concept of "winning" above all rational business considerations.

The ambiguous authority tactic is usually used just before the close of negotiations, as we saw in our car dealership example. The other side thinks they have a deal and all of a sudden they find out they have someone else, or even a whole new cast of characters, to deal with. This is also the time when the other side is most vulnerable. They've probably already disclosed their bottom line, or something close to it. Fatigue, deal fever, deadlines, and a host of other factors are working on them already.

That's one reason why the tactic is so effective. Once you've said you have to consult with another authority to approve the negotiation, the last thing the other side wants is for this mysterious other person to blow a deal that is so close to being consummated. They may start to second-guess themselves and be tempted to soften their positions a bit to help you "sell" the deal to the other authority. They actually could start making additional concessions without demanding something in return. They start *bidding against themselves.*

Ambiguous authority also sets you up to use other tactics more effectively. Remember the vise tactic—that simple phrase, "You'll have to do better than that"? When used with the ambiguous authority tactic, the combination could sound something like this: "I just don't know about this bottom line you're giving me. Personally, I think it's pretty fair. But I really believe you'll have to do better than this for me to have any chance of convincing my review committee to buy off." In effect, you're asking the other side to help you sell the deal. If the tactic works, they may look at it as "us" (you and them) against "them" (your ambiguous authority). They are now pressured to make the deal as sweet as possible so you have a better chance of selling it to your committee.

Even if they don't make outright concessions, they could pose "what-if" questions to you that will increase your information about their true positions. For instance, they could say something like, "Well, what if we offered to extend the warranty another six months? Do you think your committee would have a better chance of approving it then?" Do you see what's happened here? Simply by mentioning another authority you've shifted the negotiating range in your favor. Their new "what if" now becomes your target position, or maybe even your new minimum position. And you haven't given up a thing in return.

In much the same way, the ambiguous authority tactic can be coupled with the good cop/bad cop tactic. The ambiguous authority you introduce simply becomes the bad cop to your god cop. You use the tactic just like we discussed when we covered good cop/bad cop, with the only difference being that the bad cop is never physically present. You get the other side actually working for you (the good cop) against the ambiguous authority you have to get approval from (the bad cop).

The ambiguous authority tactic can also help you use the time pressure and time investment tactics. You can use it strategically to stretch out negotiations to bring more pressure to bear on the other side. Most contractors are convinced that the government moves slower than molasses on a winter day. The last thing they want is for you to take that so-close-to-being-done contract out that door and turn their almost-realized profits over to some government committee!

But make sure they're the ones under the time pressure, not you. It would be self-defeating to use these tactics if time is on their side.

You can also use ambiguous authority as an excellent lead-in to the caucus tactic. Having someone else you must go to for approval automatically sets up a break in the negotiations. You can use this time to make reasoned decisions about the status of the negotiations and to plan your next steps. It keeps you in control of the pace. It also gives them time to sit in that room and second-guess their positions—just as our poor car buyer did when the salesperson went to talk to "the sales manager."

To improve the effect of the ambiguous authority tactic, always try to *keep the other authority you need as vague as possible*. This prevents the other side from immediately countering your tactic. If you say, for instance, that your boss is the higher (or ambiguous) authority, the other side may simply ask to bring that person into the negotiations. They may even insist on accompanying you to your boss' office to argue their position. It's harder for the other side to put a face on something vague like "the review committee" or "my finance folks" or "my customers."

So far we've talked about how you can use the tactic of ambiguous authority. However, contractors are well versed in using this tactic too. During government negotiations, I've most often seen the tactic used *against* the government instead of *by* the government. Good industry negotiators commonly apply the ambiguous authority tactic, either alone or in combination with other tactics.

First of all, it's frustrating (at the end of the negotiation) to find out that the people you've been negotiating with don't have the final call. That's intentionally designed to fluster you. When you're flustered you're more likely to make mistakes, such as offering additional concessions that are not reciprocated by the other side.

It also allows the other side to shift the range of negotiations in their favor. What you thought was a fair, done deal (maybe you're at your target position) comes back from their ambiguous authority simply as their floor for further negotiations. Here's how they do it.

After you have revealed your target position, they cite ambiguous authority and call a caucus. They come back in and sadly proclaim their "higher ups" won't approve the deal and negotiations will have to continue under their new "marching orders." What they have really done is revise their minimum, maximum, and target positions based on now knowing *your* target position. If you want the negotiations to continue, this puts pressure on you to move yours upward as well. The whole negotiating range shifts in their favor.

Lastly, remember that negotiators in private industry are not bound by the same rules of fairness and honesty that bind you as a representative of the government. There's a chance the ambiguous authority they cite is nonexistent, as was the case in our car salesperson example. I once read of an industry negotiator who always had to consult with his "board of directors" before consummating a deal. His "board of directors" was actually his pet cocker spaniel.

I'll bet some of you reading this right now are just realizing that the ambiguous authority tactic has been successfully used against you in the past. Because this tactic has a high likelihood of being used on you again, either in your personal or professional life, what can you do about it? How do you counter it?

COUNTERS TO THE AMBIGUOUS AUTHORITY TACTIC

The best way to counter the ambiguous authority tactic is to head it off at the pass. Simply refuse to negotiate with anyone who doesn't have ultimate authority to bind their company. Remember, you control the process, including setting and running the agenda. When you send the other side a copy of your draft agenda for review, simply ask them who their negotiators will be and if they will have ultimate decision authority. Get it in writing.

If the other side shows up with a different negotiator, establish the extent of his or her authority before the negotiations begin. If that person doesn't have the final say, call off negotiations until they can provide someone who does. Even if the originally designated negotiator shows up, always reconfirm their authority before starting negotiations. Always ask the question, and never negotiate with someone who can't make the final call and sign the agreement.

Sometimes—and this is rare—the other side will still attempt to pull the ambiguous authority tactic even after you've got them to commit to having full authority to bind their firm. You'll hear something like, "Well … normally I could approve this contract. However, you've cut me so close to the bone I don't think even I can approve this without talking to the boss." What do you do now?

First, get their commitment that they will push for the deal you have agreed on when they go to their ambiguous authority. This plays on their ego and defuses some of the effectiveness of the tactic. If they commit to go to bat to support the deal as already written, they lose face if they come back with a disapproved deal. Their ego doesn't want you to think they don't have sway over their own company. You can help this along by appealing directly to their ego. Say something like, "I know you're considered the top negotiator in your company. They always follow your recommendations, don't they?"

Sometimes using this counter can actually get the other side to admit they were using the tactic, and they have authority to commit after all. Any time you can catch the other side in a tactic, they are usually so embarrassed at being caught they'll give you an extra concession without demanding reciprocity. If it's not a tactic and they actually do have to confer with another authority, you've increased the likelihood they will truly try to push for approval of the deal or risk being seen as unpersuasive. Some negotiators' egos are so huge that they would rather go into a so-so deal than lose face.

Next, after you have their commitment to push for the deal, counter with an ambiguous authority of your own. You can simply say that, because they have to get higher approval, you'll treat the agreement as a draft only. You, too, will run the "draft" by your own higher-ups for their approval. That's reciprocity, and it's only fair.

Suddenly the other side is confronted with the possibility of your side changing the deal, which negates the advantage they have in you already exposing your target position. They also now have to worry about that slow government bureaucracy tying up the contract award for an extended period of time. This can make the cost of continuing to use the tactic too high for them, and they admit they can close after all. You've just caught them in a tactic and you might get an extra concession out of it.

You also should try to lock in a definite time by which they have to give you a response. This will prevent the negotiations from dragging on and will show you are serious about a quick commitment. It also prevents them from using the time pressure or time investment tactic on you. Inform them that, at the expiration of that expressed time, they'd better have someone with authority to finalize the deal once and for all.

One last thing. Before they leave to go to their ambiguous authority, get them to nail down the exact objections or issues they have to have "approved" and why. You might not always get the answer why, but you'll usually be successful in defining what they still consider to be open items.

This does two things. First, you can tell them you now consider all the other items you've discussed and agreed to—with the exception of those items—to be closed. Get them to agree to this in writing. This will prevent them from trying to open these issues later. They can't use the nibble tactic on these issues now. Second, it gives you information regarding what is important to them, and may even give insight into their target position on these issues. Information is power, and power shifts to you.

One of the things the ambiguous authority tactic is designed to do it to get the other side to reveal its target position. When they come back from their ambiguous authority, your target position magically has become their new minimum position. That's called the bracketing tactic, and we'll talk about it next.

Chapter 20

The Bracketing Tactic

Bracketing is actually both a negotiation preparation tool and a powerful negotiation tactic. Remember back when we were talking about preparing for negotiations, I suggested you establish a minimum position (MIN), a target position (TGT), and a maximum position (MAX) for each of your issues. This approach builds in the flexibility you'll need during negotiations and you can also set your BATNA—that crucial walk-away point. In essence, you *bracket your own objectives*. So you've already seen how bracketing can be used as a tool. Now let's see how bracketing can be used as a tactic.

After you establish your MIN, TGT, and MAX positions for an issue, you immediately let the other side know what they are, right? Of course not! If you do, you've just given them your game plan and destroyed your flexibility. Remember, the other side will have MIN, TGT, and MAX positions for that issue too. If you give away your positions, watch how many times your MAX position (the absolute highest you are willing to pay) magically becomes the other side's new MIN position (the absolute minimum they will accept to do the job).

Once they have that new MIN position, the other side will establish new TGT and MAX positions based on it. Using your foolishly disclosed MAX as their new MIN, they will try to negotiate you up to their new MAX, being perfectly willing to settle for their new TGT. You have allowed them to shift the entire negotiation range upward. You just have been the victim of the tactic of bracketing.

Even the most novice negotiators usually realize that giving the other side their negotiating position is not a smart thing to do, so the chances of that situation actually happening is rather remote.

Putting the shoe on the other foot, wouldn't *you* like to know the MIN, MAX, and TGT positions of the other side before you sit down to negotiate with them? Good luck. They'll treat that information as if it were the secret recipe for Coca-Cola. But you always want to *bracket the other side's offer*. So what can we do to bracket the other side? And what do we need to look out for so we aren't bracketed by them?

Here's a golden maxim of negotiation, and the answer to both of these questions: The first side to throw out a number in negotiations usually loses. Put another way, *never* give out the first offer; *always* try to get the other side to throw out the first offer. As soon as one side throws out a number, the other side can bracket it. This number simply becomes the other side's starting point for negotiations. If the other side happens to accept immediately the first number you threw on the table, how will *that* make you feel? You'll be thinking either you made a mistake or you could have gotten away with asking for more.

I bet you've been bracketed before and didn't even realize it. Have you ever shopped for a new car? As soon as you set foot on that car lot, a helpful salesperson bounds up to you, all smiles, and says something like, "What will it take to get you in a car today?" Folks, they're not being helpful. They're trying to get you to throw out the first number so they can bracket it! Don't fall for it. If they fail to get you to commit to a number, sometimes they'll use the flank attack: "Well, what kind of monthly payment can you afford?" That will give them the same information and you'll be bracketed before you can blink. Never, in any negotiation, commit to the first number if you can help it.

You always want the other side to commit first. Who knows, you may be surprised. Their offer could be a lot better than you thought. Next, it gives you crucial information about their negotiation position. When forced to commit first, most people will lead with their MIN. Remember, the more information you get about the other side's position, the more your position is strengthened.

Finally, you can now bracket their number. That number is now a starting point for you.

As a government negotiator, you always have the decided advantage when it comes to this game of bracketing. Why? Because the government acquisition process *forces* the contractor to commit to the first number! You control the rule books. You control the process. If the contractors want to play, they have to play by your rules. The process has you send out an RFP or a request for equitable adjustment. What does that force the contractor to do? Send in a proposal. What does the contractor's proposal have to include? Right. The first number. Advantage: government.

But before you start gloating too much, here are several cautions. First, the tactic of bracketing can apply to your first counterproposal as well. As soon as you counter the contractor's proposed price, they'll now bracket your counter. Next, remember you have to be fair and reasonable to both sides. This prevents you from arbitrarily setting an unreasonable MAX or TGT position against their number and trying to browbeat them down to it. Make sure you do your homework and know the value of what you are buying. Finally, never be predictable in your bracketing increments. The other side will do their homework and prepare for it. The increments you offer in your counterproposals can give the other side important clues about how much money you have to play with and what your real target objective is. Also, *always encourage the other side to use incremental concessions*. It can tell you volumes about their position and their negotiating authority.

What if that first number the contractor throws at you blows you away by its generosity? What if it's better than you ever expected? Should you simply accept it without playing the bracketing tactic or any other negotiating games? First of all, the FAR says you can. FAR Part 15 allows you to award without discussions (negotiations) if you get that perfect proposal at that perfect price. You don't even have to establish a competitive range. You simply award the contract at the offered price. However, I would be extremely cautious before I make that decision.

If you consider the price to be unreasonably low, you must investigate why. The contractor could have made a simple math error or could have a poor understanding of the requirement. In either case, you could greatly increase the government's risk by awarding at that price. Concentrating on price alone can be false economy. If you award at an unreasonably low price, the contractor may be tempted to cut corners, and contract performance could suffer or even be in jeopardy. And remember, your ultimate goal isn't contract award. It's getting that supply or service into the hands of your customer to satisfy a need; it's successful contract performance.

Another reason you should be cautious about awarding without discussions can be learned by what contractors and professional negotiators are taught. They're taught *never* to say yes to the first offer, or first counteroffer for that matter. If you jump too quickly at the first offer the other side puts on the table, their natural inclination is to assume they offered too low or they left something out. This could trigger backpedaling. They may look for ways to put conditions on what you thought was a closed deal (remember the nibble?) or even find ways to back out of the situation altogether. Worse, they could feel they were burned enough to want to get even the next time. Now the threat of competition will limit their ability to pad future proposals, but what about modifications? Because modifications are always sole-source negotiations, competition will not be a deterrent to padding.

Finally, remember a contractor's opening position is almost never the best offer they are willing to accept.

Here's another tip related to bracketing: *Never offer to split the difference, but always encourage the other side to do so.* I've personally made this mistake in negotiations. I can't remember the exact numbers, but I was negotiating a computer services contract with a value around $2 million. Our price positions started far apart, but after long, mostly productive sessions, the contractor and I had closed the difference to around $20,000. That's where we locked up. I wasn't going to budge, and it was obvious, after many more fruitless hours of negotiating, that the contractor wasn't going to budge either. And we were only $20,000 apart.

You're probably thinking right now exactly what I was thinking then. The fairest way to settle the impasse is simply to split the difference, and that's what I offered. I told the contractor I was willing to come up $10,000 if they would come down $10,000. Clean. Neat. Fair.

That's exactly what the contractor wanted me to do, and he took me to school. I was concentrating on the difference of $20,000. He was concentrating on total contract price. My school lesson went something like this:

"Captain McIntyre, I'm at $1.5 million and you're at $1.48 million, right?"

"Yep."

"And you're now saying you'll come up to $1.49 million, right"?

"Right." (I never talked too much in negotiations, although my wife can't seem to believe this.)

"Well now, that might work. Tell you what, I'll run that new number through the corporate office [ambiguous authority tactic] and see if I can get them to agree. In fact, give me about 15 minutes to talk to them on the phone in private and we could have a deal!"

"Okay" (lamb to the slaughter).

After about an hour and a half, not 15 minutes [remainder of ambiguous authority tactic plus time pressure/time investment tactic], their negotiator came back in with a sad face and announced:

"Captain McIntyre, I'm personally embarrassed. I'm convinced your offer to split the difference was fair, and I felt sure Corporate would buy off on it. But they're convinced we can't go a penny lower than $1.5 million after all the concessions we've given up already [good cop/bad cop tactic]. But hey, we're only $10,000 apart! I just feel so bad about having to walk away from this deal over just $10,000."

"Why don't we split the difference"? (This just slipped out of my mouth automatically.)

Do you see what had happened? When I first offered to split the difference, I had unintentionally shifted the negotiation range (the bracket) upward—and they had given up absolutely nothing in return! I had also convinced myself that splitting the difference was "fair," so I was willing to split the difference again after we deadlocked again. And the funny thing is that after they reluctantly agreed to "split the difference" again, I left that negotiation feeling I had won. Who had *really* won?

So bracketing your own objectives is a helpful tool, and bracketing the other side's offer is a powerful negotiation tactic. Because you never want the other side to bracket you if you can help it, what can you do to prevent it? What are the counters to the tactic of bracketing?

COUNTERS TO THE BRACKETING TACTIC

First, as you've seen, never let the other side trick you into committing first. Never throw out the first number. If they don't have your number or position, they can't bracket it. If they try to force you to commit, use phrases such as, "You're the expert; you tell me." Or "What *do you* think is fair?" Or "You tell *me* what your company needs to make a decent profit on this work."

Next, always keep your government cost estimate secret. Never let the contractor find out how much money you think it will take to do the job or how much money you have in the bank to play with. The only exception to this is construction contracts, for which the

FAR allows you to disclose an estimated price *range* to give the competing contractors a ballpark to estimate the extent of the job. I would hesitate about even doing this, and would disclose a range only if it's the absolute last way you can ensure contractors will provide responsive proposals. Contractors will fish. They'll ask you for ballpark figures. Don't give them those figures.

Never offering to split the difference is worth mentioning again as a counter to the bracketing tactic. If you offer to split the difference, you've just given them a new number to bracket. You've also shifted the relevant negotiation range upward in the contractor's favor without a corresponding reciprocal concession from them.

Finally, if you do get pinned down and bracketed—and it happens—use logic to break the bracket. In other words, once you realize you've been bracketed, try to shift the negotiation range back down by any means you can. You could, for instance, introduce new facts in your favor or emphasize old facts in a new way. You could retreat to your ambiguous authority and trot out the good cop/bad cop tactic. You could shift some of your other "give points" to "must points" to compensate for the bracketed issue. You could even introduce new issues and demand concessions on them. Admittedly, retreating from a position you've allowed yourself to be committed to can be difficult, but it can be done.

One other tactic you could try is to deadlock intentionally on the issue you have been bracketed on, then offer to table the issue until later so the negotiation can continue. In fact, that's the next tactic we'll talk about: the set-aside tactic.

Chapter 21

The Set-aside Tactic

Deadlocks are common in negotiations, since rarely do both sides have the same goals. Both sides may also have widely different views about what they perceive as a "fair" outcome on price or any other issue. To complicate matters, some negotiators intentionally use deadlocks as a tactic to build up negotiation capital or to set up other tactics. You saw an example of this in the last counter we discussed to the bracketing tactic. Another example is the "take it or leave it" tactic that we'll talk about later.

Instead of allowing a deadlock to derail your negotiation, you first may want to use a tactic specifically designed to break deadlocks: the set-aside tactic.

Whenever the other side insists on a number or an issue you just can't live with, and you reach a deadlock, simply acknowledge their position and suggest setting it aside for a while and moving on to other issues. You get their agreement to *put that issue away until later.* Do not agree with them, don't tell them you see their point, just say something like, "I can tell this issue is important to you and it's obvious we're pretty far apart on it. Tell you what. So we can keep the negotiations moving, let's set that issue aside for the moment and see if we can't get some of these other issues out of the way." If the other side is truly interested in reaching an agreement, they'll always agree.

So. You have the sticky issue tabled. What next? Remember the order of issues tactic? You put issues in the order of least importance to you (to get the other side feeling bad about constantly saying no) or you put issues in the order of ease of agreement (to get the other side accustomed to saying yes). Now that you have deadlocked, it may be time to review your order of issues. You already have a big "no" from the other side on the issue you have set aside, so now you should rearrange your remaining issues for ease of agreement. You want to restart the momentum of the negotiation by getting agreement on many of the smaller (or noncontroversial) issues.

By tackling these other issues, both sides get into the swing of the give and take of negotiations again. And the more you agree on issues, the more the other side will be under pressure to keep the ball rolling and continue to agree.

If any of you grew up on a farm, or have visited a farm, you may have had a chance to try your hand at working an old-time water pump. When you want to fill up that water bucket from the well, you have to start by cranking that pump handle like crazy! You pump and pump and pump, encountering great resistance from that pump handle. To make matters worse, you don't get a drop of water for all your efforts—until you've pumped for a while. Then something amazing happens. The pump gets primed, the water starts rising in the pipe, and finally it starts flowing out of the spout of the pump (provided, of course, you don't have a dry well). After the water breaks the surface and starts flowing, you find resistance from that pump handle greatly decreases. You can slow down your pumping efforts and the water will continue to flow. In fact, sometimes you can keep the water flowing simply by nudging the pump handle.

It's the same in negotiations. Once you get the ball rolling, the hard part is usually over. The momentum is created and is now easier to maintain.

After you get the ball rolling again, you pull out the sticky issue you set aside earlier. Chances are, the other side is now more willing to come to some agreement on it to continue the momentum of the negotiation. After all, you've had so much success agreeing on all the other issues, right? Your chances of getting that issue resolved have now greatly improved.

Another dynamic that works in your favor when you use the set-aside tactic is the time investment factor. The same principles that make time investment work as a stand-alone tactic are working for you now. When you set aside that sticky issue, you made it possible for negotiations to continue. The longer negotiations continue, the more time the other side invests in the negotiation. The more time the other side invests, the less likely they are going to be to walk away from the table without at least something to show for all their effort and time. You have given them more of a stake to see the negotiation successfully concluded, and you have increased the chances of agreement on that seemingly deadlocked issue.

What if you perceive the other side is using the set-aside tactic against you? What do you do?

COUNTERS TO THE SET-ASIDE TACTIC

First, *don't be too hasty to counter it at all*. Setting aside this sticky issue may be just as healthy and appropriate for your side as it is for them! You've obviously deadlocked for a reason, and usually both sides have the same basic problem. You've likely reached your BATNA, or close to it, or you wouldn't have deadlocked. Chances are, the other side is in the same boat.

By using the set-aside tactic on you, the other side is hoping to restart the negotiation momentum by getting you to agree to minor, easier issues first. They will then reintroduce the hard issue after they have conditioned you to say yes and have gotten you to invest more time in the negotiation outcome, right? But this cuts both ways.

First, you eventually need to reach agreement on these other issues anyway to conclude negotiations successfully, so you're not really losing anything by it. Next, although they are conditioning you to say yes by negotiating the incremental, smaller agreements, they are doing the same thing on these same issues! They're automatically conditioning themselves to say yes too. Finally, they are investing the same amount of additional time in the negotiation as you are. So the time investment dynamic works on them too—at the very same time they are applying it to you.

Understanding these concepts when the other side pulls out the set-aside tactic can allow you to reflect the effects of the tactic back on them while resisting the effects yourself. You can reverse the effects of the tactic by simply taking it over. If they propose to set an issue aside, you can respond by saying something like, "Fine. I agree. Let's table this issue until later and see if we can't get some agreement on all these other points we have to discuss. Let's have a caucus and I'll rearrange our agenda so we can get to these other issues."

This also illustrates the most powerful counter to the set-aside tactic: *You are the government, so you control the agenda and the negotiation.* Don't let the other side take away this powerful inherent advantage you enjoy. When they pull out the set-aside, *you* get to reset the agenda and can order the revised agenda to encourage agreement on minor issues to build momentum and create a time investment. You basically hijack the other side's own tactic.

Of course, you can also disagree to set aside the issue they want to table. You control the negotiation. You may respond to their attempt to set aside an issue by saying something like, "You know, I realize this is a tough issue and we're pretty far apart on it. However, we really need to get this resolved. In fact, if we don't get agreement on this, we may be wasting our time with these other issues. I'm sure if we roll up our sleeves and put on our thinking caps, we can make some headway on this. Why don't we caucus and look for creative ways to break this deadlock?" This demonstrates to the other side, in case they had any doubt, that you control the pace of the negotiation as well as the order of issues to be discussed.

Finally, you can counter their use of the set-aside tactic by responding with your own use of the ambiguous authority tactic. This works equally well whether you agree to let them set the issue aside or force them to keep it on the table.

When we discussed that tactic earlier, you found it was important for you to establish your own ambiguous authority before going into negotiations. Now could be a good time to use it. You may want to say something like, "You're right. We're pretty far apart on this issue. In fact, I'm not sure I have authority to budge one iota from the position I've already given you. I'm going to have to go back to my supervisor to see if I have any leeway at all."

You have availed yourself of your prearranged escape route and have subjected them to the effects of the ambiguous authority tactic. Just like judo uses an opponent's own momentum against him, you have used their own introduction of the set-aside tactic to improve your chances of reaching a successful negotiation outcome.

Almost everyone involved in any negotiation process understands that bargaining is an accepted practice. In fact, it's the essence of a negotiation. Negotiators are prepared and are willing to "give" on some issues to get what they want on others and ultimately attain their goals. This underlying tenet of negotiation forms the basis for the next tactic we'll discuss: the tradeoff tactic.

Chapter 22
The Tradeoff Tactic

The tradeoff tactic is simply *always insisting on reciprocity for any concession*. To put it another way, never make a concession without getting something in return. Reducing it to dialog: "If we do this for you, what will you do for us?" And never, ever unilaterally throw the other side an unreciprocated concession as a gesture of goodwill. Never give them something for nothing. This seems so simple it should be obvious, but time and again I've seen government negotiators simply concede on "little matters" unilaterally because (1) they want the other side to like them, (2) they don't want to spoil a good relationship, (3) they want to keep the negotiations moving, or (4) they really don't mind giving on that particular point, because it's just a "little thing," isn't it?

Please resist the urge to do this. As you'll see, giving without getting in negotiations—even on minor matters—reduces your negotiation power and could allow the other side to take advantage of you. We'll look at each of the reasons I've just mentioned that inexperienced negotiators use to justify concessions without reciprocity and we will examine why their logic is flawed. First, though, let me give you a few reasons why you should always ask for a tradeoff.

The first reason is obvious. By asking for something in return, *you just may get something!* Best case, it may be something you totally didn't expect to get. Worst case, even if you get a "no," you've increased the pressure on the other side to reciprocate in the future to be considered "fair." You've also increased your information about the other side's position and flexibility regarding that position. The tradeoff tactic can work just as well even if you get nothing in return. It's the asking that's important.

This leads us into the next reason for always demanding reciprocity: By asking for that tradeoff concession, *you have increased your negotiating capital.* When you give up something without getting anything in return, you deplete your negotiating capital. Negotiation capital is simply the cumulative negotiation latitude you have created in your plan. You've already learned how to build latitude into your positions when you plan for the negotiation ("must" and "give" points; and minimum, maximum, and target positions).

You should also have a good handle on how much total negotiating room you have given all the issues—in other words, your total latitude as a negotiator. Don't deplete this reservoir of "wiggle room" without at least attempting to get something in return. It decreases your freedom to bargain and limits your other options, such as which tactics are available to use. Always decide how much ground you can give up. Put a value on it so you can ask the other side to reciprocate.

By demanding a tradeoff, you also elevate the value of your concession, if indeed you do eventually make it, by increasing the cost to the other side for asking. Remember, you have already determined your position to be fair and reasonable. There should be no "freebies" in negotiation. (Why give anything away?) Let the other side know it will be difficult for you to agree to the concession and you expect something in return to maintain fairness. If you always do this, do you think it might make them less inclined to ask for more freebies in the future? Hopefully so! It also lets the other side know you're not a pushover, which is the next reason to always use the tradeoff tactic.

If you give away positions unilaterally or fail to ask for tradeoffs when the other side asks for a concession, the other side may see you as weak and take advantage of you. Herb Cohen, in *You Can Negotiate Anything* (Bantam Books, 1982), gives an excellent example of how throwing out a concession without a tradeoff can be perceived as weakness:

> ... the typical American or Western negotiator, when confronted with a stalemate, is often willing to make the first concession to get things moving. We assume that the other party will respect this candor and collaborative spirit and reciprocate.

Actually, if you are dealing with a Soviet-style operator, the op-posite is true. During the armistice negotiation ending the Korean War, both sides stated their initial demands regarding the location of the final truce line. Obviously, they were far apart. Suddenly the United Nations negotiators, departing from appropriate adversary bargaining practices, made a quick major concession. In trying to be conciliatory with the "Soviets" from North Korea, we actually revealed our final fallback position. Instead of this being perceived as reasonableness, it gave the impression of weakness to our opponents and hardened their negotiating posture. (p. 141)

As you recall, we didn't fare too well in those negotiations. Korea remains divided to this day, North Korea is now an official member of the "Axis of Evil," and the Korean peninsula is one of the most heavily armed and volatile regions in the world.

Always demanding a concession in return for a concession is also an excellent way to stop the other side from successfully using the nibble tactic on you. If you constantly give things away without getting something in return, the other side will keep coming back to you for more and more concessions. They'll nibble you to death!

What should you ask for in return when you use the tradeoff tactic? Obviously that will depend on your particular negotiating situation. Some professional negotiators feel it's best to let the other side decide. In his book *Secrets of Power Negotiating* (Career Press, 2001), Roger Dawson puts it this way:

If you change even a word [when you ask for a tradeoff], it can dramatically change the effect. If, for example, you change this from "If we can do that for you what can you do for us?" to "If we do that for you, you will have to do this for us," you have become confrontational. You've become confrontational at a very sensitive point in the negotiations, when the other side is under pressure and is asking you for a favor. Don't do it. It could cause the negotiation to blow up in your face. You may be tempted to ask for a specific concession because you think that you'll get more that way. I disagree. I think you'll get more by leaving the suggestion up to them. (p. 78)

Other negotiators feel it is perfectly okay to ask for something specific commensurate with the value of what the other side is asking you to give up. This, of course, can also serve as your fallback position if the other side is unwilling to come up with a concession on their own. If so, you should already be prepared to request something concrete. You simply ask for one of your "give" points that you may have previously written off. Or you can increase the request of one of your "must" points above your target position or beyond what has been negotiated so far for that point. You can even be creative and experiment with any combination of these points and positions if it will add value to achieving your overall negotiation goals.

It should be obvious to you now why you should never give anything away in a negotiation without getting something in return. Let's return now to the four reasons inexperienced negotiators commonly use to justify this mistake:

"I want the other side to like me"—This is usually not verbally stated, but rather felt, by the negotiator. Almost subconsciously, the negotiator reasons that if he gives the other side a freebie, they will personally like and accept him more. It's simple human nature. Most people have an innate desire to be well liked by the people they come in contact with, especially if they will be associating with them for a period of time. Just remember that you're not representing the government and the taxpayers to win a popularity contest.

Being liked by the other side should not control your actions. What you want is their respect, and the best way to gain that is by being a principled, fair negotiator. As you've seen, you can actually lower their respect for you if you allow concessions without tradeoffs.

"I want to preserve our good working relationship"—Of course, a good working relationship with the other side can be a gigantic asset in any negotiating situation. You certainly want to create and preserve these relationships. But a healthy working relationship shouldn't

be a one-way street. In a truly healthy working relationship, both sides realize reciprocity is the key to keeping things fair and even. Just as you can't buy a trusting personal relationship with gifts, you can't create or maintain a good business relationship simply by throwing out unilateral concessions.

"I just want to keep the negotiations moving"—I admit it's tempting to want to breathe new life into a stalled negotiation by offering a concession or by giving in to a demand by the other side just to get things back on track. Hopefully you understand by now why this rarely works. You may indeed move the negotiation forward—just enough to allow the other side to accept your concession—only to deadlock again. You've also shown the other side you're willing to give things away, and they'll probably come back asking for more.

There are plenty of other ways to get a stalled negotiation moving again. The set-aside tactic, for example, is excellent. Other tactics could be trial balloons, ambiguous authority, good cop/bad cop, and time pressure. Another alternative I've heard inexperienced negotiators use is, "I just want to start things out on the right foot." Giving a concession away up front in an attempt to foster goodwill is almost always ineffective and usually boomerangs. You've started the negotiation off on the right foot all right—*their* right foot. Remember the North Korean example?

"It's just a little thing, isn't it? What could it hurt giving this away?"— Even if you feel the concession is minor, the impact of giving it away without a tradeoff could be major. As we've discussed, the impression you give to the other side could be worth far more to them than the actual concession. Remember, you derived your negotiating position through careful market research and determined it to be a fair and reasonable position prior to entering into negotiations. If you can easily give part of it away either up front or unilaterally later, and not use it as leverage to gain something of value, why did you bother to prepare it as a position in the first place?

Now let's put the shoe on the other foot. Let's say you're negotiating and you have just countered the other side's initial position with something you think is more in line with reality. They say, "Fine, but what can you do for me in exchange?" Yep. They've just pulled the tradeoff tactic against you. So, how do you counter it?

COUNTERS TO THE TRADEOFF TACTIC

First of all, realize the other side will use the tradeoff tactic against you, just as you will with them. It's part of the normal give and take of negotiating. It's the essence of bargaining. So don't be shocked or offended when the other side demands a concession from you as a condition of giving a concession of their own. Stay calm; don't get upset. And most important, *be prepared*.

You should already have thought through the answer to "If we do this for you, what will you do for us?" One counter could be to offer immediately one of your low-priority "give" points. To do this, you must have already calculated what impact this will have on your overall negotiation plan. The obvious drawback to this counter is that the other side can immediately say "That's not good enough" or, as we have learned, the dreaded, "You'll have to do better than that."

A more effective counter could be the old standard of answering a question with a question. When they ask what you will do for them in return, say "Well, what do *you* think would be fair?" In other words, let them suggest your tradeoff for you. If they answer, even if the demand is outrageous, you've at least gotten a peek as to what is important to their side. You have just increased your negotiation information.

Who knows, they may suggest you give up something that means little to you anyway. After they suggest to you what they think would be "fair" for you to give up, you can increase your information by asking, "And how do you think that's fair?" At this point, the other side usually will start elaborating, giving you even more information. They may talk themselves down from their own demand or even talk themselves out of asking for reciprocity at all.

Another way to thwart the tradeoff tactic is to counter with tactics of your own. You could use, for instance, the ambiguous authority tactic: "Gee, I don't know if I'm authorized to give up anything else. I'll have to go back and ask my boss." Or you could use the good cop/bad cop tactic: "Man, I just don't think my supervisor will go for any more concessions. She's already pretty ticked at everything I've given up. If I have to face her with this, she could go ballistic and really make things hard for us." Obviously, using these two tactics in tandem can give you a force multiplier effect.

Finally, you can simply stand firm and refuse to reciprocate. This counter is a bit dangerous because it can lead quickly to a negotiation deadlock, but it can also be used effectively. To help you decide whether to reciprocate when asked for a tradeoff, ask yourself these two questions: (1) How do I use my inherent power as a government negotiator? and (2) How thoroughly have I researched my position on this issue? How you answer these questions can help you decide whether to accept the tradeoff request, so let's talk about them.

"How Do I Use My Inherent Power as a Government Negotiator?"

Remember, you represent the government, and that gives you a measure of inherent legitimate power. Different negotiators will use this power differently (a matter of negotiation style), and some negotiators will vary how they use this power from negotiation to negotiation (a matter of tactics).

You may be one of those folks who take a hard line: "Hey! This is the government you're dealing with! We set the rules and you should be glad to have the privilege of dealing with us. Our last offer is good—it's backed by the full force of the government—and you just need to accept it or else! I can't believe you're trying to nickel and dime me here! Don't you know I represent Uncle Sam?" This like-it-or-lump-it approach works well if the other side is already intimidated because they are dealing with the government, or if there's lots of competition.

I was personally never good at the like-it-or-lump-it approach. I preferred taking the logical approach to not reciprocating: "You know, being a government negotiator I am required by law to be fair and reasonable to both sides. I have to reach an agreement that is fair to *you* as well as to the taxpayers. When I came up with my negotiation positions, I did so with this in mind. Therefore, my position as already stated is as fair and reasonable as I can be and still keep this deal—and my responsibility as a government negotiator—balanced."

"How Thoroughly Have I Researched My Position on This Issue?"

Whether you take the hard line or the logical approach, both should be backed up by the facts. You must be confident that your position is indeed fair and reasonable. Your research should be thorough enough to convince you that giving away anything more would tilt toward being unfair and unreasonable. If this is truly the case, it's easy to defend your refusal to reciprocate with the facts, and you can confidently say, "Nope. That's enough. In fact, my research shows I'm played out as far as negotiating flexibility." Yet again we see that negotiation planning is the key to success.

Ideally, you should have already asked yourself these two questions for each issue you plan on negotiating way back during negotiation planning. You should already know whether you will agree to tradeoffs for each of your major positions before you are asked the question. For example, you already have established a BATNA for each issue. If you are already there, or close to it, you will be a lot less likely to entertain a tradeoff request from the other side. Thorough negotiation planning, coupled with sound research, will take the doubt out of "should I reciprocate or not?" You now simply stick to your plan.

Your negotiation plan also had you identify issues as either "must" or "give" points. Now is the time to learn how to use this to your advantage by using the tactic of coupling issues together, which is the topic of our next chapter.

Chapter 23
The Coupling Tactic

Coupling issues together is one of the most basic and effective tactics you can use, and you're already set up to do it if you did a proper job preparing for the negotiation. Remember the prioritized list of negotiation issues you created during negotiation planning? You drew a line somewhere on that list. Everything above the line became a "must" point (objectives that absolutely have to be met). Every issue below the line became a "give" point (important objectives to strive for, but not absolutely necessary to seal the bargain).

Because you developed and prioritized your list in private, the other side has no idea what you have selected as your "must" and "give" points. You now can tie together, or "couple," certain of your "give" points with your "must" points, as if they're a package deal and inseparable. You then will present them to the other side as a package deal and negotiate them that way. You will argue long and hard for the "package" as if it is one important issue instead of an artificially constructed amalgam.

Slowly, painfully, after much gnashing of teeth, you will reluctantly relent and give up your "give" point. Because the other side has no way of knowing that you really planned on giving away your "give" point anyway, you appear to be flexible, and the other side will usually reciprocate by allowing you to have what you were trying for all along—your "must" point. The longer you hold out and the more pain you can project before you sacrifice your "give" point increases the value of your concession, and increases the likelihood of achieving your "must" point.

Obviously, you only want to couple issues that are harmonious. Never attempt to couple totally dissimilar items. If you do so, the other side will simply separate them and force you to negotiate them individually. One "give" point that you can easily couple with almost any "must" issue is price. Because you've already developed a minimum, target, and maximum position for each price issue, you have price "give" points automatically created and waiting to use!

For example, let's say your customer really needs delivery of a certain piece of machinery from the contractor by the fourth of the month—no later. You identified this as a "must" point when you planned the negotiation. You also established your prenegotiation objectives on price for the machinery, creating a minimum (best-case scenario for you) of $20,000, maximum (walk-away point) of $50,000, and a target (most likely) of $35,000. Let's say your maximum price is also a "must" point. It could also be your BATNA. Remember, the contractor doesn't know delivery by the fourth is a "must" point for you, nor do they know your prenegotiation positions on price.

You now make your minimum position your "give" point and couple it with your "must" point of delivery by the fourth of the month. You then negotiate long and hard for that equipment, priced at not a penny more than $20,000, to be delivered by the fourth of the month. Who knows? You may just get both! More than likely, however, you'll get a counteroffer consisting of a later delivery date and a higher price. Continue to insist adamantly on your "package." Only after much fanfare and time have passed will you reluctantly agree to go up to $ 35,000 (your target anyway). The contractor, seeing you have made a big "concession" in price, will be under pressure to reciprocate, most likely by agreeing to your desired (really required) delivery date.

This is admittedly a rather simplistic example. You'll rarely immediately go straight to your target, but rather taper your concession pattern, and you may have to apply other tactics to get to your "must" delivery date, but this example does illustrate nicely the power of the coupling tactic. Make a point to brainstorm with your negotiating team for possible issues that would make good coupling candidates and make this tactic part of all your negotiation planning.

Couple all your "must" points with as many "give" points as you logically can. This prevents you from carelessly giving away all your "give" points up front, leaving you with only "must" points and no flexibility. Because you don't know the other side's "must" and "give" points, it also increases the likelihood that one of your "give" points will correspond to one of the other side's "must" points—and that's a negotiating hit you're looking for! At the very least, coupling issues and negotiating them as packages can give you important additional clues to the other side's true negotiation priorities.

Coupling also has the psychological effect of giving the other side a "victory." Most negotiators are conditioned to expect concessions and they just don't feel right if they get none. When you concede that "give" point (which, unknown to the other side, you were going to concede anyway), it gives that negotiator the concession they are looking for. Think about it. When you're writing something that will be reviewed by a picky, detail-oriented boss, it's best to leave something in (purposely) you know they will cut out. They get the satisfaction of feeling they have done their job and put their "stamp" on the final copy, and you get to preserve your original intent more or less intact.

I didn't realize it then, but I practiced a form of coupling when I was going to college as a cadet at The Citadel in Charleston, South Carolina. The Citadel, being a military school, had daily room inspections. I was convinced the inspectors were not human. They had some innate drive that wouldn't let them stop digging at your room until they found *something* to give you demerits on. No matter how many hours you spent making your room absolutely perfect, they would always find something. The worst things to get caught with were "contraband" items—popcorn poppers, toasters, certain types of civilian clothes. They carried a penalty of many demerits, and sometimes even "confinement" to campus over the weekend.

The list of items The Citadel considered "contraband" was extensive, and, being far from a model cadet, I was routinely caught with contraband. I would hide my treasured contraband on top of the panels of the false ceiling. I would then clean my room immaculately, hoping the inspector's initial impression of my room would deter a more thorough search. I mean, my room was so clean you could perform surgery off any surface. Where would the inspectors go first? Totally ignoring my sparkling room, they'd take a broom handle and start poking around the panels of the false ceiling. Busted again. I actually had a friend who had so much contraband hidden in his false ceiling that the ceiling collapsed on the inspector when he started rooting around with the broom handle. Now that's justice!

Then, one day, I had been in a rush and hadn't had proper time to clean my room. The dreaded inspectors were coming and, as usual, I had contraband hidden in the ceiling (I believe it was some sort of food this time). I knew I didn't have time to clean my room and I knew I was caught Big Time. I was going to lose my food, pick up major demerits, and probably have to spend the weekend staring at the walls. The inspector poked his head in the door, immediately saw my imperfectly made bed, and said, "Improperly made bed. Two demerits," and left! I mean, he didn't even come entirely into the room. To me, two demerits wasn't even a pinprick.

Lesson learned. The inspectors would stop as soon as they found something to award demerits on. So what did I do? Next inspection, I made sure they found something small right off. I collected an appropriately impressive collection of dust bunnies, rolled them together, and left them close to the entrance of the room. True to form, the inspector immediately found the dust, awarded a few demerits for it, and left—without further inspecting my contraband-laden room. I had given the inspector one of my "give" points (my willingness to absorb a few demerits) to get my "must" point (my ability to enjoy my contraband free of confiscation and confinement).

Coupling "give" points with "must" points creates greater negotiation flexibility and greatly increases the likelihood of achieving success negotiating your most important issues. The more practice you have at using the coupling tactic, the better you will get at using it and the more cumulative flexibility you will build in to your negotiations. Expert negotiators are extremely adept at convincing you to see one issue when there actually are two issues coupled together. So how do you protect yourself? How do you counter the tactic of coupling?

COUNTERS TO THE COUPLING TACTIC

If you're up against an experienced negotiator, the coupling tactic can be extremely difficult to counter because it can be almost impossible to detect if the negotiator is truly good. The best chance you have to counter the coupling tactic lies in your negotiation preparation.

Prior to the negotiation, you have gone through your own coupling exercise with your negotiating team. You've identified common issues that the other side will likely attempt to couple because you've examined them for coupling possibilities yourself. Look for these coming back at you as packages. You know price is always a logical coupling suspect, because it almost always is a "give" point. Your experience has likely familiarized you with other likely coupling candidates, like delivery times, financing, warranties, and so forth. Be attuned to these when you sit down with the other side.

You've also used your "intel" and information-gathering resources to find out as much about the other side as possible prior to the negotiation session. This information should give you good clues about the other side's likely "must" and "give" points. If you think you know them, you will be better able to decouple these issues when you see them "put on the table" as a package.

One resource that's particularly good at sniffing out coupled items is the other side's response to your draft agenda. Scrutinize any change the other side proposes in your draft issues to discuss, their order of discussion, or the addition or deletion of issues to the agenda. This sometimes can signal the other side's attempt to couple issues.

We've all heard the axiom that the best defense is a good offense. Representing the government side, you're already well positioned to thwart the coupling tactic before it starts. You control the agenda. You control what's talked about and what isn't. Don't lose this control. Keep the initiative. Once you identify likely coupling targets, simply refuse to talk about them as packages. Set and control the agenda so all issues are treated and talked about separately.

This forces the other side to justify them on their own merits, without being able to tie them easily to other issues. In isolation, their "give" points lose much of their effectiveness as valuable tradeoffs to achieve their "must" points.

Finally, attempt to decouple issues you think have been rolled into a package by the other side as soon as you identify the tactic. Force them to be talked about as separate issues. Speed is the key here, because the package gains credibility as a package the longer it stays together.

Your decoupling process may sound something like this: "I understand delivery time is an important issue to you; however, we're talking about price right now. I've got delivery issues scheduled to be covered later on this afternoon, and I promise we'll get to it. In the meantime, how about let's stay on track with the agenda we both agreed to and finish our discussion on price? I know delivery time has an impact on your price, and we'll have time to discuss how all these issues affect each other after we get through talking about them individually."

Once you have decoupled the issues, you force the other side to talk individually about each and every point (both their "gives" and "musts"). Guess which ones they will now spend the most time negotiating and which ones they will more likely blow off or be less concerned about? Can this give you important insight into what is *really* important to the other side? You bet!

One caution, however. Always preserve the overall context of the negotiation. When you're talking issue by issue, never signal how you feel on any one point or issue the other side brings up until all their points are on the table. If you do, you lose flexibility and increase the chance of agreeing to something without getting something in return. Of course the opposite is true if you are the one laying the issue out: You want the other side to agree to them issue by issue.

The next chapter will introduce one final tactic you may want to consider before we move on to some shady tactics to watch out for: the empty pockets tactic.

Chapter 24

The Empty Pockets Tactic

Have you ever played the board game Monopoly? Remember how exciting it was to land on "Chance" and draw from that orange deck of cards? Most were good, but some would cost you money. One of the bad ones told you to pay a "poor tax." It had a picture of a very sad-looking man holding his pockets inside-out with his fingers, showing you he had nothing in them. He was showing you empty pockets.

The empty pockets tactic is simply confronting the other side with the fact that you have reached the limit of your negotiation flexibility, usually because you have run out of budget headroom. You'll say something like, "You know, I really thought we could get this deal put together, but at the prices you're demanding, I simply don't have enough funds budgeted to allow me to sign this contract. I'd love to do it, but my pockets are empty."

Time is also something you can come up empty on. As a variant to the time pressure tactic, you could say something like, "I was hoping we could finalize this contract by now, but we've simply run out of time. If we can't come to some agreement today, we'll just have to go back to the drawing board." The reason you give could be that funds are expiring or your program office has deadlines they must meet.

The empty pockets tactic puts pressure on the other side to concede within the money/time you have stipulated or risk losing the entire deal. It works especially well if they know you have alternatives, like competition or the ability to accomplish the task in-house.

Most contractors understand that the government, despite its large resources, has explicit limits on time and money for each particular acquisition. Used successfully, the empty pockets tactic forces the other side to cut to the chase, dispense with gamesmanship tactics, and reveal their bottom-line positions—or risk losing the deal. It can also trigger a subconscious sympathy response, an "I feel your pain" reaction that will make the other side more likely to go along with you.

The government primarily uses this tactic because they're usually the side forking over the money. Before you decide to use the empty pockets tactic, however, a few cautions are in order. First, remember that you must be honest. You can't bluff or lie to the other side as a government negotiator. If you say your pockets are empty, they had better really be empty! Next, this is a tactic that is best used at the end of a negotiation, rather than at the start, and then it should be used only as a last resort. When you reveal to the other side that you have no more money in the budget or time in the schedule, you have automatically decreased your negotiation flexibility. You have given the other side important information about your position, possibly even your BATNA. What if the contractor has intended to counter well below that given a little more time and pressure? You can now kiss that savings goodbye.

I have heard recently that several government agencies have adopted the practice of revealing their budgeted amounts for projects up front in their solicitation for all offerors to see. I'm not convinced this is the best thing to do. What if you get only one proposal? You might have to go into sole-source negotiations with the other side knowing exactly how much money you have to spend. What do you think the contract price will turn out to be? Darn near your budgeted amount, I'll wager. This is true even if you have established a confidential independent government cost estimate below your budgeted amount. A smart contractor, knowing your budget, will find a way to convince you to spend more than you anticipated.

Even during competitive negotiations, revealing how much money you have to play with up front allows the other side to bracket your offer, and they'll gear their negotiations around moving you up in the bracket. They could additionally be tempted to craft a solution to meet your budget, regardless of whether it's the best solution for your agency. It also makes it easier for unscrupulous contractors to violate the law by bid rigging, collusion, bid rotation, and the like.

Although it's usually used by the government side, I have seen contractors use the empty pockets tactic. Usually it will be in response to a government request for additional work at no additional cost or government requests for rework after the contractor has completed a task: "I'd love to do that for you, contracting officer, but we just didn't build enough time into our schedule [or money into our budget]." Ever heard that one? I have.

Contractor's pockets cannot only be empty of money and time, but they can be empty of other things too. They can suddenly be short on expertise, capacity, personnel, hiring ability, data rights, and so forth. And the other side, remember, isn't under the same legal obligation to be absolutely fair and reasonable to both sides as you are.

So what do you do if you think the other side is using the empty pockets tactic on you?

COUNTERS TO THE EMPTY POCKETS TACTICS

What if the other side says they just don't have the money in their budget? Or they just don't have the time or experience or plant capacity? First of all, you need to adopt the correct mental attitude toward the situation. If they don't have it in their budget, whose problem is it? Yours or theirs? It's theirs! The other side is probably hoping you'll be sympathetic to their plight, but it's *their* plight. You didn't cause it. Resist the urge to feel sorry for them simply because they didn't budget or plan correctly. Don't let them shift their burden to you.

Contractors usually use the empty pockets tactic on modification requests, after the basic contract has been negotiated and awarded.

When you agreed to the basic contract, you agreed to a certain risk-sharing relationship between the government and the contractor. Part of that agreement represented the contractor's profit, which is largely a reward for risk taken. So the contractor has already been compensated to assume the risk of not having enough of this or that.

Don't allow the contractor's empty pockets tactic to convince you they need more of what they don't have, or they need to be compensated for more because they didn't plan for enough, if the scope of the contract remains unchanged. In essence, you'd be paying them profit for a risk they now don't have to worry about—and that's not a good bargain for the taxpayer. That's why the FAR allows very few price changes when options are exercised, except for increases resulting from Service Contract Act wage changes or prenegotiated escalation factors.

It could be you're asking the contractor to do more than the original contract called for. In that case, they have a legitimate basis to request an equitable adjustment from you. They have every right to come at you with their hands open, requesting more time and money.

But what if they tell you they can't accept the extra work because they just don't have enough of something? Chances are they're using the empty pockets tactic to establish an extreme initial negotiation position. They will then be in a better position to negotiate terms more favorable to them. They're hoping you'll just be so glad they finally agreed to do it that you aren't really concerned about the cost.

Because this is often the case, you need to probe their empty pockets assertion immediately for validity. Is it *really* a deal breaker or are they just trying to get a leg up in the negotiation? They may have displayed their empty pockets for no more valid reason than to judge your initial response. How you react to a contractor telling you they can't do something speaks volumes about how important it is to you, and that gives the other side good negotiation information.

There are many ways to probe the empty pockets assertion for validity. Let's say you need an extra report done under an existing contract, but the contractor says, "Sorry, we just simply can't do it. We don't have anyone with the right skills free and available to do that right now." Immediately probe that empty pocket for validity. You could say something like, "Well I guess that's it then. Thanks for being honest with me. We'll just go find another source to do this work." Or, "So even though we have already budgeted for this report and have the funds available now, you're telling me you're not interested." Or, "Who in your company has the authority to hire someone with the right skills, and how long would that take?"

After you make a statement like this, clam up and listen. If the other side wavers at all from their "I can't do it at all" position, it's probably not a valid empty pocket.

If you find this to be the case, you now treat their refusal not as an absolute "no," but as an initial negotiating position. Feel free to use all the tactics you now know to reach a fair and reasonable conclusion. You have just drawn them into the negotiation. Ideally, they may be a little embarrassed at having to backtrack from their initial refusal to consider negotiations, and that could mean a concession without requiring reciprocity.

If the other side displays empty pockets to you, it's important to probe for validity immediately. The longer you ignore their assertion, the more validity it takes on and the harder it will be to overcome later. Don't let their assertion of impossibility go unchallenged for very long. Determine immediately whether the empty pocket is a tactic or a reality.

Sometimes your probe will reveal that the other side's pockets are truly empty. They're not using a tactic at all; they're simply stating a fact. If this is the case, counters are obviously unnecessary and other negotiating skills become more important. You may have come to an honest impasse or even a deadlock. We'll discuss some ways for breaking out of these situations later in the book.

We've just gone over quite a few good tactics you can use as a government negotiator. We've also learned how to recognize them and counter them if they are used against you. The next part of the book will introduce you to some tactics that are a little less above-board and some that are outright unethical. All of them are manipulative. Accordingly, you should rarely use these next tactics as a government negotiator sworn to be fair and reasonable. I'm not saying you should never use them, but you had better do some serious soul searching if you elect to.

Just because you shouldn't use these tactics doesn't stop them from being used against you, however—and some of them are diabolically clever and effective. Now, that's not saying all contractors out there are crafty, shifty, manipulative ogres. In reality it's quite the opposite. The vast majority of contractors you'll deal with are as hard working and honest as you are. Besides, if they are smart, they know getting caught just once playing dirty, manipulative tricks on the government creates a negative impression that is hard to live down. They're much more interested in sound, honest dealings that will foster healthy long-term relationships. They know that this is the best way to ensure continued government business.

I've personally seen a dramatic drop in manipulative tactics during the last decade. The Competition in Contracting Act, FASA, and the Clinger-Cohen Act have led the way in replacing the old contractor-government adversarial stereotype with mutually respectful, true partnering relationships between government and industry. But I'm a realist and you should be too. There may be a few bad apples lurking out there, and you have a responsibility as a government negotiator to protect the taxpayer. So I've included these tactics in this book not for you to use, but for you to be able to recognize and counter.

Part Five

Tactics to Watch Out For

Chapter 25

The Climate
Control Tactic

One important rule of negotiation is always to have home court advantage. When you schedule a negotiation at your facility, in addition to putting the other side a little more ill at ease, you gain control over certain things you otherwise couldn't. Like the thermostat. I've known instructors who make the temperature in their classrooms a little on the cold side to discourage students nodding off, and I've known contractors who use their ability to control the physical climate in the negotiating room as an effective negotiation tactic in much the same way.

Prior to the negotiation, they make the temperature in the room a little too hot or a little too cold on purpose. It's not too noticeable, but a little uncomfortable. As the negotiation drags on, the visiting team can't help but be affected by this climatic ploy. They start to get uncomfortable. They may not even realize why they're uncomfortable or, best, it only registers subconsciously that they are uncomfortable. In either case, they are imperceptibly pressured to come to some sort of agreement—even if it's not the best deal they could get—more quickly to get out of that uncomfortable situation as soon as possible.

At the very least, the other side can become distracted by being too cold or too hot, and lose some of the focus they vitally need to be applying to the issues being discussed. It's simply hard to concentrate well when you are uncomfortable.

Even if they consciously realize they are too hot or cold, they are a little hesitant to bring the situation up to their hosts. They are guests and they don't want to offend. Besides, their hosts don't seem to be bothered in the least by the uncomfortable room temperature. That's because they planned for it. You see, the climate control tactic is a group tactic. The team leader who planned the tactic has already prepared his team by warning them to dress appropriately.

So if you perceive the other side is trying to manipulate you into a quick deal by using the climate control tactic, how do you respond?

COUNTERS TO THE CLIMATE CONTROL TACTIC

The easiest counter is simply not to give up home court advantage. If at all possible, insist on having the negotiation at a facility you control. This will put you in charge of the thermostat. One of the big advantages of being a government negotiator is that you control the negotiation process. This includes the agenda and the venue. There are many benefits to conducting negotiations in a facility you own or are familiar with. The ability to thwart the climate control tactic is just one of them. The only hand that should touch a thermostat in a negotiating room is yours.

There may be times, of course, when you're the guest team and the other side controls the negotiating room. So if you can't control the thermostat, what can you do? First, prepare your own team. Tell them that because you don't know whether the room will be too hot or too cold they should dress accordingly. Have them layer their clothes, so they can easily bundle up or shed clothes as appropriate. Nothing dramatic; you don't want to do a striptease in front of the other side. Dress coats and button-down sweaters can easily be donned or removed. Light jackets can be carried easily and can be unobtrusively on hand should they be needed.

Realize people have different comfort levels. Even if the host is not trying to pull the climate control tactic, the room may be uncomfortable for some. I've been a classroom instructor for a while now and I don't believe I've ever had a single class agree on the right room temperature. Some students are always too hot whereas others say they're too cold to think. Some then pipe up and say,

"Don't change a thing. The temperature's fine!" Preparing your team by reminding them to layer their clothing automatically takes care of these biological differences and ensures that all members of your team will be able to concentrate on the negotiations, not on getting comfortable. It also effectively thwarts the climate control tactic if it's being pulled on you.

Another simple counter is to request that the host adjust the room temperature. Of course, this only works if you or your team members realize they are uncomfortable. How you ask is important, however. *Who* asks is more important. Just as you control everything else in relation to your team, you as team leader need to control the asking. Keep in mind that the exchange I describe next can be used for any adjustment in the physical negotiation surroundings, not just for temperature changes.

One of the worst mistakes I made as an instructor was to ask the class, "Hey, is the room temperature okay in here? Is everybody comfortable?" I bet you already know what I got: 15 minutes of pure pandemonium. Immediately 30 people started talking at the same time, each with a different view of what climatic changes should occur. Soon the class settled into the "I'm as cold as an ice cube" faction, the "I'm roasting like a hotcake" faction, and the "I'm fine, don't change a thing or you'll mess me up" faction. (I'll talk about the "don't bother me, I want to go back to sleep" faction in another book.) An unofficial spokesperson magically arose to champion the cause of each faction and to rally the troops to the cause. Not only had I lost control of the class and wasted valuable instruction time, but I had neatly and very publicly maneuvered myself into a no-win situation.

Whatever decision I now made was going to please only a third of the class. The other two thirds would feel slighted by me at best and ignored by me at worst. In an honest attempt to be nice I had divided the class against itself, alienated a majority of them, and still not solved the problem. In fact, some of the students probably didn't even know they had a problem until I opened my big mouth. Worse, I had generally lost credibility with the class as an effective leader.

If my class was my negotiation team, how many basic rules of negotiation did I violate? How about "Never lose control of your team" or "Never allow your team to show disagreement in front of the other side," to name a few? Don't let this happen to you.

Talk to your team beforehand, during the negotiation preparation stage. First, assure them they can come to you if they are uncomfortable with the room temperature. Then, lay out the process: They come only to you and only in private. At your next caucus, you will then talk among your team in private and agree on a course of action (thermostat up or down, for example). This can be done by voice vote, secret ballot, squeaky wheel, or whatever. Once the decision is made, everyone must cheerfully agree with it, or at least give the other side the impression they cheerfully agree with it when they get back in the room.

You, as team leader, will then approach the other side's leader and request the climate change. I recommend approaching their team leader in private with your request, which won't put them on the spot with their own team members and will lessen the chance they will want to consult with their team before complying. You may say something like, "We really appreciate the fine way you've prepared for us today. There's just one small thing. We believe it's too cold in there. I'm sure your folks are cold too. We request you bump the thermostat up at least three degrees. Once the room heats up a bit, we'll continue. We'd really appreciate it. You-all are doing a great job, and thanks!"

How you phrase this is important. Notice you use "we" instead of "I" or "some folks on my team." This presents a unified front and demonstrates to their leader that your team won't be divided on this issue. Next, you make the problem a common one that's mutually shared by both teams by asserting that if your folks are cold, the other team probably is as well. This allows their leader to comply without feeling like he has made a concession without getting something in return.

Then, you *request* the change—politely but assertively—rather than just *ask* for it. If you ask, you could get a "no," and that's not what you want. It also shows you have resolve and won't be easily manipulated.

Notice also that you are specific in your request. You request that the thermostat be raised "at least three degrees" instead of simply "up" or "a tad." This makes your request more actionable and more difficult to be ignored or modified by the other side. You then signal that negotiations will not continue until your request is complied with. You've done it nicely, but the message is clear.

Finally, notice how you open and close your request with compliments and pleasantry. In his book *The One-Minute Manager* (William Morrow, 1982), Spencer Johnson calls this a "correction sandwich" and introduces it as a pattern to reprimand subordinates. During negotiations, I've found this to be an excellent approach when you have to give the other side bad news, or you want to call their attention to something you want changed and they probably won't like it.

I call it the "negotiation sandwich." You start with honest praise and compliments, then bring up only the behavior or situation you want them to address, then end with praise and compliments. You sandwich the negative between two positives. The positive language you have used to surround your negative request makes it easier for the other side to swallow. You improve the chances of having your request complied with without damaging your working relationship with the other side.

So don't let the climate control tactic freeze you out or burn you up. With a little preparation, or, lacking that, a little kind assertiveness, you can effectively negate the tactic if it is used. Even if it isn't used, your preparation or assertiveness can set up your team to concentrate better on the issues at hand.

The climate control tactic works largely on a subliminal level, subconsciously forcing negotiators to make poor snap decisions and generally to lose their ability to concentrate. The next tactic we'll talk about also taps into and plays with the subconscious—the strength in numbers tactic.

Chapter 26

The Strength in Numbers Tactic

Have you ever done any public speaking? Your throat may get dry, your ears may ring, you may have trouble concentrating, and you may even approach a panic attack. You may have peeked out at the audience before you start and have seen just a few seats occupied. "No problem," you think. "I can do this!" The next time you look out, however, half the room is full and you feel butterflies in your stomach. The more the room fills up, the worse it gets. By the time you take your place at the podium or hear yourself introduced, you're in full-scale stage fright!

If this describes you, don't feel alone. You are just one of the millions of Americans who rank fear of public speaking right up there with fear of death. Is it a rational fear? No! The crowd is simply made up of single individuals, each one of whom you would have no problem carrying on a conversation with one on one. But together—whew! They become a monster ready to devour you! This is, of course, your mind playing tricks on you.

Crowds affect the brain on a subconscious level. Your brain tells you, "Hey, you're outnumbered here and they're the enemy! You'd better fight or fly!" Our brain convinces us that these individuals, when amassed in a group, become much smarter than us, much more critical of us, and extremely imposing. They are to be deferred to and feared.

This fear can be triggered in groups as well as in individuals. Our early ancestors were affected by it. Let's say you're a club-swinging member of a caveman community that's banded together to defend your caves from a rival faction. When the other side comes over the hill, however, you notice they have twice as many club swingers as your side does. That's right. Dry mouth, ringing ears, wobbly legs. You may even start thinking, "You know, our caves aren't that great anyway. Why don't we just give them the caves? We'll be fine sleeping under some brush. It's better than getting bopped over the head, and we'll have a better view." Throughout history, rival groups, armies, and even nations have been affected the same way. They have deferred to the concept of strength in numbers.

Throughout the years, cagey negotiators have found a way to turn this subconscious fear of being outnumbered into an effective tactic. They know that simply outnumbering your team by the physical number of bodies triggers subconscious fears of inferiority from your side and tilts the negotiation almost imperceptibly their way. They do whatever it takes to ensure there are more of them present in the negotiating room than you.

For the tactic to work, it's essential for them to find out beforehand how many team members the other side will have so they can plan to have more. If they are the host, it's relatively easy. The host usually prepares a draft agenda and sends it out to the other side some time before the negotiation event. As part of that draft agenda, they will innocuously ask how many folks you plan on bringing so they can make sure they have enough seats prepared or refreshments ready for them and so forth. Although that's nice, it's not the real reason they asked. They want to get a nose count from the other side so they can have more people present in the room for the negotiation.

If they are not the host, the job's a little harder. But they'll try to get a nose count of your team any way they can. They may ask, for instance, what type of experts you'll be including (lawyers, program people, and so on) so they can make sure they have corresponding experts who can "talk the issues."

The strength in numbers tactic doesn't require overwhelming force to work. One or two extra people will do. It doesn't even matter if these extra people contribute or even know anything about the negotiation subjects. Remember, this is a mental tactic.

Their physical presence is all that's needed. I've seen a negotiation team leader, when the other side showed up with more people than anticipated, scurry down the hall collaring anybody he could find, asking, "Hey! Are you busy right now? Good! Just come in this room, sit down, shut up, and look smart!"

What triggers our inferiority when we are confronted with a larger negotiation team? You may start thinking, "Whoa! Look at how many people they're bringing to the table. They must consider this negotiation much more important than we do. They're probably much better prepared than us. They probably have different slants on each issue and a dedicated champion for each. They undoubtedly have come up with important things we haven't even thought about. We're going to get clobbered in this negotiation!"

Consciously or subconsciously, or sometimes both, the negotiation has already tilted in their favor before it has even started. We start off playing defense. Because we are physically weaker, we feel emotionally and intellectually weaker.

How do you respond if you think you're being bullied by the strength in numbers tactic?

COUNTERS TO THE STRENGTH IN NUMBERS TACTIC

As with any tactic, the best way to counter the strength in numbers tactic is to not give it a chance to be used at all. Representing the government side, you will normally be the host, and you'll control the agenda and the venue. You're the one who will send out the draft agenda and force the other side to give you a nose count of their team. You also will pick the room in which the negotiations will take place, and you can use the physical seating limitations of the room (or your arrangement of it) to mandate the maximum number of folks the other side can bring.

You set the rules. Simply set a rule that the other side can bring no more than, say, five team members.

If the negotiating teams are going to be small, and the room can easily accommodate extra players, there is a chance the other side might show up with one or two extra people. It may be they honestly believe these folks are needed or they might be playing the strength in numbers tactic on you. At this point, you can add team members of your own, if they are available. If they are not available, you can either elect to start the negotiations anyway or reschedule when your additional players are available.

You might say something like, "I see you brought your attorney and your vice-president of sales. We weren't expecting that or we would have made sure our lawyer and program manager's schedules were clear for today. Just to make sure we can cover all the issues and truly get agreement from everyone at once, I'm going to reschedule our meeting for tomorrow, when our folks are available. That way, we can make sure we can wrap this thing up in one session."

I've heard some people ask, "Why don't you just tell them their lawyer and VP (or whatever extra people they have brought) aren't needed and that they can go home, or just not allow them into the negotiating room?" You could do this, but I don't recommend it. It's a little too dictatorial and it could alienate the other side. They could have honestly brought these additional folks because they thought they were needed and could contribute to the discussion. If you exclude them, and only them, it could send the message that you think they are not important.

It could also be read by the people who picked them to attend that you think they have bad judgment. Because these are the folks who are staying for the negotiation, you don't want to start off on that wrong foot.

Good relationships are essential for effective negotiations, and kind gestures play a large part in cementing these types of relationships. There are some gestures, however, that just appear as kindness. In reality, they are deadly effective negotiation tactics designed by the other side to trip you up. One of these is called the walk in the woods tactic.

Chapter 27

The Walk in the Woods Tactic

I know that the walk in the woods tactic is effective, because it has been used against me. Very successfully. In fact, I didn't recognize the tactic or how well it worked on me until long after the negotiation ended. It's normally pulled out well into the negotiation and usually after you've deadlocked on an issue, or perhaps the entire negotiation has stalled. It's rarely recognized by untrained negotiators because it's disguised as a kind gesture, a great idea from the other side to break the deadlock. You need to learn to recognize this tactic. Here's how the tactic unfolds.

You're the team leader for the government side. After a fairly successful negotiation, you're deadlocked on a particularly thorny issue. You've gone back and forth with the other side perhaps for hours with no resolution or even movement. It's looking hopeless. You and your team are getting tired. Suddenly the team leader from the other side pushes back in her chair (body language tactic), rubs her face with both hands in a tired way (another body language tactic), sighs deeply, looks directly at you, and says something like, "You know, we're sooooo close to getting this thing done. And we've been beating up each other on this one gnarly issue for the past two hours. Quite frankly, my people are flat tired. I know your folks are probably pretty beat up and tired too. Tell you what. Let's put our teams on break and let's just me and you, one on one, get together somewhere—maybe the cafeteria for a cup of coffee, maybe outside for a breath of fresh air—and see if there's any way we can jointly work out some way to get this thing moving again."

In essence, she's asked you to take a walk in the woods with her. Remember every fairy tale you've ever read? Where do all the bad things always happen? In the woods.

When their team leader makes this suggestion, her folks heartily and vocally agree, and your folks join in too. After all, they really *are* tired and a break sounds like heaven to them right about now. To you, it *does* sound like a logical approach to solving the problem, your folks are behind the idea, and you secretly want a breath of fresh air or some coffee anyway, so you agree. You go for a walk in the woods with her.

What has she just done to you? She's effectively isolated you from your entire support infrastructure. You have all these smart people on your team precisely because they have expertise, skills, and knowledge you don't have. They cover your weaknesses with their strengths. But they can't do that when they're not there, and you can't pull on their talents. She's also maneuvered you into a neutral location where you're not surrounded by the trappings of your legitimate power.

You're now out of familiar territory. She's now got you where you are isolated, unsupported, on unfamiliar ground, and at your weakest.

And she's got it planned. She knows exactly what she's going to say, how she's going to say it, and what she wants you to agree to. It wasn't just a spur-of-the-moment decision she had to meet alone with you. She's planned for it. Her smart folks she left on break with your smart folks have already prepped her for this precise moment, so she still has the benefit of their expertise. She has minimum, maximum, and target positions and planned tactics to get you to agree to her team's way of solving the deadlock. And she knows she has a good chance of having it her way. You're about to get hammered.

I bet some of you are thinking back right now and realizing you've been the victim of the walk in the woods tactic in the past, and haven't know it until this moment. Don't feel bad; remember, the same thing happened to me. How is it that reasonably intelligent folks like us can get pulled into the walk in the woods tactic so easily?

First, the other side timed it right. They waited until you and your team really needed a break. At this point, everyone—your team included—thought it was a great idea. Even if you didn't particularly like the idea (and you probably did), you are hesitant to go against the grain. They also waited until you had deadlocked on an important issue and spent considerable time trying to resolve it. Eventually everyone is desperate for some sort of solution, and they presented an appealing approach to solving the problem and getting on with things. Everyone thinks, "What a great idea!"

Finally, they appealed directly to your ego. When they offered to work it out with you alone, they were reinforcing and inflating your concept of your own self-importance as team leader and your ability to make decisions. "Hey, they know I'm the mover and shaker of this group" you think, and you like the compliment. No wonder it's a very effective tactic.

The walk in the woods tactic has a couple of lesser variations that are just as effective. One is for their team leader to pull you aside during a normal break or at lunch to discuss an "important issue" or a negotiating sticking point. Maybe they'll offer to drive you to lunch, getting you alone in the car with them. In any case, it has the same effect: It isolates you from your team and you are unprepared.

Another variant is for certain members of the other team to do the same to their counterparts on your team. They'll pass it off as a "technical point that really only you and I are concerned about" or "something only the two of us are able to discuss from a technical standpoint." Other team members are unconcerned because, after all, they're "just doing that techie talk thing." In reality, they're attempting to isolate your team members either to gather more information or to convince them to come around to their way of seeing an issue.

When the negotiation starts again, they're hoping they have an ally from your side; they'll divide and conquer, using that person to force a wedge between members of your own team. We already know one of the worst things that can happen is to show dissension within your own team in front of the other side.

The walk in the woods tactic is so effective because it's not easy to recognize as a tactic, unless you're trained to look for it. Once you know it exists, however, it's relatively easy to counter. So, how do you counter it?

COUNTERS TO THE WALK IN THE WOODS TACTIC

The advice you've learned from countless fairy tales is the same advice you should take in negotiations: Stay out of the woods. Bad things can happen there. You counter the walk in the woods tactic by simply not letting yourself, under any circumstances, be isolated from your team by anyone from the other team. Your strength is in your team; absolutely refuse to be isolated from it.

You can say something like, "That's a great idea to put our folks on break. In fact, you read my mind. I was just about to call a caucus so I could go over how to break out of this deadlock with my smart folks. I'm sure you have some suggestions to mull over with your team as well. But I like the idea of a break too. Let's go ahead and break for 15 minutes, then meet with our teams for the next, say, 30 minutes. We'll come back together here at exactly two o'clock. Hopefully, by then, we'll be refreshed and have some ideas to discuss to get back on track."

When you are on breaks or at lunch, make sure you are not available to be button-holed by anyone from the other side. Surround yourself with your teammates during breaks; eat lunch with your team. It's okay to mingle with folks from the other side during breaks or lunch, but never put yourself in a position to get caught alone or cut out from the group.

Never continue the negotiation during breaks or lunch. Use this time to take your mind off the negotiation and mentally refresh yourself and your team members. If the other side attempts to bring up negotiation issues during these periods, playfully steer them to other subjects.

Finally, familiarize your team beforehand about the dangers of one-on-one discussions with the other side during breaks in the negotiation. Explain the dangers it poses to team unity and to safeguarding team positions and information.

Each member of your team should be aware of the walk in the woods tactic, because each of them could be a potential victim. Train them not to allow themselves to be isolated from the rest of the team. An added benefit of this could be improved team cohesiveness as you spend more time together, not just in the negotiation room but on breaks and at lunch as well.

Chapter 28

Emotional Tactics

Although I'm sure you've been told not to allow it to happen, negotiations can get emotional. I've seen some negotiators get extremely emotional. People are people and they have certain "hot buttons" that can bring out a range of emotions in a variety of manifestations. Anger, fear, rejection, sadness, elation, guilt, exasperation, embarrassment, and plain boredom are human emotions that are not easily turned off or forgotten simply because you're supposed to be in a professional negotiation situation.

Many times, the emotions are pure. Sometimes, however, they are simply being used as a tactic. In either case, the use of emotion in a negotiation can have a powerful impact on the outcome, so you'd better be able to know how to deal with them. In this chapter, we'll talk about how various forms of emotion can be used as tactics.

ANGER

Anger is possibly the most powerful and volatile emotion we humans can have. Remember the last time someone was angry at you? Not just mad, but really, really angry? How did it make you feel? Intimidated? Threatened? Frustrated? Defensive? Apologetic? Scared? If the person who was angry had the capability to act based on their anger, I'll bet your reaction—whatever it was—was magnified many times over. Displays of raw anger bring out innate defensive mechanisms in all of us that are in themselves hard to control, but usually give the angry person some benefit. Negotiators discovered this early in history; feigned anger as a tactic has been around for a long, long time.

In 1960, Nikita Khrushchev led the Soviet Union during a particularly bitter and dangerous point in the Cold War. Angered by a

Philippine United Nations delegate who charged that his country had swallowed up Eastern Europe, he launched into his now famous "We Will Bury You" tirade against all things capitalistic and Western. He started out angry and got angrier. He yelled, puffed, panted, and ranted. At the climatic moment in his speech he actually pounded the table with his shoe!

What effect do you think this had? Countries allied with the Soviet Union saw a leader of strength who didn't mind standing up to the capitalists. Western countries were horrified that a man so prone to lose his temper controlled the largest nuclear arsenal in the world. Countries targeted for intimidation by the Soviets felt helpless and more inclined to give in to Soviet threats. Countries on the fence thought they had better throw in with the crazier of the two sides to avoid annihilation. It was a very effective, memorable speech, and the raw display of anger helped further galvanize the world into two camps. The Soviets picked up allies, rattled the Western world into forms of appeasement, and gained concessions from countries that were not aligned but scared stiff. Khrushchev's shoe-pounding anger was very effective.

But was it real? When enhanced by experts, photographs of Khrushchev pounding his shoe clearly showed he still had both of his shoes on! Where did the other shoe come from? Speculation is he borrowed it and kept it handy for just such a moment. It wasn't real anger; it was an intentional tactic designed to bring about the results it did. Here, anger was used as a tactic to manipulate.

Now, I've never had a contractor pound a shoe at me across the negotiating table, but I have had negotiators use anger as a tactic against me, and it can be used against you. It's thankfully not common in government negotiations now, but it still can happen. To complicate matters, this anger can be a tactic or it can be real.

The other side can flare up in anger when you do such things as counter their proposal, insist on something you believe is fair and reasonable, change the requirements of the solicitation, or any number of other things. They may get angry about a side meeting some of your team members had with some of their team members. They may be angry about comments they heard you or someone on your team say about them or their company. They may shout, stand up, get red in the face, claim you're unfair, threaten to call off negotiations, threaten other types of retaliation, or even walk out of the negotiation room (we'll talk about that one later).

When confronted with raw anger, your defenses naturally go up. Most people feel uncomfortable with conflict and you might have a tendency to backpedal, to rethink whatever you did to make them so angry. You may get apologetic and give unilateral concessions. It may be particularly effective if the other side displays their anger at you in front of your own team. You then have status, standing, and peer pressure to add to your worries. Anger shown at you in public places or in front of others can cause embarrassment. It could trigger you to make concessions to get out of the embarrassing situation. In any case, it puts you on the defensive.

Anger displayed toward you can also simply throw you off balance, frustrate you. Worse, it can trigger your own anger in response. At the same time, it can increase the relative power of their negotiation position. They force you to see defusing their anger as one of your new negotiation objectives, one that you are willing to trade for a concession. They've created something from nothing. Sounds like a tactic to me!

So, how do you counter when the other side uses anger as an emotional tactic?

Counters to Anger

Anger is an extremely hard tactic to recognize because there are some really good actors out there. Are they trying to pull a tactic on you or are they *really* angry? Fortunately, you don't have to be an expert in discerning the difference, because your response to both actual and feigned anger is about the same.

When someone is angry at you or something you've done, your natural tendency is to get angry back, to take it personally, which immediately sucks you in to their anger and makes you less rational. So if you're confronted by an angry negotiator, the first thing to do is force yourself not to take it personally. I know that's a lot easier to agree to while calmly reading this book than it is when actually confronted with it, but it's essential to maintain control of the situation and the negotiation. Simply refuse to get personal and don't get angry back.

Continue to treat the angry negotiator with courtesy. Control your own temper and hear them out. Resist the urge to retaliate, even if you have just cause to do so. Let them blow, and never interrupt them while they are in their angry tirade. Don't confront them on the issues as they bring them up, even if their facts are incorrect. Hear them out without defending your own position. If you interrupt or try to defend your position in the middle of their anger, their anger will just increase. This takes practice, because it goes against basic human nature to defend ourselves.

In his book *Secrets of Power Negotiating* (Career Press, 2001), Roger Dawson puts it this way:

> At my seminars, I sometimes ask a person in the front row to stand. As I hold my two hands out, with my palms facing toward the person I've asked to stand, I ask him to place his hands against mine. Having done that and without saying another word, I gently start to push against him. Automatically, without any instruction, he always begins to push back. People shove when you shove them. Similarly, when you argue with someone, it automatically makes him or her want to argue back. (p. 35)

As you patiently listen to your opponent's tirade, take notes about what he is saying and let him see you taking notes. This shows him you are listening and you aren't writing off their position; you are concerned. It also gives you a focus point to help you better control your own anger and your desire to retaliate. Make sure to control the other members of your team and don't let any of them interrupt or get angry either. It's best to prepare your team before the negotiations by instructing them how you want to handle anger if it comes up so they'll know to keep quiet too.

When your opponent's anger is spent and they've blown all they can blow, read back the essence of what they said to them. You may say, "So, I understand you are concerned about …. Do I have that correct?" This reaffirms to them that you have been listening. Notice what you *don't* say. Don't say, "I understand you are angry because …." I've personally found angry people don't like to be told they are angry, and this action sometimes bumps up their anger level a couple of notches.

Don't attempt to defuse their anger with humor. Although you may be tempted to break the tension with a joke or a humorous comment, this usually backfires. Notice also that you don't agree with their position. You just let them know you *understand* their position. After you have read back or restated their position to them, you give them a chance to respond. This makes sure you have their position correct and it also give them another chance to blow off more steam if there's any left. You want them deflated of as much of their anger as possible.

Some respected authors suggest using the "feel, felt, found" formula to respond to anger. It would go something like this: After they blow, you respond by saying something like, "I understand exactly how you *feel* about this. Many people I know have *felt* the same way. But you know what I've *found?*"

Personally, I have not found this approach to be too useful. The "feel" and "felt" parts of the formula are okay, but the "found" part can present problems. First, you're usually not prepared to fill in the blanks with anything insightful after you say "You know what I've found?" You need time to formulate an answer, and snap judgments can just irritate the problem. Next, the other side, if they are truly angry, is in no mood to listen to you right now. They could care less what you have "found." They're still angry. They might even perceive you are being condescending or trying to lecture them, which will just spiral their anger upward. You need to put some time between their anger and your next response.

So, after they have blown all they can blow, call an immediate caucus. You may say something like, "I see this issue is very important to you and I understand how you can feel that way. I need some time to talk to my team about what you have brought up. Why don't we take a 30-minute break, and start back at 2:30?"

This does several good things. First, it allows a cooling-off period. True anger is usually brief, and the more time that passes, the less angry the person becomes. Time defuses anger. The other side will be less angry when the negotiation continues, and they will be more likely to listen to you. Next, it gives you and your team time to cool off too. The most professional negotiator in the world is still human. Although you may be good at controlling your temper, your blood is probably up at this moment too, and you need to cool off to be more rational with your response. A break additionally gives you and your team time to craft an appropriate, logically thought-out response. When you go back, you'll now have something to put behind the "here's what I've found" in the "feel, felt, found" formula.

Finally, if their anger was really a tactic, it lets the other side know it won't be a fruitful tactic. By calling a break, they have been unsuccessful in pulling you into bad decision making based on emotion rather than logic.

When you caucus with your team after the other side's angry outburst, try to identify the root cause of the anger. Don't focus on the angry negotiator's emotional outburst and how to smooth it. You'll just get sidetracked if you try to "handle" or placate their anger. Anger is just the symptom; you want to address the underlying cause of the anger.

Separate the people from the problem. Get a full understanding of your position, their position, and why the difference of opinion came about. You want to diagnose the problem and resolve the conflict to get the negotiation back on track.

Here's one last point about handling an angry negotiator. You don't want their anger to stall the negotiations for any longer than is absolutely necessary for both sides to cool off and for you to craft a thought-out response. Restart the negotiations as quickly as possible. As we've learned, time defuses anger. But if you let too much time pass unnecessarily, anger can reignite and grow even stronger.

When you called a caucus, you promised the angry negotiator you would start back at a certain time. Make sure you honor that commitment. If you don't, the other side might think you are putting them off, are unconcerned with their issue, or (even worse) have no logical response to their position.

How to Defuse a Protest Before It Happens: An Example

Handling anger effectively takes practice, and I've blown it a few times. I've allowed myself to get immediately defensive and argumentative when confronted by angry contractors, and it usually got worse from there. I learned more effective techniques for handling anger by taking quite a few lumps over the years. Let me give you a situation as an example of how to handle anger properly and how *not to*.

Every time you award a competitive contract, there's one very happy contractor. There are also several very disappointed contractors—the ones who didn't get the award. Losing a contract can be devastating to a contractor. Not only have they spent a lot of time, energy, and money for nothing, but they may have forgone other lucrative opportunities while competing for the contract they didn't win.

Often, a losing contractor may have to lay off employees or take other belt-tightening measures. Sometimes, winning or losing a contract can literally make or break their entire business. If the firm that lost is convinced they should have won, disappointment can turn into anger. Anger can turn into the thing all government contracting professionals dread—a protest.

Government acquisition regulations allow contractors who are dissatisfied with a government award decision to file an official protest of the action and request a remedy of the action. Protests must be submitted in writing to the CO. If your agency receives a protest, generally all actions on that acquisition have to stop until the protest is resolved. For the price of a postage stamp, the protesting contractor can stop your acquisition dead in the water. Even if you eventually win the protest, the effects on your program can be devastating. You want a protest about as much as you want a root canal.

The first inkling you may be receiving a protest usually comes right after you have made your award decision and a losing contractor finds out about it. You'll get an irate telephone call out of the blue with pure anger on the other end. You'll hear things like, "I can't believe you awarded this contract to so-and-so! You very well know we should have won that contract. You're being totally unfair and this is my official notification that I'm officially protesting this action right now!" The tirade may or may not come with a string of explicatives, but it's obvious to you the caller is *angry*. Sometimes, you have to hold the phone out from your ear to keep your eardrum intact.

First of all, you don't really have an official protest yet. Remember that the official protest must be in writing. How you handle that first irate phone call could make the difference in whether you actually receive an official protest. Your first impulse will be to dig in and defend your award decision. After all, *you* made the award call and they are challenging *your* personal judgment. You'll be tempted to get angry back and justify to them why you did what you did. It's human nature.

That's the absolute worst thing you can do at this moment. They are in no mood to listen to you or your positions right now. They're operating on pure anger, and any attempt you make to defend your decision at this time will only drive their anger further. If you argue with the contractor at this moment, you can almost be assured you're going to get an official protest in the mail.

Although they may be personally assaulting you, don't take it personally. Hold the phone out so you preserve your hearing and simply let them blow. Let them get their emotion out. Don't interrupt them; don't try to comment on what they are saying. They won't listen. If you interrupt them and challenge their position with attempts at reasoning, you'll just upset them more. Let them let off steam. Sometimes that's all they want to do. I have defused a contractor's desire to file a protest just by allowing them to blow off steam.

Every now and then, pull the phone close enough to say "I see," "I understand," or "Uh-huh." Make sure to take notes as they blow. When they are spent, read back to them what they have said (you can delete the expletives). You might say, "Let me see if I understand. You're upset because …. Do I have that right?"

What does that tell them? That's right—you're listening to them. Sometimes that's all they want—someone to listen to their frustration at not having won. If they know you have listened and understand their gripes, their need to officially protest may dissolve. Notice you don't say "I agree"; you just say, "I understand." You have shown them the courtesy of listening to them and understanding their position.

Even after they have spent their anger, never try to address their concerns during that first phone call. I learned this lesson the hard way several time before I "got" it. They're still in no mood to listen or to accept your reasoning over theirs right now. If you try, you're almost guaranteed to get them angry again and assure yourself an official protest from them just as soon as they can write and mail the letter.

Put some time between that phone call and your response. You might say something like, "I see how you can feel this was unfair. Many contractors have felt the same way. You've brought up some things I need to talk over with my smart folks before I can answer them intelligently. Let's set up a time tomorrow for me to call you back and address your concerns. How does 9:00 AM sound to you, or would you prefer it to be later?" That's right. You're creating time for their anger to defuse. By letting them select the callback time, you're also letting them save a little face by having some control over the situation.

Once you've set the callback time and hung up the phone, get your team together. Try to identify the root cause of the contractor's anger and how to respond to it in a logical and effective way. I strongly recommend your legal counsel become a part of the discussion at this point. Every word of your response should be vetted, not only to strike the right tone with the disappointed contractor, but to avoid creating legal tangles you'll regret later should the situation actually result in an official protest.

Finally, make sure to call them back when you promised them you would call back! Nothing will infuriate them more at this point than the perception they are being ignored. You can almost guarantee a protest if you don't call them back when you said you would.

During the callback, either present them your vetted answer or, better yet, make them familiar with the process of requesting a postaward debriefing. This will show them there's an official channel open to them to have a detailed meeting during which the government explains why that contractor didn't get the award. Coach them through the process of requesting this. Now you've put even more time between their anger and the solution, and you've bought your side extra time to prepare as well. The postaward debriefing process outlined in the FAR was designed, among other things, to defuse protests, and it's very effective at doing so.

By using this simple process, I was able to reduce drastically the number of protests I received. Of course, sometimes you'll get a protest anyway (despite your best efforts), but I found these techniques to lessen the likelihood. In any case, this same process can be used effectively any time you are confronted with anger—whether real or a tactic.

Although anger is the most volatile emotion or tactic you'll have to deal with, it's not the only one you may have to handle. You may confront other emotions, either real or used purely as a tactic, in any negotiation situation. The basic way of handling these other emotions is quite similar to how we've learned to handle anger, but each emotion has peculiarities you need to be familiar with. Let's look at some of these other emotions and how to handle them.

PERSONAL ATTACKS

Personal attacks can come in many different forms and may be either direct or subtle. Thankfully, they are rare in today's environment and, in my opinion, extremely counterproductive. The other side may appear to be personally (and sometimes vocally) insulted by a position you've chosen or a proposal you've tabled. They may challenge your knowledge and professional competence. They may criticize the quality of your work, your track record, or even your work ethic. They may say your actions have personally offended them in some way. They might make snide and insulting comments about the way you dress, the car you drive, or your inability or unwillingness (as a government negotiator) "to get a *real* job" (this one was used on me several times).

They may attack your basic intelligence and even call you ignorant. They can be personally discourteous to you by deliberately not making eye contact, showing up late for meetings, and interrupting you when you're talking. They may take cell phone calls or conduct other business in the middle of your negotiation session with them.

These jabs can be applied all at once or subtly over time. In everyday life situations, people that treat you this way are usually simply trying to cover up or compensate for their own feelings of inferiority.

Most experienced negotiators you'll run into, however, would never have gotten to their current position by feeling insecure. They're professionals, full of self-confidence in their abilities. They don't insult just to insult. They're trained never to utter a single word during a negotiation unless it is calculated to bring some advantage to their side. So if negotiators start with the personal insults, you can usually bet it's a tactic they're using to gain a certain advantage.

What are they trying to do? Personal attacks used as a tactic are an attempt to break your concentration, throw you off balance, and make you feel uncomfortable. They try to get you to focus on yourself and your shortcomings instead of on the issue being discussed. They're trying to make you feel less confident as a negotiator and as a person.

Once sidetracked, you can't devote 100 percent of your mental ability to achieving your negotiation objectives. They're hoping you'll start concentrating on the insults and how to fight back, and not on the issues at hand. They're trying to make you, personally, part of the problem. And this gives them an additional bargaining chip, one additional thing to "fix" by possibly (and sometimes subconsciously) receiving a concession from your side.

It's also calculated to be a direct attack on the thing your innate being naturally desires to protect the most—your ego. Your ego is your own mental picture of how you look to other people, and you usually see it as a fairly rosy picture. It gives you a general sense of well-being and allows you to function normally. When your ego is challenged, it can trigger automatic reflexes from deep within you to defend your "picture." These reflexes can cause you to get angry and defensive. Consequently, you could get sucked into defending yourself or striking back personally at them. Your focus partially shifts to rebuilding or protecting your ego instead of negotiating a best-value deal for the government.

Finally, personal attacks can be used as an attempt by the other side to gain a power advantage in the negotiations. Remember our discussion of bargaining power? The first power we talked about was the power of legitimacy, and you saw that you automatically possess most of that power because you are a representative of the government. The other side knows this and will sometimes use personal insults to attempt to level the field. By attacking you personally, they attack your power of legitimacy and your ability to use it effectively during negotiations.

We also discussed expert power, which is held by the side that knows the business better. If you are a noted expert in your field, or have a reputation as a skilled negotiator or analyst or whatever, the other side may attempt to level the playing field by personally attacking your competency. Because you chose your entire negotiation strategy based on your assessment of the relative powers of the sides, these kinds of attacks, if successful, can weaken or even undermine your whole negotiation position.

So if you come under personal attack, how do you respond?

Counters to Personal Attacks

If someone from the other side attacks you personally, your first counter is simply to recognize it's probably just a tactic. This will tame your natural desire to fight back and defend yourself, which is what they're trying to get you to do. Take a deep breath, smile, and persevere. (OK, you don't *have* to smile if the personal attack is singularly vicious, but don't let them know they're getting to you.)

Whatever you do, don't get pulled into counterattacking, losing your temper, or defending yourself. *Don't fight back.* Your single goal at this point is to put the negotiation back on an impersonal footing. Your simple refusal to react to the attack will dilute its intended purpose, preserve your relative power position, and signal to the other side that further personal attacks will bear no fruit for them.

Some negotiation experts will advise you to call a break immediately after the other side launches a personal attack. The reason, they say, is to break the emotional attention and interrupt the emotional momentum. After all, it's awfully hard to counterattack against an empty room.

Although calling a caucus is a good counter to an angry negotiator, I don't recommend it to counter a personal attack. In my experience, I've found that calling a break at this point might be perceived by the other side as confirmation that their personal attack tactic is working. You may be signaling to them that they are getting to you. Encouraged by this, they may simply continue the attack after the negotiation is resumed.

My advice is to keep the negotiation moving by immediately focusing back on the impersonal nuts and bolts of the negotiation issues. Doing this not only lets the other side know immediately that they're not going to get away with personal attacks, but it also can cause them to lose face (which translates to loss of negotiating power) by seeming petty.

The one exception to this is if you feel your own emotions uncontrollably welling up. Then, by all means, call an immediate break. Remember, the last thing you want to do is to get pulled into the attack cycle. If you must break, use the time to calm down, refocus on the issues, and bring the negotiation back to an impersonal basis when you resume.

In some cases, you can actually turn personal attacks into an advantage in the negotiation. If they claim they're personally insulted by your negotiation position, ask them what they would consider not insulting. If they call you unfair, ask them what they would consider fair. In both these cases, you're pulling a reversal on them—putting them on the spot to reveal more information about *their* negotiating position. This gives you more information, which, as you've learned, gives more negotiating power to your side. It also forces them to refocus on the impersonal issues of the negotiation.

If they personally attack your knowledge or professional competence, my advice is simply: Don't respond in any way whatsoever. Just play it off. Immediately say something like, "Okay, now let's get back to business." Don't even acknowledge the attack; act as if you never even heard it. Resist the urge to counter with the tactic of silence.

Although silence is a potent tactic in many circumstances, it's usually counterproductive in situations like this. It may signal to the other side that they have "got your goat" and may simply encourage them to continue the attack. Immediately refocus on the issues. The same goes if they attack your personal appearance, social status, politics, religion, affiliations, personal possessions, choice of acquaintances, and so forth. Defuse the tactic by ignoring the tactic and pressing on. Remember the saying you learned in elementary school: "Sticks and stones may break my bones, but words can never hurt me!"

Personal attacks on your reputation, work quality, or your track record as a negotiator, however, should not be totally ignored, even if you realize they are just being used as tactics. These are direct attacks against your power of legitimacy, and you must take positive steps to reassert your position of control over the negotiation gently but firmly. If you let these kinds of attacks pass without comment, the other side may perceive you as weak or, worse, in agreement with their assessment. This could encourage them to keep up the pressure.

Immediately respond to attacks like these by letting them know you disagree with their assessment and returning the focus back to the impersonal issues being discussed, in the same sentence. You may say something like, "Well I sure don't know where *that* came from, but let's get back to business" or "Obviously, you've received some bad info, but I'd like to hear from you what you think is a fair solution to this problem."

The key is to end the sentence with a refocus back on the issues. This gives them the message that you don't agree with their comments, without giving them an opening to respond to your challenge of their comments. You maintain the moral high ground and prevent the attack from continuing.

Personal attacks in the form of discourteous behavior (such as tardiness, inattentiveness, or cell phone use) also can't be ignored. Unless you respond in some way, you are only encouraging the other party to continue this disruptive and discourteous behavior. Let the person know the behavior is unacceptable, but in a non-confrontational or non-scolding way.

You might say something like, "Hey, listen. I know the world doesn't stop just because we're having this negotiation, but I was under the impression this contract was as important to your company as it is to us. And, just like you, we have other things scheduled, and your [tardiness, inattentiveness, disruptive phone calls, and so on] is threatening to disrupt our other important activities. Can we agree to focus on the issues at hand or should we reschedule these negotiations for a later date?"

Personal attacks are rare in government negotiations, but you must be prepared in case you encounter them. By recognizing the tactic and using the counters we've discussed (don't fight back, keep the negotiation moving, push the negotiation back to an impersonal level, keep control), you can defuse the intended effects of a personal attack and keep the negotiation moving to a successful conclusion. As you've seen, you can even turn a personal attack against you into a negotiation advantage!

GUILT

Unlike anger and personal attacks, which are rare, making the other side feel guilty about something is a common emotional tactic, even in government negotiations. Why? Because it works! Just think about your own personal life and you'll see how effectively it works.

Have you ever had someone put a "guilt trip" on you? Parents put guilt trips on grown children for not calling them enough. Grown children put guilt trips on their parents for not sending them enough money when they're at college. Children still at home make parents feel guilty by proclaiming, "All the other parents let *their* kids do it!" Spouses use guilt trips on their mates: "Gee, hon, after all I do for you around here, I didn't think it would be too much to ask ...." Neighbors put guilt trips on other neighbors, "If Stan were home (another neighbor), he'd let me borrow *his* lawn mower!" Bosses make raise-seeking employees feel guilty by citing the financial woes of the company. Even well-known charities grow profitable by invoking guilt: "For the cost of just one cup of coffee a day, you can feed this poor, adorable-looking, starving orphan!"

Were any of these guilt tactics ever used successfully on you? Have you used any of these guilt tactics successfully yourself? If you're honest, you probably said yes to both questions, and you can immediately think of several occasions when either guilt giving or guilt receiving has influenced the outcome of something in your personal life.

When someone makes you feel guilty, it immediately works on your emotions. You often have an uncontrollable urge to cast off the guilt by "making it right" or somehow mollifying the "injured" party. Guilt has an unnerving effect on us all, and we've all felt it. And we also know from personal experience that making someone else feel guilty greatly increases our chances of getting our way.

It works the same way in negotiations. The other side may try to make you feel guilty about something you have done, haven't done, a position you've taken, or any number of other things. These guilt trips are usually timed to come right at the end, or close to the end, of the negotiation. They may sadly tell you your final offer will absolutely bankrupt their company; they'd love to accept it, but they don't want to be the one personally responsible for bringing doom, gloom, and unemployment down on "all those good folks and their families." They may say no other government negotiator has ever been this unfair to them or driven them to so low a price.

How about this one: "Just because you have the full force and power of the mean, huge, and uncaring federal government behind you, you're taking advantage of me as a small, defenseless contractor just trying to make a decent living." Or this one: "You've surely beat me down in this negotiation. When I go back to my boss with this deal, I'm sure to be fired—and I have five children to feed!" Or this one: "I know we're late on our promised delivery date and we're absolutely mortified by it. But, come on! You know we'll make it right in the end. What's wrong? Don't you trust us?" Obviously, the list of guilt-giving opportunities is endless.

What do they all have in common? They are all designed to make you feel bad—in a word, guilty. They're hoping you'll respond emotionally to the guilt trip by softening your position or maybe throwing in an additional concession or two. They're hoping to hear the magic words, "Well, maybe we could…." The guilt giver plays up the perception of your absolute dominance and control of them and their very livelihoods. From that lofty position, it's easier for you to throw a few more bread crumbs their way and not feel like you're giving up much of relative value. Besides, it alleviates your feeling of guilt. What a deal! What a deal, indeed—for *them!*

Counters to Guilt

Just like anger and personal attacks, the best way to counter guilt trip tactics is simply to recognize them for what they are—tactics. Once that's firm in your mind, you're less likely to be emotionally affected by the guilt tactic and less likely to blunder into unilateral concession giving. You don't even have to acknowledge verbally that you recognize it as a tactic. Your next responses will make it clear to them that you're not buying it.

Immediately, test the validity of their claim. The better you have prepared for the negotiation, the easier this will be, because you probably already have accumulated information to refute their claim. Are they *really* going to lose their job if you don't soften up? Is the company *really* going to fold if they don't get this deal? Do they *really* think you don't trust them? The best way to test for validity is by probing with open-ended questions. For instance, you might respond with something like, "Did I hear you say your company may fold if you don't get this deal? How can a company that pulls in gross revenues of $626 million a year go bankrupt from just one contract?" Or something like, "Wow! Do you really think they'll fire you? I see here you are a substantial shareholder in the company. Wouldn't it be superexpensive for them to have to buy you out?"

Here, your previous work at intelligence gathering before the negotiation started will pay you dividends. If you don't have the facts to throw back at them, you can still test the validity of the guilt trip with open-ended questions such as, "Can you describe to me exactly how accepting this contract as-is will put [you, your company] at risk"?

In either case, you've let them know you're not buying the guilt trip, and you've put them on the defensive to back up the reason they think you should feel guilty. If you're lucky, you may get the added bonus of gaining additional useful information by what they say when they respond to your probing questions!

One caution. When you probe for validity, resist the urge to be cute or probe with snide comments. I tried this once. A negotiator had insisted my "hard-line" position would put his standing in his company in jeopardy. Without thinking, I rattled off something like, "Sounds like that's your problem. Why are you trying to make it mine? Besides, I bet your expense account alone is larger than my entire annual salary."

Now, I have to admit it felt good saying that—and it certainly countered the guilt tactic—but it also blew the negotiation. I had damaged our working relationship so much that we could never really get back on track. The negotiations stalled and spiraled downhill from there. In the end, neither party really achieved their objectives. I had won the battle but lost the war.

After you have recognized the guilt trip tactic and tested it for validity, you then steer the negotiation back—as soon as possible—to focusing on discussing the issues. Separate their guilt-giving issues, which are usually personal, from the true negotiation issues at hand and focus on the latter.

You might say something like, "I understand you're personally concerned about that, but I don't see the bearing it has on coming to an agreement on the issues we're discussing. Let's concentrate on getting those solved." Or, "I don't see how that relates to what we need to get done here today." If they make you feel guilty for not trusting them, an appropriate response could be something like, "It's not a question of trust. Trust isn't the issue here today. We can deal with that later. Right now, let's get back to the real issues and solve the problem we have at hand. In fact, coming to an agreement on this will probably help us establish mutual trust." Whatever response you make, be sure it divides the emotion away from the issues and forces the discussion back to where it belongs: on the negotiation issues only.

A final way to deal with a guilt trip is to put the other side in the driver's seat. Pull a verbal reversal. After they lay the guilt trip on you, ask them, "If you were me, how would you respond to what you just said?" Or, "How do you think I should respond to your last comment?" This puts them on the spot, forcing *them* to confront what they're trying to make you do. Usually, you'll get a response back something like, "Er … um … ah … I didn't really mean to … ah …. I mean I don't actually think … um … well, what I meant to say was …." You may end up *truly* feeling guilty after you hear them stammer around for a while!

If they're trying to make you feel guilty about a position you've taken on a particular issue, you might say, "Well, what do *you* think would be a fair solution?" In both cases, you've gone from the defensive to the offensive, and you've done it in an environment *that they created*, which almost compels them to respond with a concession, an agreement to your terms, or at the very least additional information that could be useful to your side. Don't fall prey to guilt!

FRUSTRATION

Have you ever dealt with someone, either in your personal or professional life, who just gives up all of a sudden in a fluster? You're dealing with a sticky situation or negotiation and you may have deadlocked on a thing or two, but their sudden capitulation catches you totally off guard? You were sure a little more tough give-and-take would solve the problem—things were looking up for your side—and all of a sudden the other side, in a flustered manner, says something like, "Well, I just don't have time for any more of this. Why don't you just figure out what's fair and get back to me?" They then hurriedly start gathering their papers and make a quick exit. They don't storm out angry, and you can tell they're not mad; they just seem plain frustrated and maybe a little bit exasperated. Sometimes they don't physically leave, but you can tell their minds have. They mentally move on to other things having nothing to do with your negotiations.

You're left wondering what just happened, and not really realizing if it's good or bad for your side. On the one hand, you may think it's a good thing. You must be such a fine negotiator they just couldn't hold their own with you. You overpowered them with your skill and wit! You've frustrated, maybe even exasperated, people you thought were good negotiators—and that must be good, right?

Or maybe they're so busy with other important irons in the fire that fighting over your little deal, championed by such a fine negotiator as yourself, suddenly takes a back seat to their other priorities. They must have finally realized you're not going to be a pushover, so they're moving on to other battles that will be easier to win. That's also good, right?

Then, after this brief phase of self-congratulation, you start to realize that it might not be so good after all. For one, there's no one left in the room to complete the deal with. They're either physically or mentally gone, and it takes two to tango. Hmm. And just before they left, they essentially put you in charge of the entire negotiation—*both* sides of the negotiation, theirs and yours! Hmm indeed. Could it be they did this on purpose? As reality sets in, you start to conclude you might be the victim of a superslick emotional tactic—the frustrated negotiator.

Of course, it's not always a tactic. Even good negotiators get genuinely frustrated at times, as I'm sure you have. But whether it's a tactic or the real McCoy, the frustrated negotiator's impact on you is the same. First, it throws you off balance. They may have shown some signs of rising frustration, but you never thought they'd get so flustered that they'd just give up. And off balance isn't a good place to be if you're in a negotiation. To make matters worse, they gave up before the important issues of the negotiation were settled, so you haven't really won anything. Everything is still in limbo. They didn't agree to your position; they just gave up on finding a negotiated solution.

To make matters worse, they threw the entire weight of finding a solution onto your shoulders. They took themselves out of the game after tagging you and making you "it." Do you see what unenviable position that leaves you in? Instead of having the balance of two different people engaging in the give and take of negotiations, you're now forced to be—at the same time—both sides. They've set you up to negotiate against yourself. Who's the only party who can lose that one?

Here's the problem. You know you can't simply stick with your own last offer; they still have to agree to a final solution and they obviously don't like it. In fact, it's the thing that got them so frustrated in the first place. If you negotiate against yourself and cough up a concession or a new solution to the issue, they'll have a legitimate excuse to reject it because they weren't involved in coming up with it. You did it without them. You're left guessing what you can give them that they might accept. And you're worried about making it appealing enough so they won't think you're taking advantage of them.

Finally, the emotion they displayed in becoming frustrated or exasperated has an emotional effect on you too. They want you to feel sorry for them because of all the pressures and deadlines they're under. You may be tempted to soften your position to make them feel better, show them you're a fair person, and get them back to the table. Under these circumstances, most negotiators will give up more than they planned, and certainly more than they need to.

Counters to Frustration

Displaying intentional frustration is a manipulative tactic designed to play on your emotions, so the best way to counter it is to recognize it for the tactic it is and not let it get to you as intended. The worst thing you can do is to sit placidly back and let their frustration play out to its logical conclusion—sticking you with both ends of the negotiation decisions.

The sooner you can peg the tactic, the sooner you can derail its intent. And you don't have to guess whether the frustration is real or feigned. Like most emotional tactics, your response to frustration is the same no matter if it's real or play acting.

The first chance you logically can, find a point to interject yourself into their bluster. Calmly and slowly tell them you understand their problems and you sympathize with the pressures they face. The "feel, felt, found" formula we introduced earlier is an excellent model to follow here.

You might say something like, "Man, I really can understand why you're feeling frustrated, especially someone with all your responsibilities. In fact, I don't see how you keep from getting overwhelmed. Actually, I've felt the same way on quite a number of occasions, and I'm maybe feeling a little that way myself now. But you know what I've found? I've found if I *really* focus on one thing at a time—like concentrating on getting over this issue we're dealing with right now—it breaks the problem up into more bite-sized chunks and I don't feel so overwhelmed. Do you think we can do that now or would you rather take a break and start back again later?"

Of course, there are many ways to say this and you should use your own personality and what you know of the other person and the situation to guide you, as long as the results are achieved. And what are the results? First, your calm, measured tone will have a settling effect on the situation. If the negotiator is truly frustrated, your steady voice and expressed empathy will calm them down. If they are playing the frustration tactic, this same measured response by you will signal to them that they've been busted and that they won't get away with playing the frustration tactic on you.

Next, you offer them a solution. You outline how to beat their frustration by breaking the problem into digestible chunks and focusing on the trees, not the forest. You also offer them the alternative of rescheduling the negotiations for a less chaotic time in their lives. If they are honestly frustrated, this may seem like you've thrown them a lifeline. If they are playing the frustration tactic, you have coolly negated its intended effects.

Please note here that you shouldn't attempt to solve the underlying problems that are purportedly causing their frustration. If you start working on those problems, even though your actions are well intentioned, the other side may perceive you've taken ownership of those problems. They're now magically your problems, not theirs. Of course, if their frustration is simply a tactic, there may not be any real underlying problems to solve, so you'd just be chasing your tail anyway.

Offer to solve the frustration, as we talked about earlier—not the underlying problems that caused the frustration. You probably already have enough problems of your own to deal with without taking on some of theirs too.

The one thing you can't do is let the frustrated negotiator remove himself from the responsibility of continuing the discussion and decision making, and throw it all on you. You must keep these frustrated negotiators in the game. Their attempt to stick you with all the decisions is, at best, a copout and, at worst, an emotional dirty tactic.

The spouse who gives up on an argument with the famous words "Whatever you say, dear" hasn't solved the problem. They've just created an atmosphere for the problem to grow and fester, and for the deadly effects of resentment to creep in. You shouldn't want that in your personal relationships and you certainly don't want it when you're negotiating for the government. You've got to force the other side back into the give and take of the negotiation.

You might say something like, "I understand you're frustrated right now, and I'm hearing you say you want me to fix it, but I can't solve this problem by myself. I need your input, especially because you're able to look at things from a different angle than I can. Hang in with me and let's put this issue to bed in a manner that satisfies both our sides."

Simply refuse to come up with a solution on your own without their input. As you've seen, any solution you craft unilaterally can simply be vetoed by the other side as soon as it's proposed. Tell them you're not going to do it on your own. If that means rescheduling the negotiations, so be it.

Your ultimate goal is to get the negotiation back on course as soon as possible. Calm the frustrated negotiator and sympathize with him. Let him know he's not going to get away with his tactic, then reel him back in to a discussion of the issues you need to resolve. Demonstrate to him that the only way he's going to get any result out of the negotiations is to continue to negotiate.

CONFUSION

Personally, I don't think there's anything more frustrating than having to deal with confused negotiators. Have you ever experienced this? They're flustered, they're disorganized, they ramble, they spend a lot of time looking for and juggling papers, and they jump from one subject to another without having fully discussed anything. They eventually circle back to incomplete issues, take a few more swings at them, and then race on toward other things.

There is no rhyme, reason, or discernible pattern in their negotiation process; they're all over the board. Out of the blue, they may introduce new issues you see as having nothing to do with what you're talking about. Or they may clumsily reopen issues you thought were already laid to rest, bringing up new facets. They may present you with a long list of possible solutions or ways to agree to an issue. They're just disorganized and, well, confused.

Trying to follow or even keep up with a confused negotiator can be like trying to nail Jell-O to the wall. It just can't be done. Pretty soon, you're flustered and just as confused as they are. You'll find that you've lost track of where you are in your own negotiation plan, your negotiation objectives are out the window, and you're now totally unsure of what a fair outcome for your side even looks like. The negotiation you planned so well now looks unsolvable and insurmountable.

What you thought was simple has become incredibly complicated. You start to wonder how any company in their right mind would hire someone this confusing to represent them in major negotiations.

It could be true that the company has indeed made a personnel mistake and the person is truly confused. More likely, however, you're dealing with a skilled negotiator who knows quite well what effect their confusion will have on you. Generating confusion can be a powerfully effective negotiation tactic if it isn't recognized and dealt with quickly.

Have you ever noticed that confusion is contagious? By acting confused, the other side knows they have a high likelihood of drawing you and your team into confusion as well. Now both sides are confused. The only problem is, they're feigning confusion as a tactic. They're not really confused, and now you actually are. They've just gotten a leg up in the negotiation.

Because you are thrown into confusion by the erratic actions of the confused negotiator, your clarity of purpose blurs. Your decision-making ability diminishes; you don't know which issue to focus on and try to resolve. You have to focus on following and understanding the confused negotiator as he twists and turns, instead of focusing on your agenda and successfully completing the negotiation.

Because the confused negotiator has thrown so many issues on the table, your team cohesiveness may also fragment as individual members of your team chase after different issues in isolation. In extreme cases, this may even cause divisions and differences among members of your own team in the presence of the other side—and we've already discussed how disastrous *that* can be! Worse, your confusion can turn into frustration, then to exasperation, and you may lose your rationality as a negotiator. If this happens, chances are you're going to get hammered in that negotiation.

In essence, you have lost control of the negotiation. That's the ultimate goal of the tactic—to force you to pass the initiative to the other side and go into a confused, defensive crouch. By virtue of your position as a government negotiator, you have the built-in advantage of being in control of the process. This brings great power to your side and the other side knows it. The confusion tactic is their attempt to unseat you and assume control of the process of the negotiation. If their tactic works, they have caused a state of confusion in you, and they know a confused mind is more easily led.

Confusion is an unnatural state and the confused mind starts looking for assistance to come back in balance. The other side will be more than happy to provide that assistance, to guide you back to a state of clarity. They will start setting the agenda they want and you'll be more than happy to march to their tune.

Now that you're confused, you're also more susceptible to the effects of other tactics the other side may use. Sometimes they'll use the confusion tactic as a precursor to the frustration tactic we've already discussed. It makes the ultimate use of this tactic more believable and effective. If they have been successful in splitting your team on some of the issues, they can hit you with the divide and conquer tactic. They'll split your team and defeat you. They can also hit you with the good cop/bad cop tactic, with their good cop graciously coming in and restoring order.

At this point, you may be so grateful *someone* is taking control of the confused negotiator (their bad cop) you let them do it, and pass the agenda setting (and control of the negotiation) to the other side. You may even side with and assist their good cop, the one person at the table who seems to bring clarity back to the negotiation. Now they have an additional member on their team—you!

Another version of using confusion as a tactic doesn't require the other side to appear confused at all. They may simply lay out so many different options as possible solutions to a particular issue that the sheer magnitude of the choices overwhelms you and throws you into confusion. You're like a kid in a candy store who goes hungry because you don't know which candy to choose to eat first. After they have numbed your mind with the many different and complex ways of solving the problem, they'll reassure you that they are the experts and can guide you to the right decision for your particular situation. They may say something like, "I know the options seem overwhelming, but we're the experts. We've successfully led many clients through the decision-making process to the one solution that is custom tailored for them."

If they're successful, you'll bow to their expertise and let them sell you exactly what they want to sell you, and usually at the price they want. You're just grateful someone came in and made the difficult decision for you.

Counters to Confusion

The best way to deal with a confused negotiator and to prevent the effects it can have on you is simply to stay firmly in control of the negotiation process. Don't let their confusion or erratic behavior trick you into ceding control to the other side. It takes two to tango, so refuse to dance with them. Preventive medicine is best here. If you sit back and let the confused negotiator weave his web of confusion, even for a few minutes, you may have already lost control. Act at the first sign of confusion from the other side. You might say something like, "Whoa! You've thrown a lot on the table here. Let's slow down and resolve these issues one by one. Now, as I was saying about your overhead rates …."

Draw them back and force them to refocus on the issues set by your agenda, not theirs. If you have already lost control, reestablish it as quickly as possible once you realize what's going on.

You should have already developed an excellent tool to keep you in control and keep the negotiations focused—your agenda. The agenda is your plan of action for the negotiation and it orders the issues so the event moves along in a smooth, logical, methodical way. Whenever the other side starts to drift off track, bring out the agenda and get them back on it.

You've already learned that you should develop a draft agenda well ahead of the negotiation and send it to the other side for review and comment. You then finalize the agenda and send the other side a copy before the negotiation starts. This means they have already had input in establishing the agenda and have agreed to it. Simply remind them of their commitment and get them back to playing by the rules they agreed to play by before the negotiation started.

Another effective strategy many experienced negotiators use to stay focused on the issues, but at the same time capture other possible issues the other side may table, is establishing an issues "parking lot." This is preventive; you establish the parking lot and go over the rules for how it will be used well before the negotiation starts. If you must, you can establish it after the need arises, but it's best to set it up as part of your negotiation planning so everyone knows the rules up front.

Here's how a parking lot works. If an issue comes up that someone feels distracts from the main course of the negotiation, that issue may be "parked" in the parking lot to be resolved at a later time. Either side may nominate issues to be parked, but the lead negotiator for the government team (you) has sole authority to make the call to park the issue or not. Issues subject to parking could be off-agenda issues, new issues, or significant permutations, options, or complicating factors of existing issues. The gist of the issues is briefly jotted down, usually on sticky notes, and placed on a board or similar area labeled PARKING LOT where both sides can always see them.

Once the issue is parked, both sides can then mentally move on with the negotiation, knowing these issues will be discussed later and not forgotten. A preset time, either at the end of the day or the end of the negotiation, is reserved in the agenda to address the parked issues. Keep this time to no more than a half hour to an hour.

During that time, you first briefly go through all the parked issues to make sure they're still valid. Some issues may have already been resolved as a result of the normal negotiation process. Others may not seem so important now and the side that parked them may no longer want to pursue them. Still others may have been rolled up in other issues still to be discussed in the main negotiation. If a parked issue is no longer valid for any of these reasons, remove that issue from the parking lot. Now you're left with just the valid issues to tackle, and simply take them on one by one.

As the parking lot issues are resolved, remove them from the parking lot. Stick to the limits you have preset for parking lot issues. If you have many parked issues, don't try to resolve all of them during your allotted parking lot time. Some issues may have to be postponed for the next day's parking lot time or may need to be brought back into the main thrust of the negotiation.

That's how I set up and handle an issues parking lot. If you find that different processes, procedures, or rules work better for you, by all means do it your way. The key is not the process, but the ability to "park" issues to keep the main thrust of the negotiation going and keep you in control. Establishing a parking lot sets up a framework to unclutter the flow of the negotiation, robs the other side of much of the effect of using the confusion tactic, and helps the truly confused negotiator regain and maintain his bearings.

Finally, you may want to consider calling a caucus if things get too confusing, or if you need to take back control or counter the other side's use of confusion as a tactic. Even though you may need this time to resolve your own confusion, always imply that it is for the other side's benefit. You might say something like, "It seems like you're a little confused here. Why don't we caucus for a half hour so you and your team can refocus on exactly what you want and think through how to present it to us in a logical way. Don't forget to take a copy of our agenda with you so you can see where things fit in."

This approach lets them know that you are still in control, and you believe they are the side that's confused and must take action to return to clarity. They're the ones that must fix it, not you. Notice that you also called the agenda "our" agenda, not "the" agenda, which further reminds them they agreed to stick to it.

Of course, your team should use the caucus time to reevaluate the new issues, your effectiveness, and your next steps and tactics. You may, for instance, use this time to set up a parking lot if you haven't done so already. When you return from the caucus, immediately reestablish control of the negotiation by requesting their solution or restatement of the confusing issue or issues.

If someone tries to confuse you in a negotiation, fight back by staying firmly in control. Stick to your agenda and remind them they agreed to do the same. Consider establishing a parking lot for distracting issues. Finally, call a strategic caucus if you get confused or if you want to signal to the other side that you're not falling for their confusion tactics.

FEAR

Fear isn't usually the first thing that comes to mind when you think about government contract negotiations—maybe hostage negotiations or negotiations to prevent or end a war, but not government contract negotiations. However, fear can sometimes play a part, either for you or against you, when you're negotiating with a contractor. Fear can swing the advantage to either side, depending on which side is feeling fearful and reacting based on that fear.

Let's first talk about the possible fear you may have in dealing with the other side and how to overcome it. We'll then explore how you can use the other side's fear of not getting a contract—or not performing well if they do get the contract—to your advantage.

Do you know someone who gets stage fright? I'm not talking about way back in elementary school plays or junior high school recitals, but in your workplace. Someone who, say, freezes up during a presentation or a briefing, or seems befuddled and incoherent in a meeting when called on to speak? Someone who anguishes over an upcoming speaking engagement, maybe even losing sleep and being unable to eat? Is that someone you? If it is, don't worry. You're in good and plentiful company.

For some, it's not just speaking in front of large crowds that invokes this fear; a small crowd will do just fine, thank you! Like the crowd you find in a negotiation room or in a government-only meeting. Usually this fear stems from a fear of being embarrassed in front of other people, and it can be very real and debilitating. It can be magnified by the thought of having to engage in negotiations with representatives of a large, "prestigious" company.

The fear may seem to be confirmed when the other side shows up. You may think, "Here I am, just a lowly little GS umph-dee-dumph about to confront some high corporate shark muckety-mucks that eat people like me for a snack. And man, look at the way they're dressed. That suit could probably cover two of my house payments and those shoes alone could get me out of credit card debt!" You may tend to be cowed by a perceived gap in position and knowledge, and your fear escalates.

As the person entrusted to form, organize, and lead a team through a successful negotiation, this fear can seriously diminish your effectiveness as a leader and negotiator, and put in jeopardy your ability to reach a fair and reasonable outcome for the government. You can't afford this. You need to master your fear, but how? Now if you're the bold, outspoken type who relishes the thought of orating to the masses and crossing swords with the dauntless, feel free to skip the next few paragraphs. But if the thought of expressing your ideas in front of more than two people makes you break out in hives, read on!

Overcoming Your Fear

The opposite of fear is confidence, and the best way to build confidence is to plan and understand your negotiation thoroughly.

Build a sound negotiation plan using the techniques in this book and with the help of your teammates. Rehearse the plan and ask questions until you are confident you understand the rationale behind the plan and the process of carrying it out. Talk with your teammates from the program side to ensure that you have a passable knowledge of all the possible technical issues that may arise.

Knowledge is power, and power erases fear. Consider what-if scenarios and likely strategies and counterstrategies the other side may use, and be comfortable with how you plan to deal with them. Once you are confident of your plan, the negotiation will become simply executing a process you are very familiar and comfortable with. The better prepared you are, the less anxious you will be at the negotiation table.

Don't think of the negotiators from the other side as insurmountable dragons simply because they wear fancy suits and have impressive titles. Because you represent the government side, in all likelihood you know more about what your customer needs than they do. You're the expert. They have come dressed up specifically to impress *you*. You control the process; you set the rules. When the dance starts, the other side has no choice but to dance to your music.

Think back to kindergarten. Who had more power in the world than the little boy or girl that brought a big, fresh chocolate chip cookie out to recess with them? Every boy and girl within seeing or smelling distance, no matter what their playground pecking order status, was soon trying to be that kid's best friend. When you're negotiating for the government, remember: You have the cookie. They want the cookie. That puts you in the driver's seat.

Remember also that you never have to be alone in a negotiation. We've already gone over how to build your team of experts, and you will bring most of these smart folks right to the table with you. You have backup. You have friendly forces you can defer to, caucus with, and rely on. Even a solemn nod or muttered "uh-huh" or "that's right" from someone on your side while you're speaking can give you a boost of confidence.

If you have set yourself up to use the ambiguous authority tactic we discussed earlier, and I strongly recommend that you do, you also have a retreat route. Simply knowing you have a way out if things go badly or you gum things up can be a huge confidence builder.

Finally, confidence in public speaking—even in front of small groups—improves with practice and experience. The longer you're in the game, the more confident you'll be as time goes on. To shorten the cycle, you may consider seeking out speaking or team leadership opportunities in less threatening environments, such as joining a Toastmaster's club, and you should read the many good books available on public speaking and team leadership.

By the way, don't try too hard to lose all your fear. Most recognized public speaking experts agree that a little tension before a meeting can actually enhance your performance. A little nervousness makes you more likely to concentrate and less likely to take foolish risks. You want a few butterflies in your stomach; you just don't want so many that your stomach ends up in your throat!

What the Other Side Fears

In all likelihood the other side is just as fearful as you—not necessarily about the negotiation itself, but about the outcome. Remember, you have the cookie and they want the cookie. They are negotiating with you because their company wants to sell you something. If they don't get you to come to an agreement in the negotiation, they don't make the sale. If they don't make the sale, their company loses revenue. And revenue is the lifeblood of any company.

In all likelihood, they have already spent much time, energy, and money chasing this rabbit up to now. A company can expend great effort and dollars making their bid/no-bid decision, calculating anticipated rates of return, assessing competition and the probability of getting the contract, analyzing risk, preparing their proposal, assembling their negotiation team, and preparing for the negotiation. These are all sunk costs that they are under tremendous pressure to recoup. And that's not counting lost opportunity cost—the cost of having to forgo pursuing other contracts because they've tied up their resources chasing yours.

Even in a sole-source situation, the fear of not getting the contract, and not being able to recoup this sunk cost and invested time, is always there. You don't have to do anything to create this fear.

Another fear that's always present when any company does business with the government is the fear of the requirement or the program being canceled. Face it. If you're a contractor, dealing with the government can be a risky business! Nothing is certain until the money is obligated by the CO (basically, when the contract is signed), and many strange things can happen to the requirement before that happens. If the requirement is canceled, not only does the company get nothing, but they also lose all the time, money, and effort they have sunk into the project up to that time.

Even you have no control over some of the reasons a requirement might be canceled:

• Congress fails to authorize the program.

• Congress authorizes but fails to fund the program.

• Congress pulls the money for the program to put somewhere else.

• Your agency reallocates funding away from the program.

• The needs of the government or your agency change.

• Technology changes.

These are just some of the problems the other side has to be concerned about when they come to the negotiation table. They're also concerned about the requirement being canceled as a result of things that are in your control, such as your inability to reach what you feel is a fair and reasonable price. If that's the case, the FAR requires you to cancel the solicitation. You can never make award of any contract if you can't make a positive statement that the price is fair and reasonable. You may eventually resolicit, but this takes additional time, and time is money to a contractor.

They may also be concerned that you will find a higher priority socioeconomic set-aside candidate to reserve full or partial award for. The larger they are as a business, the more they are fearful of this possibility.

The other side is also fearful of what I call *requirement drag-on*. This is when the government requirement isn't canceled, but it mysteriously enters a state of suspended animation. This could be the result of funding problems, requirements definition problems, a change in the scope of the requirement, or any number of other causes. I once competed on a federal requirement that dragged on fully a year after the contract was supposed to be awarded as a result of (as far as I can guess) a spat between the customer, the host contracting activity, and that contracting activity's legal counsel.

These scenarios are what create so much fear in the contractor's mind. The government is usually tightlipped about the cause of the delay. Because the requirement hasn't been canceled, and if it is lucrative enough in their eyes, the contractor will continue to chase it—not knowing when (if ever) a contract will actually be awarded. They are trapped into continuing to tie up scarce resources, talent, and dollars chasing a rabbit that hasn't gone away but has become extremely elusive.

Perhaps the contractor's biggest fear is competition. If the other side knows there's competition for the contract, they are forced to cut costs and offer maximum performance solutions in an attempt to beat the competition and win the contract. They are forced into a much-diminished power position in negotiations. And still there's no guarantee.

Even if the company keeps all their smart folks up at night for weeks slashing costs and improving their proposal, even if they keep well within bounds in the negotiation, they still could lose the contract and all their effort will have been for naught. Sometimes they may even have to be concerned with competition from within the government itself, if you have the capability to accomplish the task in-house.

Sometimes the other side may be just as fearful about winning the contract as they are about losing it. If they win, they now must perform as promised within the cost constraints they agreed to. If competition forced them to promise the moon at cut-rate prices, they may have a real fear that they simply can't do it. They can't do all they said they were going to do within the price they locked themselves into and still make a profit. This may lead them to trim costs as they perform, which endangers the quality of their performance under the contract. If they can't perform, or if they perform badly, they stand a good chance of getting a poor past performance rating from the government.

The FAR requires a past performance report on every completed contract over $100,000 (the threshold is higher for the Department of Defense), and contractors are extremely concerned with keeping these reports positive. The government uses past performance as an evaluation factor in the award of most contracts, so one bad past performance rating on one contract can significantly reduce that company's chances of winning more government business in the future.

Contractors are also fearful of the unknown. No solicitation or proposal can anticipate everything. There is always the risk of unanticipated events, glitches, oversights, price increases for labor or materials, mission changes, personnel changes, and so forth, cropping up. Any one of these can threaten the contractor's technical approach, contract performance, reliability of cost estimates, and even the future of the contract. In a fixed-price environment, the contractor has to assume many of these risks.

They are also fearful that the government might not be telling them the whole story—all the facts. Someone on the government team, usually from the technical side, may be holding back crucial information the contractor needs to assess risk and price their proposal properly. This, as you can imagine, has led to much litigation over the years.

Finally, the contractor may fear damaging their long-term relationship with your agency by something they do either in negotiations or later in contract performance. If they're too overbearing or argumentative in negotiations, even if they believe they are right, their actions may taint the government's interest in dealing with them in the future. So they may have huge pressure on them to be agreeable during the negotiation. They also know they can do damage to the relationship by disappointing the government in contract performance or by becoming too unyielding in the face of inevitable government-directed changes or disagreements.

Good contractors know they can't live by one contract alone. They need to feed their families next year and the year after that. Maintaining a good relationship with their primary customers is the best way they can ensure future business, profitability, and survival.

Using Their Fear to Your Advantage

As you can see, the smug, confident, well-dressed contractor negotiators sitting across the table from you quite likely have a deep current of fear running under the surface. You can turn these fears into perfectly acceptable negotiation tactics that will lend more power to your side and assist you in finalizing an agreement that is truly fair and reasonable for both sides. In fact, you can increase the effectiveness of many of the negotiation tactics you have learned up to now by realizing that these fears exist. Simply realizing that the other side has pressures and fears can reduce your stress level and make you a better negotiator.

Some of the tactics you have already learned automatically reinforce fears the other side may have. For instance, using the tactic of silence is an excellent way to stoke fears the other side may have. You may be silent simply because you just don't have anything to say at the time, or you may be using silence as a tactic, but they don't know that for sure. Your silence can amplify all the fears we've just talked about.

When you're silent at key points during the negotiation, some of the questions that may run through their minds are: Are you holding back on some important information we need to know? Are you offended by our offer? Are you contemplating the benefits of retaining the work in-house? Are you mentally comparing our latest offer with a competitor's offer? Did we price our offer too high? Are you contemplating canceling the solicitation rather than pay our price? And on and on.

That's why the tactic of silence is so effective. You compel them to multiply their fears irrationally until sometimes you even get an unanticipated unilateral concession.

Another tactic that can compound their fear is the order of issues tactic. By arranging to negotiate the issues by difficulty of agreement (the toughest, most important issues first) instead of ease of agreement (the easiest, least important issues first), you signal to the other side that you have the power. This will play on their fear that your power comes from the power of having options, only one of which is their proposal.

Throwing your most important issue out up front is almost like saying, "Tell me right now, before we waste each other's time, are you going to be able to give me what I want or not?" In the other side's mind, the implications of an "or not" answer could mean you will move on to other options. This fear could pressure them to give concessions early, establishing a pattern that will be difficult for them to get out of as negotiations continue.

You can also try the time pressure tactic. You might drop the hint that you have little time remaining to award the contract before your funds expire. Remember, though, you can't mislead or lie to the other side; you must actually be in a tight time situation.

You can use a slight variation of the vise tactic. If you don't immediately get a concession after you say the magic words "you'll have to do better than that," look at your watch, sigh, and say something like, "I was hoping we could wrap this up by now. I've got other folks to talk to." Of course, the perception they'll get is that those "other folks" are their competitors.

You can also hint that awarding the contract and having the work done is more of a "nice to have" than a "need to have." Other tactics that compound fear well are the use of caucuses, the ambiguous authority tactic, and the empty pockets tactic.

However, the most effective way to leverage the other side's fear is by invoking the power of competition. The more options you have, the more power you have. The combination of them knowing they're in competition for the contract coupled with your attitude of subtle indifference to striking a deal with them really will turn their screws. Throw in a few well-timed tactics, or a hint that you may well reconsider and do the job with in-house people, and you strengthen your position. Show them you are firmly in control and absolutely serious about achieving the best value for your customer and the taxpayer.

I'll caution you one more time, though. You can't intentionally lie to the contractor as part of any negotiation strategy you use. I advise against stretching the truth even a little bit. If you tell them you have other folks to talk to, you'd better really have other folks to talk to.

You also are prohibited from what car dealers call "shopping the bid." That's when you beat the car dealer down to their lowest price and then take that price to their competitors and ask if they can beat it. Although that's perfectly okay to do in your private negotiations, the government calls this *auctioning*, and you're not supposed to do it when you're negotiating for Uncle Sam. You can't reveal a contractor's proposed price to anyone who doesn't have a valid need to know and keep on the good side of the Procurement Integrity Act. You can be tough, but you always have to be completely honest.

Chapter 29

The Walkout Tactic

I'm sure you have heard of, seen on TV, or even personally experienced a negotiator get up and walk out in the middle of a negotiation. They may do it in anger, frustration, with a flourish, or coolly and smugly. They may take their entire negotiating team with them, just some of their team, or they may be the only one on their team who walks out. They may punctuate their exit by terse words like "I'll see you in court!" or "Well, I guess we have nothing else to talk about." In all cases, it's usually very dramatic, attention getting, and pivotal in the negotiation process. In all likelihood, it's also just a well-planned tactic.

The walkout tactic, like the good cop/bad cop tactic, is so commonly used that it can almost be called overused. Smart negotiators continue to use it, however, because it works.

The walkout tactic is rarely used as a stand-alone tactic, but is usually combined with other tactics. For example, the other side often uses the walkout tactic as the culmination point of the good cop/bad cop tactic, with the bad cop storming out of the room at a crucial moment. This, of course, leaves the good cop in the room to complete the tactic (see Chapter 16 for an explanation of how the good cop/bad cop tactic works).

It can also be used in tandem with the anger tactic to increase its effectiveness. But perhaps the most effective use of the walkout tactic is when it's combined with the frustration tactic. Reread, in the last chapter, how the frustration tactic is used and the results it's designed to get and you'll see why it's so effective.

Unless it's being used simply as a set-up for the good cop/bad cop tactic, the walkout tactic is intended to shock, embarrass, and confuse your team. By walking out, the other side has created, out of thin air, another issue to use as a bargaining chip to gain concessions from you. By projecting their willingness to walk away from the deal, they greatly increase their negotiating power. You start thinking, "Well, they probably have other options—other contracts to chase—if they're so willing to leave us high and dry like this!" In your mind, it increases the value of what they are trying to sell and you almost subconsciously can't help but want it more.

Getting them back to the negotiating table now becomes *your* problem and you'll feel pressure to throw them a bone (a unilateral concession) to have them sit down with you again. You start bidding against yourself.

COUNTERS TO THE WALKOUT TACTIC

When you're negotiating with experienced companies, you can rest assured that they won't send an ineffective negotiator to deal with you. Only an ineffective negotiator will actually get angry enough to storm out of the room before the deal is closed for his company. You can always safely assume the walkout is a carefully calculated tactic being played by a professional negotiator.

As you have learned, the best counter to any tactic is simply to recognize it as a tactic, which immediately takes most of the sting out of it. Look for telltale signs their walkout is a tactic: Is the whole team leaving? (If not, you're being set up for the good cop/bad cop tactic.) Are they leaving something in the room, like a briefcase? Are they leaving before they have a ride back to the airport or well in advance of their scheduled departure time? (If so, they're definitely planning to return.) Do they have competition for the contract? (If so, you can almost be assured it's a bluff).

Let the other side know you recognize their dramatic walkout as a tactic. This is a counter that has to be sprung quickly, because you have to catch them before they storm out of the room or out of earshot. Don't let their bluster or dramatics bamboozle you into stunned silence. As soon as you see them start packing up or rising to head out the door, call their bluff. You may say something like, "Oh, come on, Susan! You're not going to play the walkout tactic on me are you? I thought you knew I was better than that! How about let's call a 15-minute caucus instead and get back together and crunch this thing out? In fact, your team can stay in here and I'll take my team to the other room. I need to talk to them anyway about your last point. I'll be back in 15. Is there any reason you won't be here then?"

A variant could be, "Oh, come on Carl! Don't hit me with the walkout tactic! I know you have options and you know I have options, but I really think we can pull this off together. I need a break anyway to talk about your last point with my team. We're going down the hall and we'll be back in 15 minutes. How long do you think you need?"

Let's analyze what you've done with either of these responses. You've immediately let them know you recognize their actions as the walkout tactic in a way that transmits to them that you know how to deal with it and that you won't let it be effective against you.

I suggest you call the potential walker by their first name, as I did in the two examples; it seems to work better. I don't really know why. Perhaps the personalization associated with hearing their first name causes them to hesitate, but it does work better.

You then immediately call a caucus, which serves several useful purposes. First, it allows you to ignore the tactic. Second, it forces the other side to continue to be engaged in the process of the negotiation. Lastly, it allows you to reassert control of the negotiation. Remember, *you* are in control of the negotiation. If you allow the other side to walk out, you have ceded control to them and lost power in the negotiation.

When you call a caucus, you signal to the other side that you don't consider the negotiation over and they'd better remain engaged.

However, instead of challenging or demanding they continue, you offer them the escape route of a caucus, which lets them save face in front of their team and greatly improves the chance they'll come back to the table.

Notice also in both examples that when a caucus was called, you mentioned that you have alternatives other than their company if they go through with a total walkout. Even if you're in a sole-source situation, you always have the option of doing the work in-house, by separate contract, or electing to not do the work at all (depending on your customer's needs). Try to make this fact known as subtly as you can, to remind them that you have options.

Notice also that both examples struck some sort of conciliatory chord. Putting in something like "I really think we can pull this together," "I don't think we're that far apart," or "I'm sure we can crunch this out" signals to them that you are still open to creative solutions to satisfy both parties' interests.

After the conciliatory words, let the other side know why you called the caucus. Notice that in both examples, it's to let *you* have time to talk with *your* team. This strengthens their perception that you are firmly in control of the negotiations. It also gives them something to think about. Here are just some of the things they may be thinking about: Why do you have to talk with your team? Are you planning on walking out too and did we beat you to the punch? Do you have a solution favorable to our side that you need to air with your team? Are you going to talk with your team about completely pulling the plug on the whole negotiation? Are you going to meet to consider and maybe even recommend a competitor or another course of action? Have we seriously offended you? Are you going to contemplate releasing some additional information that will be useful or vital to us?

The bottom line is that they now must guess why you want to talk to your team in private. This usually reverses the intended effect of the walkout tactic and gives them a solid reason to remain engaged in the negotiation. They'll be curious enough to stick around to see what your team is going to come up with.

Finally, notice that both examples set a definite time to reconvene and asked an open-ended question that requires a response from the other side. Actually, the definite time is negotiable, and that's just the point. If they start negotiating about the return time, they're still negotiating. If they're still negotiating, they're still in the negotiation!

Let them have any reasonable time they feel they need, but establish a definite return time before you allow them to leave. Don't let them say "We'll get back to you." That puts them in control, not you.

Very rarely, a walkout could be for real. Maybe the other side has reached their BATNA or the return on their investment just isn't there under the current conditions. If so, the counters we've just discussed may not work. If they're going to walk, they're going to walk, especially if they are in a superior bargaining position.

I've never had this happen in a competitive negotiation and I've experienced it only once in a sole-source negotiation. But it can happen. Sometimes the parties just can't get together. Sometimes it just doesn't work.

In the case of my sole-source walkout, the other side knew they had all the power. They were sole source and they knew we *had* to have what they were offering, and quickly! We just couldn't agree to a fair price and they got up to walk away. I tried all the walkout counters to no avail.

As a last-gasp measure, I had their lead negotiator sign an official document I quickly typed up stating that the negotiations were concluded because of the parties' inability to reach an agreement and the CO's (my) inability to establish successfully a fair and reasonable price. I mentioned that I would be sending this memo to his superiors at their corporate headquarters.

I was hoping this would make them come back to the bargaining table, but it didn't work. Obviously, they had planned for an impasse and they were using the walkout to hammer down their own terms. Ultimately, we had to agree to them. You can't win 'em all!

Chapter 30

The Lock-in Tactic

Lock-in tactics can come in the form of ultimatums or threats. They can also come in the form of actions the other side has already taken that they now want you to ratify after the fact, or actions they have taken that have intentionally restricted their negotiating room. In all these cases, they are attempting to solidify (or "lock in") their position, forcing you to be the one to give in so that the negotiation can continue. Most of the time, they aren't actually *that* locked in to the extreme position they're claiming; they just want you to think they are. That's what makes this tactic something to watch out for!

THE CLASSIC LOCK-IN TACTIC

In their book *Getting to Yes* (Penguin Books, 1991), Fisher and Ury retell Thomas Schelling's classic example of a lock-in tactic. There are two dynamite trucks playing "chicken" with each other on a narrow one-lane road. As they head toward each other with great speed, it becomes a test of wills as to which driver will be the first to "chicken out" and turn off the road to avoid a collision. When the trucks get dangerously close, one of the drivers pulls off his steering wheel and tosses it out the window!

What kind of signal is that to the driver of the other truck? If you were that driver, what would you do when you saw that steering wheel fly out of the other truck? You see the driver of the other truck as having few options left, and you'd better be the one who makes the hard choice—quickly—because you still have more options. The other driver has actually strengthened his bargaining position by intentionally weakening his own control over the situation.

In contract negotiations, an example of a lock-in tactic is when the other negotiator has vowed to his upper management to get no less than a certain percentage increase from the government for the next year of contract performance. He has even made this vow directly to the rank-and-file employees of the company, setting high expectations in their minds for future raises. To make matters worse, he has been very public about these declarations, perhaps even picking up local media coverage. Now the general public is involved and may have expectations too. Money isn't the only thing the other side may try to lock in; it could also be environmental issues, noise issues, or any other conceivable issue that affects your negotiation position.

In the latter example, the negotiator has intentionally attempted to set the negotiation range before the negotiation even starts. Because he has publicly committed to getting no less than such-and-such when he negotiates with you, you perceive that he will lose credibility and perhaps even his job if he's unable to get it. He has also publicly "sold" his position to many people, setting expectations about the negotiation before it even begins and perhaps even winning support for his position.

In both examples, the other side has intentionally made extreme commitments, making it seemingly impossible for them to backtrack. This makes it extremely difficult for you to move them from that position. You're almost put in the position of giving a concession up front just to get the ball rolling! Also, because their position is so locked in, any concessions they do make will come at an extreme price to you.

Lock-in tactics can also be used as rallying cries and morale builders for the other side's team. The negotiator can use them to ensure control and unity over his own team, giving the team members focus for the negotiation and a common commitment to accomplish a certain result.

An excellent example from history comes from Cortez's conquest of Montezuma and the Aztec nation. In 1519, Cortez landed his small force of about 600 men on the coast at Vera Cruz with nothing less than total conquest of the Aztecs as his goal. But there were problems. He had only 600 men and Montezuma had thousands and thousands of warriors. Montezuma controlled the terrain, the food supplies, and the virtually impregnable fortress city of Tenochtitlan (current-day Mexico City), surrounded by water. Because of the terrain, simply getting to Tenochtitlan, even with no opposition, would be a daunting task.

Put yourself in the position of one of Cortez's conquistadors. Would you look at the odds and try to convince him to settle for a little local loot and a safe boat ride back to Cuba, your base? I probably would have. In fact, some of his men started to grumble and even talked of mutiny when they learned of his plan. It seemed like suicide. When his men looked to him for his first order, do you know what he said? "Burn the boats." The rest of the exchange may have taken place as follows:

"Huh?"

"Burn the boats."

"Excuse me?"

"*Burn* the boats."

"Ha! That's a good one, boss!"

"BURN THE BOATS!"

"Sir, maybe I misunderstood you. Did you just tell us to burn the boats?"

"Yep."

"You're kidding, right?"

"Nope."

And they did. Retreat was no longer an option. Cortez had taken that option off the board. The only remaining option was to conquer or die. Do you think this had the desired effect of motivating his soldiers to accomplish the task at hand? Sure did. In 1521, Cortez and his men conquered Montezuma, Tenochtitlan, and all of the New World for Spain, all starting with only 600 men and some charred boat timber.

THE FAIT ACCOMPLI

Have you ever heard the expression "It's easier to beg for forgiveness than ask for permission"? Have *you* ever done that? If you have, you already know how the lock-in tactic called *fait accompli* works. Fait accompli (French for "it is done") is when the other side assumes you'll agree to what they want to do beforehand, and they go ahead and do it before any agreement is reached. They then present you with these facts (the "fait accompli") and hope you'll simply accept what they've done instead of going to the trouble of negotiating about it. Because the deed is already done, both sides are already locked in to the result.

As angry as you may get, it doesn't change the fact that the other side has unilaterally taken away most of your options and severely decreased your negotiating position, your power over the outcome. You have lost an incredible amount of negotiating wiggle room and usually you're left with just haggling over the final price.

Recently, my wife Jill was both the victim, and then the perpetrator, of the fait accompli tactic. Because I am eternally on the road, Jill is the bill payer and the boss of the house, including keeping up the yard. She had been having a few minor spats with our yard maintenance folks during the past few months. Nothing major, just little disagreements over the quality of their service. When the next monthly invoice arrived, however, Jill noticed that the company had unilaterally elected to increase our monthly yard maintenance fee by $15. That's the fait accompli tactic. The company was betting Jill would just accept the increase (thinking, maybe it's normal, maybe their expenses have risen, and so on) instead of going to all the trouble of complaining and fighting over (i.e., negotiating over) such a small increase.

They bet wrong. Obviously, they didn't know Jill too well! Although she's never had a lick of formal training in negotiations, she's a better negotiator than I am. She promptly pulled the lawn maintenance contract, studied it, and saw it contained no clauses authorizing the company to bump up the price for any reason whatsoever. Now what to do? She knew the company expected her to do nothing (not happening) or maybe, at most, call and complain a little. (Jill? A little? Get real!) She also knew they were probably prepared to wear her down if she did call. So she didn't call. She simply used the fait accompli tactic right back at them. She wrote out the check for the usual amount, marked "paid in full" on it and the invoice, attached the check to the invoice, mailed it, and waited to see what would happen.

What happened? Absolutely nothing. For a while, the invoices kept coming in billing us the extra $15, and Jill kept paying the invoices less the $15. Soon, the invoices went back to the original contract amount. She hasn't had a single call from the company, and they keep cashing our checks and providing us lawn service as if nothing has changed. As I mentioned earlier, in the sport of wrestling, this is called a *reversal* and you get points for it. Go Jill!

In the world of government negotiations, however, the fait accompli tactic is a dangerous game for a contractor to play. In yard maintenance, if you do something without permission and later ask for payment it's called *fait accompli.* In government contracts, it's called an *unauthorized commitment.* The rules are different. If the contractor volunteers work without authority, direction, or encouragement from the government, you can simply say, "Thank you for your contribution to the United States of America. We didn't tell you to do this and we're not paying for it." The government is the sovereign, and the sovereign makes the rules.

It gets a little more complicated if the contractor's fait accompli was directed or egged on by someone in the government. It's still an unauthorized commitment, but now the CO has a choice. He can either elect to stick the contractor with the bill or ratify (make good) the unauthorized commitment. Even if the act is ratified, however, it interrupts the contractor's cash flow. They may eventually get paid, but it could take awhile.

In light of these dangers, smart contractors rarely knowingly use the fait accompli tactic. We still have our share of ratifications in the federal government, but most don't come from intentional use of fait accompli.

THREATS

I have rarely seen direct threats used in government contract negotiations. Contractors rarely use them because of the huge disparity between their position and the position of the federal government. It would be like an ant threatening an elephant; it rarely works. Government negotiators (good government negotiators, that is) rarely use them because they are highly intimidating and not really considered good-faith negotiations. Remember, you have to be fair and reasonable to both sides.

A direct threat is when one side warns the other, in no uncertain terms, of harsh consequences if they fail to agree to their terms. An example of a direct threat is: "If you don't pay me the price I'm demanding for this contract modification, I'm telling you right now I'm going to court!" No mincing of words, no attempts at niceties or compromise—just in your face.

Direct threats are also rarely used because there are plenty of better ways to get your point across just as effectively—probably more effectively. For example, veiled threats and concerned warnings work much better and are more commonly encountered. These toned-down versions of direct threats simply imply bad consequences instead of threatening them, and show concern about the negative effects the event will have on the other side. They still get the same point across, only in a kinder, gentler way.

When someone feels intimidated or directly threatened, their defenses go up pretty quickly and position lock-in usually occurs. With the veiled threat or concerned warning, your defenses don't go up nearly as fast because the other side is trying to convince you that they feel your pain and want to help you avoid it. Also, a direct threat usually is fairly specific while a veiled threat usually alludes to broad, unspecified consequences. Because the consequences are so nebulous, the threatened party's imagination can magnify them and make them much more menacing than they really are. All the nasty stuff that *might* happen is more intimidating than the one specific thing that *could* happen.

With the direct threat, the threatened party at least knows what the consequences will be and can plan, strategize, and make calculated decisions accordingly. The more fuzzy the consequences, the less control the threatened party has over handling them.

Let's examine the direct threat compared with the veiled threat/concerned warning by using an example. The example is rather long and complex, but its intent is to cover all the bases and give you a good look at the benefit of using veiled threats/concerned warnings over direct threats. It's based on an actual negotiation situation I once faced.

You're negotiating with a contractor who has messed up royally on a major cost-reimbursement contract vital to national defense. They've had overrun after overrun and don't seem any closer to achieving the contract objective than when they first were awarded the contract. You've tried every remedy possible, both informal and formal, with no result. Your agency has just informed you they will be providing no more funding for the project. If this were a fixed-price contract, you'd have every reason to terminate this contractor for default. Because it's a cost contract, however, you're stuck with the terminations clause for cost-reimbursement contracts, forcing you to pay the contractor a sizeable sum just to get out of the contract.

You're mortified at the thought of paying this contractor even more money after the way they have wasted so much taxpayer money already. You devise a government strategy that uses a no-cost settlement agreement instead of a termination, thus avoiding the expensive termination costs. The problem is that you have to convince the contractor to accept it. They know the terminations clause as well as you do. They've done the math and they're expecting that hefty termination settlement. Let's see how a direct threat would work in this case.

Direct Threat Approach

"Contractor, if you don't go along with this no-cost settlement agreement, I'm going to force you to do it. I'll withhold payment of any remaining money due you under this contract, forcing you to take us to the appeals board. I guarantee you the appeals board will see it our way, and you'll end up spending a lot of time, energy, and legal fees for nothing!"

How do you think that's going to play with the contractor? How would *you* react? If I were the contractor, it would make me just that much more anxious to go to court and prove you wrong, especially because you were so blunt and rude about it. Even if I think I'll lose, I might do it just out of principle. Also, I now know your strategy so I can better prepare to deal with it. By threatening me directly, you have given me your game plan. Now let's see how a veiled threat/concerned warning might work.

Veiled Threat/Concerned Warning Approach

"Contractor, we all knew how difficult this project was going to be to pull off, but you know as well as I do that you pretty much blew it. I just don't think it's fair to pay you more money to get out of a contract that you messed up this badly. I sure wish you'd accept this no-cost agreement. It's your call, of course, but if you continue to press for termination costs, I'll have no choice but to deny them. You won't like that and we'll probably end up in court.

Now I don't really know who'll win on this issue when it goes to court, but I'm prepared to lose. If the decision goes against us, I'll gladly pay you any amount the court orders. We have the money; we're the federal government. If we do go to court, however, I'm concerned about the impact it will have on your company, no matter who ultimately wins.

Last time I looked, only 10 percent of your total annual sales comes from the federal government; the vast majority of your profit is from consumer sales. You've built up a great reputation in the marketplace for your consumer goods.

Right now, only a few people in the world know how royally you messed up this contract so vital to the defense of this nation, and they're all right here in this room. If we go to court, it will be front page news in the *Washington Post*, the *Wall Street Journal*, the *New York Times*, and the *Los Angeles Times*. It will probably get follow-up coverage on some television talk shows and news magazines. Although I wouldn't want this to happen, I don't see how we could prevent it. I'm concerned about the impact this negative publicity could have on your well-earned reputation and your survivability as a company able to continue to help us with our contracting needs in the future, aren't you?"

Put yourself in the contractor's shoes. Would you react differently to this approach than to a direct threat? Did it give you something to think about and, more important, something to lose? The threat is implied, not direct, and the consequences will not come directly from you, but from other vague sources and will be in the nebulous form of damaged reputation and lost sales. You're simply helping the contractor by pointing out the grave consequences of the situation and offering them a way out—your settlement agreement!

"TAKE IT OR LEAVE IT"

I'm sure that sometime in your career, or sometime in your personal life, you've either used the phrase "take it or leave it" or you've heard it used against you. It's a very familiar form of lock-in tactic designed to get you to commit, under pressure, to terms usually more favorable to the other side than your side. It allows the other side to signal to you that they are perfectly willing to walk away from the deal (although usually that's the last thing they *really* want to do).

Experienced negotiators usually deliver this form of lock-in tactic close to the end of the negotiation, because it's a lot more effective after they have softened you up with the time investment tactic. If they simply start the negotiation out with "take it or leave it," you have no investment in them and it's very easy for you to take them up on the "leave it" part and turn to their competition. We'll talk about one exception to this a little later.

The other side will usually try to strengthen their take-it-or-leave-it stance by backing up their demand with some sort of documented evidence or other facts to add legitimacy to their ultimatum. They may say that their bosses have allowed them to do only so much, which is combining the take it or leave it tactic with the ambiguous authority tactic. They may say they would like to do more, but it's "just not in our budget" or "we just don't have any more money or resources we can allot to this project."

Most experienced negotiators you will deal with, however, know better than to use the exact phrase "take it or leave it" because of how harsh it sounds. It instantly ruffles feathers, creates bad will, and can be very counterproductive to the negotiation process. They'll use more subtle statements like, "I'm sorry. Company policy is that we never negotiate" or "Sorry, but that's our walk-away price. We can't do it for anything less than that" or "We never deviate from our published prices." I'm sure you've heard some of these. They're just softer forms of the take it or leave it tactic.

Of course, if you're dealing with a sole-source contractor, "take it or leave it" may be something you hear word for word. This is especially true when you're negotiating important modifications to existing contracts, which, by definition, are sole-source. For commercial items, changes in terms and conditions (modifications) can't happen unless both sides—you and the contractor—agree to them, so "take it or leave it" may be a logical course for a contractor to take. The more competition you have, the more alternatives you have, the less likely you will be directly threatened with "take it or leave it."

Earlier, you found that the other side will usually use the take-it-or-leave-it tactic close to the end of the negotiations, because it's more effective after they have gotten you to invest time and energy into the effort. Here's the one exception I mentioned.

Sometimes the other side may intentionally use a form of the take-it-or-leave-it tactic (usually couched in softer tones) right at the start of a negotiation. Certain car dealerships are notorious for using this version of the tactic. Have you ever seen a car dealer that advertises something like: "THE STICKER PRICE IS THE PRICE YOU PAY! WE DON'T HAGGLE OVER PRICES! OUR STICKER PRICES ARE ALREADY THE MOST DISCOUNTED, BEST DEAL YOU CAN GET! WE DON'T LIKE TO NEGOTIATE HERE!"

In government negotiations, it's usually the contractor who says, right up front, something like the following: "Our GSA contract prices we quoted you are our absolute rock-bottom prices and we never negotiate them. We just don't like to negotiate."

Folks, don't be fooled! Anybody who says they don't like to negotiate really *loves* to negotiate and is usually very good at it. Look what using the "we don't like to negotiate" tactic does for them. First, it plays on many individuals' natural reluctance to haggle. Most consumers, and many government negotiators, simply feel uncomfortable negotiating. Not to worry—the nice old contractor will make it easy for you. You loosen up, feel less pressured, and tend to trust that person more. They have now set the stage to hit you with manipulative tactics almost at will. You're less guarded and not looking for them. Also, it's hard for you to believe, even if you have a hint you're being played, that the nice person who's not making you haggle would really do this to you. You're a sitting duck.

Second, the we-don't-like-to-negotiate tactic is used as a trick to get you to give away your entire negotiating range up front. The other side may say something like, "Listen, at ABC Company, we don't like to haggle with the government over prices. So just tell me how much you think it will take to get this deal done and I'll let you know if we can do it for that amount." Folks, they're trying to get you to give them the first number. Remember what you're never supposed to do in negotiations? Right: Put the first number on the table! If you fall for this, you'll give them your government cost estimate, or your maximum, minimum, or target position. Then what will the other side do? They'll use the bracketing tactic on you before you can blink an eye.

Finally, a we-don't-like-to-negotiate or the take-it-or-leave-it stance taps into our natural temptation to test it to see if it's really what they mean. The other side is banking on it. You're usually tempted to test them to see if they're really serious. The other side may say something like, "Listen, our proposal price of $125 per hour is the absolute minimum we can do to hope to break even on this contract. I understand you want us to come down to $75 per hour, but that's impossible. It's got to be $125 per hour or nothing. Take it or leave it."

An inexperienced negotiator may be tempted, in the spirit of keeping the negotiations going, to test their firm stance by a small concession. It may go something like this:

Government Negotiator: Okay. Maybe I *could* come up from $75 per hour to $80 per hour, but that's the absolute best we can do.

Contractor: Nope. $125 per hour. Take it or leave it.

Government Negotiator: I understand your position and I know you have to make a profit for this to be worthwhile. How about $95 per hour?

Contractor: Nope. $125 per hour. Take it or leave it.

Government Negotiator: $110 per hour?

And so forth. By giving the first concession in response to the contractor's take-it-or-leave-it stance, the inexperienced government negotiator signals their willingness to give concessions if the contractor just sticks to their guns and doesn't move. Pretty soon, the government negotiator has given away practically their entire negotiating range without getting a single concession in return. Not a good negotiating day!

COUNTERS TO THE LOCK-IN TACTIC

Whatever guise lock-in tactics take (classic lock-in, fait accompli, direct or veiled threats, or "take it or leave it"), your negotiating arsenal must include counters to break the effect of the tactic and get the negotiation back on track. Sometimes the hardest part is to divine whether the lock-in is being used as a tactic or whether it's a real bottom-line position. This is important, because you handle the two very differently. If the other side locks in because that's really all they have left to give, and if your side can't live with it, you're headed for a true, honest deadlock.

So how do you know the difference? The best way is to have your homework done. The data gathering you did way back when you were planning the negotiation becomes worth its weight in gold now. The more you know about the other side's position before you sit down to negotiate, the better able you will be to determine whether they're bluffing. For instance, the other side may lock in to a published price list from which they say they can't deviate, but your negotiation preparation has uncovered several occasions when they were flexible on pricing to other agencies. If this is the case, you have them dead-to-rights in an attempt to use the lock-in tactic.

Also, remember the other side will usually attempt to bolster their lock-in tactic by citing facts, figures, and other information in an attempt to gain credibility for their position. If you suspect the lock-in tactic, immediately tests those facts for validity. You could find they have reached their true bottom line, or you could find your facts tend to contradict theirs and they're playing a tactic. By knowing as much as you can about the other side, you have a better handle on what they stand to lose if the lock-in doesn't play out their way.

An example of a validity test could sound something like, "Are you sure the OSHA regulations won't let you do this job with less than three people present? I had my team research the regulations last night and our attorney reviewed them this morning. They couldn't find anything in them that mandates that many people for that particular job. Where are you getting your information?" Notice that you have requested that they validate their own facts and figures, and at the same time you have let them know you've done your homework.

One caution about testing their facts for validity: You need to do it as soon as possible. A delay in responding to or challenging their information could be interpreted as your tacit acceptance of the information as factual. The longer their information sits on the table, the more valid it becomes. If this happens, the other side has transferred their problem to you, and now it's either a joint problem—or worse, your problem! You have enough problems of your own without having to help them solve theirs, especially if they're made up!

Another effective counter to lock-in tactics is to use the ambiguous authority tactic yourself to lock in your own position. Hopefully you've created an ambiguous authority before the negotiations started, and you've let the other side know you have one. Now you simply use that ambiguous authority to counter their lock-in and present them with a dilemma. You may say, "I understand you're saying you need at least $200 per hour and I'd sure love to give you that much, but I'm pretty sure my review committee won't go for it. I'm not even sure if it's in our budget. How do you suggest I sell them on the idea?"

Notice that you've not only used your own ambiguous authority to provide you a retreat route, but you've phrased it in a way that's almost certainly going to pull more information about their position from them or force them to back down if they are really just bluffing. In rare cases, they may actually be able to give you the additional information that does indeed justify their position. In all cases you win, because you now know more about their position than you did before.

You can also try to escalate their lock-in position to the other side's *own* higher, or ambiguous, authority. If they're smart negotiators, they, like you, have already created an ambiguous authority of their own. Sometimes it's a true higher authority and sometimes it's just a made-up authority, but it doesn't matter. Simply use it to go up their own chain with their own demand.

If they say they don't have authority to approve a price decrease or a longer warranty, ask them who in their company does. Ask to talk to that person. If they hem and haw and show reluctance to elevate the issue to their own bosses, it's almost a sure bet they actually *do* have the authority and are just using a lock-in tactic. If they actually do have to consult a higher authority, but hesitate, that's even better. This causes them to lose face in the negotiation, diminishing their power position, and clues you in that their position probably isn't as locked in as they are letting on.

Finally, if they actually let you escalate the issue to their higher authority, that's a good thing too. Generally, the higher you escalate issues in a negotiation, the more room for compromise you find. Higher echelons are usually more concerned with general customer relations than with the bottom-line result of one contract negotiation (that is, of course, if they're not playing the good cop/bad cop tactic on you). As an added touch, you might want to try a little flattery. You may say something like, "Could you check with your boss to see if your company has any flexibility on this? I'm sure if anyone can convince them, you can!"

If you want to play the counter a little softer, you might try the trial balloon tactic, coupled with the "feel, felt" (without the "found") formula. It could go something like this: "I understand you feel you can't give any more on this issue, and I've felt the same way on a lot of issues I've negotiated, but what if we look at a longer delivery period? Could that have an effect on your pricing structure?"

Another nonthreatening way to confront the lock-in is to ask the other side what it would take for them to change their position. Either way, you're set to get more information and break the effect of the lock-in. You've shown you are flexible, and if they don't reciprocate, they're set up to look inflexible.

You can also counter the lock-in tactic by simply ignoring it. Blow it off as if you didn't even hear it. If you simply refuse to acknowledge it as a locked-in position, it doesn't lock you in. I know it sounds simple, but ignoring a lock-in does several things, all good for your side.

First, it gets the other side wondering why you've ignored it! Here they've gone to these great lengths to present you with a lock-in position and it simply bounced off your back. Why? Do you know something they don't? Have you already made up your mind to walk away? Have you got a better deal from their competitors? Did they misread you and this issue isn't actually that big for you? And on and on. Their imagination will lead them into attempting to defend their position more and more, and this will give you more information about their position.

Second, it strings the perceived threat out in time. And the more time that passes after a threat is delivered, the less potent that threat becomes. The other side will be under more and more pressure to make good on the threat, and that's usually the last thing they want to do. Usually they'll back down and modify their position if you simply let enough time pass without responding. Put them off. Time is always on your side if they throw the lock-in tactic at you.

Finally, ignoring a lock-in lets the other side know you'll not be intimidated into making rash, panicked decisions during the negotiation. Pressure tactics aren't going to affect you. You don't play the game that way and you're certainly not going to play their game. You will not be cowed into making concessions under duress and will discuss revising your position only if they can prove the merits of their case.

Chapter 31

The Decoy Tactic

If you remember, the coupling tactic is when you combine one of your "give" points (something you'd like, but can do without) with one of your "must" points (something you've got to have) and represent them as a package deal to build negotiation flexibility. You really eventually plan to concede on your "give" point to get your "must" point. Even though you're willing to let your "give" point go, both your "must" and "give" points are actual negotiation objectives you have.

Not so with the decoy tactic. With this tactic, the other side either makes up a phony issue or forcefully presses an issue they really don't care about to distract you from the real issue. They've also created a false issue they can later "give up," but only in return for a real concession from your side.

The decoy tactic is a tactic only the other side can use. Remember, you represent the government side, and this position comes with some restrictions. You are ethically required to be fair and reasonable to both sides, which means that you can't make up imaginary issues to mislead the other side; you can't lie. If you tell the contractor delivery time is your most important issue, for example, it really has to be. Of course, the other side isn't bound by these same rules, so they are free to use this tactic if they choose. Accordingly, the decoy tactic is one you can't use, but you have to be able to recognize it when it's used against you so you can effectively counter it.

Let's say you've awarded a food services contract for a large dining hall or cafeteria and you've negotiated a great bottom-line price. The contractor really had to cut their profit rate to the bone to make it through the competition and to survive your expertise at the negotiating table. The base plus two option-year contract is two days into performance, with the contractor doing fairly well. Then the contractor hits you with a problem.

In the solicitation and resultant contract, you promised to provide the winning contractor's employees locker space at the facility so they would have a place to store their personal items, change of clothes, and so forth. The lockers you've provided are one foot deep, wide, and high, and can be locked, although you didn't describe them in that much detail in your solicitation. You just said locker space would be made available. You also neglected to offer the competing contractors a site visit of the facility before award.

Now the contractor's management folks have hit you with a written complaint that the locker space you are providing their employees is entirely inadequate. In fact, they say, when you stated locker space would be provided they took it to mean the "industry standard" of two feet wide by five feet high with a bar for hanging clothes. They state that their workers are extremely upset about the small size of their lockers and they think you have breached the contract by not providing what you promised them in the first place. They're seriously contemplating filing an official claim against your agency to force you to provide "adequate" lockers for their employees.

Whoa! You thought everything was rosy and now look at the problems you're having on this supposedly "simple" contract! You talk with your legal folks and don't exactly get a "warm fuzzy" that you're entirely right on the locker issue. If it turns into a dispute with an official claim filed, the courts could indeed agree with the contractor; there's really no predicting the outcome. From experience, you know how much energy, time, effort, and money are spent defending a claim—even if you win in the end—and your agency's budget is pretty skimpy this year. You start doing research into your options.

Your engineers tell you that, because of the configuration of the building, installing the larger lockers will cost you umpteen thousands of dollars and will require shutting down the facility during the installation for health purposes. Both of these are nonstarting issues for you. You can't afford the huge one-time hit to your budget and you can't shut down the facility because of constant need. To make matters worse, your helpful attorney reminds you that if the contractor files a claim and wins in court, the court may indeed order you to do just that.

You're desperately casting about for other options when the contractor calls with a wonderful solution. Although the employees are steaming about the lockers, the contractor thinks he can talk them into living with the existing ones if they can just have a little boost in their hourly pay as compensation. They give you the figures and it adds up to a little bit less than what it would take for you to renovate the facility to provide the new lockers. In addition, the cost would be spread out over the entire three years of contract performance, preventing your agency from taking that big one-time hit this year when you can least afford it.

Thank goodness the contractor came in with this solution to your problem. Thank goodness they can persuade their employees to forgo the larger lockers. Thank goodness they're actually looking out for your interests and are willing to work with you. This is great!

Or is it? In truth, the contractor could care less about the amount of locker space his employees have. He just wants to get more net profit out of a contract he was forced to cut to the bone to win in the first place. The "wonderful solution" of raising the employees' wages to compensate for the small lockers was always the real goal of the contractor. When employee wages are raised, the contractor will add overhead, G&A, and profit, and will increase the profitability of the contract. The size of the lockers was simply the decoy issue.

The contractor put exaggerated emphasis on an issue that didn't really concern him that much to trade it off for a concession by you that he really desired but had little chance of getting directly. You're now officially the victim of the decoy tactic.

COUNTERS TO THE DECOY TACTIC

The hardest part about countering the decoy tactic is being able to recognize that the tactic is indeed being used against you. By its very nature, the tactic is designed to trick you into believing that the issue the other side is pressing is, in fact, an important issue to them, when in fact it really isn't. So how do you know the difference? Doing your homework is the key.

The better your market research, the more you will already know about the other side's goals (what's really important to them and what isn't). The more you know about the other side's circumstances, the better you'll be able to judge whether they're *actually* concerned about an issue or whether they're (1) just creating an issue out of thin air to wrangle a concession from you that they really want and couldn't get otherwise, or (2) puffing up an issue that is relatively trivial to them to get the same result.

Let's take the contract with the locker size problem, for example. You've done your market research and you know this company has a reputation for not really taking care of their employees. Employee turnover is at the highest rate in the industry, and the company is infamous for trying to get away with paying the lowest hourly wage possible and giving their employees the least fringe benefits possible. It's obvious that their focus is on the bottom line at the expense of their employees. Knowing this, you're ready to call their bluff when they hit you with the locker size issue.

Unless they have had a sudden change of heart, it's going to be hard for them to convince you they truly have their employees' best interests in mind. Your market research shows you better. You know it's probably a decoy tactic and the real object is to get more money out of the contract for the company.

Once you recognize the decoy tactic, what do you do next? You have several options here. The first is simply to ignore the decoy issue once you figure out it's a decoy. Look for the underlying issue the other side is trying to divert you from and focus on it. In our locker size example, you may say something like, "Is the size of our lockers really the only thing you're concerned about? Is there anything else bothering you?" What you're fishing for is getting the other side to open up and start talking more about the real issue rather than the decoy issue, which will give you the information you need to develop a strategy and tactics to negotiate the real issue successfully.

Another option you have is to tackle the decoy issue head-on. Let the other side see that you recognize it as a legitimate, important issue to be dealt with in isolation. When you do this, you don't give the other side an opportunity to introduce a "fix" to the decoy issue that gives them what they really want. You go on the offensive, introducing your own preferred fix to the decoy issue; this takes the initiative for fixing the decoy issue away from them.

If they try to introduce the real issue, you say something like, "Well, an increase in wages is a separate issue. Let's table it for the moment and resolve this issue you have just brought up about the size of the lockers. What if we ...." You then insert the solution you think would be best for your side. Even if they don't accept it, it flushes out their position so you're in a better position to deal with it.

As an alternative, instead of suggesting a solution to the decoy issue at this point, you may well want to use the ambiguous authority tactic. You might say something like, "I understand locker size is an important issue to you and you're dissatisfied with the current situation. How about let's get your position in writing and I'll take it to my boss and see what I can to for you."

You can then follow it up with the good cop/bad cop tactic. You may say, for instance, "Well, I took the locker size issue to my boss [your "bad" cop] and although I really fought for you, she'll only allow me to give you some kind of relief if your company reciprocates. She's convinced the contract is clear and in our favor, and she'll consider enlarging the lockers only for a reduction in contract price of around umpteen dollars. However, I'm sure she'll be reasonable and accept something other than a price reduction if it's fair. Can you think of anything else you might be able to offer?"

You've isolated the decoy issue, turned it into a real issue (the very thing the other side didn't want), and twisted it to your advantage by using the tradeoff tactic. You'll give on the lockers, but only if the other side gives you something in return.

This process successfully sidetracks their attempt to get to their real issue of getting an increase in the contract price. Instead, they now have to concentrate on overcoming your ambiguous authority, good cop/bad cop, and tradeoff tactics, and hold the status quo on the contract. Not only have you negated their decoy tactic, but you now have *them* in a defensive crouch. If successfully played, they will be more than happy to simply settle for the original deal, which is what you wanted in the first place. Once the other side finds their attempt to decoy you has blown up in their faces, they will be a lot less likely to try it again in the future.

Chapter 32

The Sweep Tactic

The sweep tactic is a group tactic that must be well planned in advance. All the other team members are used to set up the other side for the sweep; then, at the crucial moment, the team member playing the role of the sweeper swoops in out of nowhere and completes the tactic.

We talked about the role of the sweeper in Chapter 10. Because the sweep tactic involves some minor level of deception, it should generally be considered off limits for a government negotiation team to use. Of course, the other side isn't bound by your same ethical rules. Consequently, the sweep tactic can and sometimes is used by the other side during negotiations, so you'll have to know how to spot it and counter it. Here's how it works.

Before the negotiation starts, people playing the role of sweeper pleasantly mingle, shake hands, and say "hi," but don't get too involved in any conversation. When the negotiation starts, they take their place at the end of the table. They continue to smile, nod, and generally show good, attentive body language, but they don't participate in the negotiation. If they've been assigned traditional sweeper duties, they may (once in a while) summarize the proceedings, but that's it. For the most part, they hang pleasantly and silently at the fringe of the negotiation. Pretty soon the other side forgets they're even there.

Now comes a big negotiation issue your team already knows will be contentious. Sure enough, when discussions start up, both sides polarize quickly around their positions and the duel is on. The negotiations around this issue get hotter and hotter, and neither side is moving an inch. The role players on both sides kick in and add their acts to the melee. The teams are deadlocking, the technocrats are "technocrating" against each other, and the good and bad cops are putting on passionate performances. Pretty soon it's obvious the negotiations have deadlocked on this issue.

You're at an impasse, but your team leader insists on continuing the negotiation. So both sides continue to knock their heads against the wall, trying to get around this one sticky issue. And it goes on and on. Pretty soon the other side is shot, frustrated, and desperate for something—*anything*—to get them out of this deadlock and move on with the negotiation.

All of a sudden, from the far side of the table, a lone soft voice is heard saying, "Wait a minute! I think I have a solution!" All heads turn in surprise to the far side of the table, tracing the voice to the person they didn't even realize was still in the room—the sweeper. With the other side's attention now concentrated and their curiosity piqued, the sweeper then puts forth an astoundingly simple but brilliant "breakthrough" solution to the nasty problem.

At this point, the other side is so desperate for a solution to the issue that has deadlocked them for so long that they will usually jump at the proposal, even if it's not the best deal they know they can get. The sweeper comes in and literally "sweeps" the deal.

Of course, the spur-of-the-moment solution the sweeper comes up with to break the deadlock isn't a spur-of-the-moment solution at all. Instead, it's a preplanned position that favors the sweeper team's side. In fact, the very deadlock that brought about the sweeper's solution was, itself, manufactured. It was a group effort by the sweeper's teammates to position the other side for easier acceptance of the sweeper's proposal by wearing them out and creating the illusion of a hard-line, immovable position.

To create the deadlock, the team usually puts forth their maximum position and never budges from it. What the other side doesn't know is that the sweeper has been given the team's target position and waits for just the right time to spring it as the ultimate, fair solution to the deadlock.

The other side, not realizing that the sweeper's brainstorm solution is in fact the team's target position, sees a chance for gain. All they know is that up to now they haven't been able to budge the other side a bit. Now one of the other side's own team members has tabled a solution that "gives" a little from that iron-clad position. The introduction of even this little bit of movement on the issue, especially from someone not heard from before or tainted by the heated arguments, lures the other side into swift agreement.

After all (they reason), if they don't lock in this concession before the other members of the team turn against and invalidate their own teammate's break from the hard line, the chance may evaporate. By playing on this fear, the sweeper and her teammates "sweep" the other side into agreeing with their opponent's already prepared target position without having to give any additional concessions. And get this: They even think they have scored a coup in the negotiation!

Even if the sweep tactic doesn't lure the other side into jumping on the sweeper's proposed solution, it has a high chance of giving the sweeper's team additional information about the other side. Invariably, as soon as the sweeper has caught everybody's attention and proposed her prearranged "breakthrough" solution, that solution will elicit unsolicited comments from less disciplined members of the other side's team.

These spur-of-the-moment, unguarded, instant reactions give the sweeper's team crucial insight about the other side—their position, how flexible they are, if they're all on the same page, and so forth. Before the other side's team leader can pull in the loose cannon teammate, he will have already revealed information that now can help the other side. That's the sweep tactic and it works like a charm.

COUNTERS TO THE SWEEP TACTIC

Luckily, this is a tactic you don't have to worry about countering too often because it's not used that much. To be effective, the sweep

tactic requires detailed planning, much rehearsal, impeccable timing, and good acting. The time and expertise involved in setting up
the tactic works to preclude its use except in high-dollar, complex
negotiations. Additionally, it requires a relatively large negotiating
team to execute properly. You need several members to dig in and
set up the sweeper to work the play.

Of course, there's always the exception to the rule, and you may
find yourself the victim of the sweep tactic sometime in your career. If you suspect the sweep tactic is being used against you, how
do you counter it?

As we have seen time and time again, preparation of your team and
early identification of the tactic are the keys to taking the "sweep"
out of the sweep tactic. When you were preparing for the negotiation, part of that preparation included briefing your team (Chapter
3). During that briefing, you made it clear to all team members that
you, as team leader, will control all conversation during the negotiation session. Nobody talks unless you tell them to. You maintain
firm control of your team by setting up that control beforehand
and reinforcing it continuously. This will lessen the possibility of
letting loose uncontrolled outbursts and reactions that the sweep
tactic is intended to elicit from your team members.

As team leader, you should never give in to the impulse to put your
jaw in gear before engaging your brain. You're also responsible for
ensuring that your teammates do the same. When the sweeper or
any member of the other team raises an issue, proposal, or solution
you have not had time to prepare for, immediately call a caucus.
Take a break in the negotiation without giving the other side any
clue regarding how you feel about the new information. Before
you leave, you may want to have the other side restate their proposal to make sure you understand it, but don't let them see your
reaction to it and don't vocalize any snap judgments.

The caucus allows you and your team to process the new information in private, without the threat of giving away your inclinations

and intentions by reacting unguardedly in front of the other side. Simply doing this will go a long way in decreasing the value of the sweep tactic as an information-gathering tool for the other side.

The caucus also buys you time to analyze the new information in a rational, dispassionate way. Remember, the sweep tactic is designed to force you into a quick acceptance of a "solution" the other side has proposed. The tactic is used to maneuver you into accepting this "brilliant" solution by creating an artificial deadlock, hoping you'll jump on the solution out of gratitude or sheer frustration.

Calling a caucus breaks this flow. It gives your team a breather and puts time between the negative impacts the deadlock has created among your team members, allowing a more reasoned evaluation of the actual merits of the proposed solution. It lessens the chance you'll make a snap decision in the heat of the negotiation that you'll regret later and it takes the wind out of the sweep tactic.

You can also counter the sweep tactic by being able to recognize the likelihood that it will actually be used by the other side and planning for it accordingly. In other words, do your homework before the negotiation. We've talked about this as part of planning for the negotiation, and now you see yet another instance where it can really pay off. Do your research on the other side's negotiation habits. Talk to folks who have dealt with them before. Find out if they have a reputation for using the sweep tactic and, if so, how they set it up.

If you determine that the other side is likely to use the sweep tactic, warn your team members beforehand about how the tactic works and how best to counter it. This may even allow you to preplan some counters, such as the vise tactic or the tactic of silence. For example, when their sweeper executes the sweep by proposing the solution, you say "You've got to do better than that." Then shut up; don't elaborate. Wait for them to make the next statement. In the uncomfortable silence that follows, they may just start bidding against themselves and modifying their own last offer.

Finally, you need to be alert when the negotiation starts and progresses. The very nature of setting up the tactic automatically throws off telltale clues that the other side is intending to use it.

Did the other side bring an unusually large contingent for the negotiation? The larger the team, the more likely that the sweep tactic may be used. Before the negotiation starts, can you spot one of their team members assuming the classic sweeper role? During the negotiation, does one of their team members seem to hang back and not take part? Is one of their team members, other than the team leader, periodically summarizing the progress of the talks, but not doing much else?

If so, you may just have identified their sweeper. Of course, this doesn't necessarily mean the sweeper will actually use the sweep tactic, but if the other side does elect to use it, you now know where it will be coming from.

Chapter 33

The Deliberate
Mistake Tactic

The deliberate mistake tactic is definitely a tactic you cannot use as a government negotiator. It involves deliberate deception and is therefore considered negotiating in bad faith—and you can't negotiate in bad faith, lie, or intentionally mislead a contractor in negotiations. It's an unscrupulous tactic that thankfully isn't used much by the other side either because it's just plain unethical and sometimes even illegal. However, you may run in to someone who will try to use it, so you'd better know how to spot it and how it works.

There are two general versions of the deliberate mistake tactic: phony facts, and deliberate omissions and errors. We'll look at both.

PHONY FACTS

The most common use of the deliberate mistake tactic is when the other side intentionally misrepresents facts, misrepresents their authority, makes up phony facts, or deliberately misstates their intentions. Quite simply, they lie and mislead you to gain an advantage in the negotiation.

Everyone's heard of the used car salesperson who assures the prospective buyer, "This car was owned by a little old lady who only drove it to the store and back once a week, and she took care of it as if it was one of her own children." In fact, the car may have gone through several owners, none of whom the salesperson knows, nor does he know how they drove or treated the car. The car could have been used as a getaway car for a bank robbery, or the engine may have blown, or the car is about ready to fall apart.

Of course, this is a simplistic example, and most states have laws on the books to protect buyers and take care of such unscrupulous salespeople. Although the government has similar laws to punish folks who intentionally lie to the government, the phony facts version of the deliberate deception tactic can be harder to spot in government negotiations.

For instance, a contractor might say something like, "This is the lowest per-hour labor price we ever offer. It's the same and only price we always charge all our government clients." In reality, this contractor could be deceiving you into accepting a high per-hour labor price that they, in reality, have lowered for other government contracts in the past. Or they may say something like, "I promise you we will keep our highest quality people dedicated to this effort." In reality, they plan on pulling these folks off the job as soon as they get contract award and replacing them with the "scrubs."

Another example is a contractor who intentionally submits false charges or inflated numbers in a request for payment or contract adjustment. Often these requests are quite lengthy, very technical, and mind-numbingly mathematical. They're boring, tedious, just plain complicated, and hard to read or to follow. The other side may hope that you take one look at the complicated mess, decide that the contractor must know what he's talking about, figure you have better things to do with your time, and approve the payment or adjustment without further scrutiny. It happens all the time.

These are just a few examples of how the other side can try to pull you into a bad deal by intentionally misrepresenting facts. They'll usually pick things that will be hard or impossible for you to verify, or are convoluted and complicated. They're relying on either your lack of knowledge or the sheer volume of work to scare you from digging deep enough to uncover the truth.

The other side may also intentionally misrepresent the extent of their authority. Let's say, for example, you're trying to counter the possible use of the ambiguous authority tactic before a negotiation begins. You ask the other side's lead negotiator, straight out, if they have the authority to consummate the deal or if they have to defer to their "home office." They assure you that they have sole authority to close the negotiations on behalf of their company.

In reality, they know they don't actually have that authority, but must go back to their company if they don't reach certain negotiation goals. They flat-out lie to you. Sure enough, when you think you have a deal put together, they hem and haw and eventually tell you they must confer with their home office before they can strike the deal. "Wait a minute!" you say. "Didn't you tell me before all this started that you had sole authority to complete the deal?"

At this point, they can give you any number of excuses, such as "I honestly thought I did, but was mistaken" or "I did when we began, but company policy has changed" or "The new boss insists on it and I need my job!" You suspect the excuse is baloney and they intended to pull this stunt from the start, but it's just a strong suspicion; you have no way of knowing it as fact. Whatever excuse they come up with, it's going to be extremely hard for you to prove that deliberate deception actually occurred.

The other side might also attempt to deceive you by making up phony "facts" out of thin air to support their position or convince you to make decisions favorable to them based on these made-up "facts." They might point to nonexistent or highly concocted and doctored surveys, engineering analyses, market research data, and the like. They might assure you that a certain component they make has never failed, when in fact it has. They might claim phony startup costs, mobilization costs, or labor charges for work never done. They might claim acceptance of their product or service by certain regulatory groups or industry authorities that either don't exist or have never heard of them. The list is endless.

Finally, they can hit you with phony facts by deliberately misstating their true intentions. They may say something like, "If we win this contract, I assure you it will be our company's absolute number one priority!" when they actually intend to relegate your contract to the back burner once award is clinched. Or, "You don't have to worry about awarding us this computer hardware contract. Our company plans to support this particular hardware platform for at least 10 years. You'll have no problem getting hardware/software maintenance or spare parts for the system." In reality, their company already has plans to retool a new or totally different platform as soon as possible, leaving you with a dinosaur system that is impossible to maintain.

Actual intentions are hard to prove up front, and the company can always argue that the situation has changed, forcing them to back off their earlier assurances. These situations remind me of the Civil War colonel giving his troops a rousing pep talk right before committing them into a desperate frontal assault against the enemy: "Okay boys! I want you to go in low and go in fast. Keep your heads down, conserve your energy and ammunition until you reach the target, and, remember, in the midst of the battle, I'll be behind you (far, far, far behind you)!"

Counters to Phony Facts

The most obvious and easiest way to counter the phony facts version of the deliberate deception tactic is to know the real facts yourself, which comes from good negotiation planning backed up by thorough market research. Do your homework. Know the situation. Become an expert on what you're buying before launching into the negotiation. Of course, it's perfectly okay to rely on the other members of your team, such as your technical experts, to get a handle on the real facts and the true situation.

If you know the real facts cold, you can immediately challenge the other side's facts, figures, and assumptions if they appear to be phony: "I hear what you're saying, but according to my research ...." should roll off the tongue quite nicely, provided that you prepared with the proper research. If you can catch them in a little fabrication or stretching of the truth early on, negotiation power will shift dramatically to your side and you will now dominate the entire negotiation. They'll be on the defensive from this point on and will know that you expect them to prove everything else they claim. You won't trust them—and they'll know it.

If the other side hits you with facts you haven't prepared for, but you think are a little fishy, you have every right to challenge them and request background data or evidence to support their claim or assertion. You have every right to demand proof. Ask for their supporting documentation—and put higher credence on evidence that comes from outside their organization from independent sources.

You don't have to accept everything the other side is telling you if it doesn't sound quite right. You haven't risen to the position of authority and responsibility you now have by being an idiot. Trust your instincts. Verify their claims. Call a caucus and don't reconvene the negotiation until the other side produces documentation that convinces you of the truth of their assertions. Caucus again when the documentation is received so your team can examine it and verify it without the pressure of being in the negotiation room with them. Take as long as necessary. Don't be rushed.

If you determine that the other side has used doctored "facts," you must respond quickly and decisively. Intentionally lying or misleading the government is not a healthy thing for anyone to do, and you represent the government. You've got to turn that behavior around quickly and not let it negatively affect the price the taxpayer is paying for the stuff the government buys. Call the other side on the incorrect information. Let them know that you know it's not valid.

Offer them a chance to rethink their position or correct their mistake, or to show you further evidence supporting their position—and refuse to continue the negotiation until they do. After they have revised their information, you then can resume the negotiation from that new perspective.

Notice, at this point, that you don't blatantly yell "Liar, liar, pants on fire!" or accuse them of any wrongdoing. You're still giving them the benefit of the doubt. It could have been an honest mistake, they could have been fed bad information, or they may honestly believe what they are claiming. Your reaction merely calls their representation of the facts into question, regardless of their intent, and gives them an opportunity to amend their position. Most people (honest or not) are concerned about their reputation, and just calling them on an inaccuracy will have a huge effect.

First, they now know you're watching. They are on notice that they won't get away with intentionally stretching the truth, making up stuff, or being sloppy. Second, they're now on the defensive and they know it. They'll spend the rest of the negotiation double-checking their facts and figures, reassuring you with additional (and useful) information, and generally trying to reestablish their position as a trusted contractor. With good or ill intent, they know they have to earn their way back into your good graces. They may even give away a unilateral concession or two.

Finally, they know what effect the situation is having on your relationship with them. You and your team are now on notice to give all their arguments, facts, and figures a little more scrutiny in the future—for the remainder of the negotiation and for all business deals afterward.

Sometimes, although rarely, the other side might not react to your challenge of their facts in a shamed and defensive way. Instead, they might let you know quickly and in a surprised manner that they can't believe you don't trust them. When you legitimately challenge their facts, ask for more supporting data, or confront them with different data of your own, they may say something like, "What's wrong? I thought we had a good relationship here. You don't trust me after all we've been through?" They'll sound truly hurt, and say it in an accusatory fashion. They may be sincerely hurt, but they may also be intentionally trying to put you in a no-win situation.

Most people want other people to see them in a good light; they don't want other people to think badly of them. By playing on this innate emotion, they may be trying to get you to reassure them that you really do trust them. If you do, you've just watered down your own position, put them back in control, and all but accepted their version of the facts. Your alternative is to be untrusting and look like an ogre.

The best way to get out of this corner is to take trust off the table as an issue. Let the other side know that trust is not the issue. The issue is getting to the real facts so both sides can come to a fair and reasonable agreement that's in the best interests of all concerned. Turn the negotiation back on track by saying something like, "It isn't a question of trust. I'm sure we both want to make a decision based on the most accurate facts available, especially because both of us are going to have to live with the agreement after it's reached. I just want to make absolutely sure we've got our facts straight so we can start this relationship off solidly and on the right foot."

You don't say you don't trust them, but you don't give ground either. You treat trust as a separate issue.

We can't leave the subject of phony facts without talking about the huge legal arsenal you have as a representative of the government if you have been lied to or deceived intentionally. If it's absolutely clear that their phony facts are intentional, or if you have relied on deliberately phony facts to the detriment of the government, you at least need to be aware of the laws that protect the government and their impact on the other side.

Once you see these laws and their penalties, you'll understand why deliberate deception is rarely used by contractors. Uncle Sam doesn't like to be lied to, and he has set up some powerful tools to deal with those who do lie.

Let's look at some of the laws that protect us from being lied to. But first, know that I am not an attorney. I certainly don't have an attorney's knowledge of the laws or their application, so please don't take the following discussion as 100 percent legally correct. Mine is just a layman's summary.

Thankfully, you don't have to be an attorney to do your job as either a government negotiator or a CO. You've got those smart folks on staff. If you believe you've been intentionally lied to, or believe that a person has committed fraud against the government, go get these smart folks. Let them guide you through the nuances of the following laws:

1. *False Statements Act (18 USC 1001)*—This act sets up criminal prohibitions against providing false statements to the government. It provides for fines and up to five years in jail.

2. *Possession of False Papers to Defraud the United States (18 USC 1002)*—This law makes it a criminal offense to possess any false, altered, forged, or counterfeited writing or documents knowingly and with intent to defraud the government. So, it's not only a crime to use them, but even to have them!

3. *Major Fraud against the United States (18 USC 1031)*—This law makes it a criminal offense to execute or even attempt to execute fraud knowingly against the government, and it provides for fines up to $1 million and up to 10 years in jail.

4. *False Claims Criminal Offense Statute (18 USC 287)* and *Civil Statute (31 USC 3729*, also known as the *False Claims Act)*—The civil version alone, what we commonly call the False Claims Act, provides for a civil penalty of not less than $5,000 and not more than $10,000, plus three times the amount of damage the false claim caused the government. Per occurrence! You don't have to be criminally prosecuted to get hit by this one.

5. *Mail Fraud (18 USC 1341)* and *Wire Fraud (18 USC 1343)*—These are both criminal statutes that can be applied in addition to and in conjunction with all the other laws we've mentioned. So, if a person commits fraud, they get hit with the fraud statutes. If they commit that fraud through the mail or by telephone, they can get hit with these as well.

6. *Program Fraud Civil Remedies Act of 1986 (31 USC 3802)*—Even if the government can't or doesn't prosecute fraud criminally or

with a civil suit, it can levy administrative penalties. This act sets administrative remedies for false claims and false statements. It provides for administrative penalties of $5000 *per false claim or statement*.

7. *Truth in Negotiations Act (10 USC 2306a and 41 USC 254a)*— Commonly known by its acronym TINA, this act covers defective pricing on certain types of contracts. It covers things like cost or pricing data, certified cost or pricing data, and information other than cost or pricing data.

In addition to criminal, civil, and administrative statutes, other actions can be taken against folks who give the government phony facts on purpose. On conviction of bribery or other certain conflicts of interest, any awarded contract with that person or company can be voided and rescinded by the government. It's like it never existed. The use of this tool is somewhat narrow, so consult with your legal folks and FAR Part 3.7 for advice and detailed information.

The guilty parties can also find themselves in the tenacious hold of the government's Excluded Parties List System, described in FAR Part 9.4. The heart of this system is the Excluded Parties List, commonly called the *debar list*. Making intentionally phony statements to the government is one of many transgressions that can place a contractor on this list.

A contractor can be suspended for up to one year, debarred for up to three years, or otherwise made ineligible for specific times a particular piece of legislation calls for. A contractor on the debar list is ineligible to receive any government contract awards for the period of time they are on the list, unless your agency head specifies in writing a compelling reason to do so. Even if a contractor is merely proposed for debarment, they can't receive awards. They can't even act as representatives for any other contractor doing business with the government. You simply can't do business with them at all.

If you're a contractor and your main source of income comes from government business, what do you think would happen to your company if you were disallowed from doing business with the government for three years? Yep. You're probably history.

If you survive being posted on the Excluded Parties List as a company, your prospects for future government business will be dim, even *after* you come off the list. The two main reasons for this are the government's requirements to (1) award only to responsible contractors and (2) collect and use past performance information on contractors:

Responsibility—FAR Part 9 requires that contract awards be made only to responsible prospective contractors (FAR 9.102(a)). The CO must use seven general standards of responsibility to make this judgment call, two of which are that the contractor must have (1) a satisfactory performance record (FAR 9.104-1(c)), and (2) a satisfactory record of integrity and business ethics (FAR 9.104-1(d)). Although the FAR gives the CO leeway in applying these standards to determine responsibility, do you think an appearance on the Excluded Parties List—even a previous, expired appearance—will help the contractor's case? Probably not. Good luck being found responsible.

Past Performance—FAR 42.1502 directs all COs to prepare an evaluation of contractor performance for each contract over $100,000 at the time the contract is completed. (The threshold is higher in the Department of Defense.) This information is collected and stored in a database, and is then used by COs at the front end of the process of awarding new contracts. It helps them select future prospective contractors for contract award. In fact, past performance must be evaluated in every negotiated acquisition expected to exceed $100,000.

Your past performance report is a subjective judgment call on how well you think the contractor did on the contract overall. Among other things, you should talk about "the contractor's history of reasonable and cooperative behavior and commitment to customer satisfaction, and, generally, the contractor's business-like concern for the interests of the customer" (FAR 42.1501). If a contractor has a reputation of intentionally giving the government phony facts, it should show up in their past performance report. If you've had a contractor feed you phony facts during negotiations, either for award of the contract or during modification negotiations, you should report this in their past performance report. Bad reputations are hard to live down.

DELIBERATE OMISSIONS AND ERRORS

The second version of the deliberate mistake tactic is the deliberate omission of material facts and the making of "accidental errors" that aren't really accidental at all. Deliberate omissions can occur when the other side intentionally leaves out a material fact that has a significant bearing on the negotiation. They also occur when the other side knows you're thinking things are one way, when they know for a fact they're not that way at all. They don't share your assumptions, but their silence leads you to believe they do. "Accidental" errors are usually math mistakes made on purpose, in anticipation that you won't scrutinize them and will accept the deal along with the math error skewed in their favor.

Let's say, for instance, that you ask a prospective contractor to provide you with information on all federal contracts they have performed during the past three years as part of your past performance data collection and evaluation. The contractor provides you with seven contracts and telephone points of contact for each. You call the references and verify that the contractor did a good job on all seven contracts and make an award decision to that contractor accordingly. What the contractor didn't tell you was that they royally messed up two additional contracts during that period. They chose to omit that important information deliberately.

Another example of a deliberate omission could be when the other side submits résumés of key personnel that are so sterling and pedigreed they make your eyes water. The fact they omit is that they intend to pull these folks as soon as they get the contract award and replace them with less qualified personnel. Where are these brilliant people going? You'll find they're lending their résumés to other proposals to win the contractor more business. Unless you have something like a key personnel clause, you could be stuck with the second stringers.

Sometimes the other side knows you're interpreting something either in your own requirements document or their proposal one way, when they know it's really something different altogether, and they will inform you of the correct interpretation and demand compensation for it only after the deal is sealed. They deliberately allow you to think your assumptions or facts are correct by being silent and not correcting them.

Let's say, for instance, you've asked for 2,400 pairs of alligator clips. They know that you're thinking a pair is two individual clips, as in two earrings making up a pair. So you're expecting a total of 4,800 individual alligator clips. What they don't tell you is that they're interpreting the requirement for a pair of alligator clips to be like a pair of pants, or a pair of scissors or pliers. They only intend to deliver 2,400 individual alligator clips.

When they deliver only 2,400 clips and charge you the full contract price, you're livid! You confront them and they claim that the requirements document is ambiguous. An ambiguity is a word or phrase that can have two logical, but different, meanings. Ambiguities are always legally construed against the drafter of the language. Who wrote the requirements document? The government did. This means that the contractor's interpretation that a pair is a single clip will stand, if it's a reasonable interpretation.

You've just been the victim of the deliberate mistake tactic. The fact that they knew what your interpretation was all along will be difficult (if not impossible) to prove.

Finally, the other side could intentionally commit errors in their proposal, hoping you won't catch them. Math errors in their favor are the most common, although not the only thing they can play with. Delivery dates, milestone dates, discount terms, warranty provisions, levels of support, mean time between failures, mean time to repair, and so forth, can also be the subject of intentional "goofs."

Usually the contractor will sandwich the error between mind-numbing gobs of other boring data, hoping you'll be discouraged from taking the time to dig deep enough to discover it. Or they'll bury it in an out-of-the-way or unusual place, like a footnote, or put it in a section that talks about something totally different. If you don't catch it, it could become part of the contract and then you're legal bound to it.

Counters to Deliberate Omissions and Errors

This form of the deliberate mistake tactic is harder to counter than phony facts. First, it's harder to catch the deception. If the other side gives you phony facts, at least they've put something on the table and out in the open that you can analyze, verify, and challenge. With deliberate omissions, they simply haven't told you something they should have. With intentional errors, they've usually buried them so deep you need picks, shovels, and a strong miner's headlamp to ferret them out. You have less to go on and a smaller, more elusive target to catch and verify. Sometimes you have no target at all.

Second, even if you perceive or actually know they're intentionally not telling you something or have made an intentional mistake, it's harder to do much about it. Most of the legal and contractual remedies we discussed when we dealt with phony facts require you not only to catch the deception, but to prove it was deceitful.

If you call the other side on the carpet for a deliberate omission or error, all they have to say is something like, "Oops! You're right! How silly of me to forget to mention that, and how stupid of me to make that math error. I assure you they were honest mistakes and I'm going to fire that junior person that gave me that information. I'll correct them right away. My bad." If you can't prove that the mistake was intentional, most of your arsenal goes away.

You still have some arrows in the quiver, however, and most of them are the same ones you use to counter the phony facts version of the tactic. First, know your facts cold. The more you know about the situation, the more likely you are to spot key omissions and errors. If you catch them in an omission or error, put them on the defensive for the remainder of the negotiation. Let them know that their "carelessness" has caused you to question the credibility and accuracy of everything they tell you from that point on. What else have they left out or messed up? Request more backup or corroborating data. Make them work and dig. Make them regret being so "careless."

Because you can't really prove they meant to do it, you don't challenge their ethics or honesty. You can, however, certainly make them regret using the tactic (if it is indeed a tactic and not an honest mistake) by revisiting and reverifying everything you've agreed to so far and by scrutinizing everything yet to come in the negotiation.

If you already have an awarded contract and the negotiation is over a modification, the fact that the contractor "carelessly" omitted material facts or committed "stupid" errors can and should be reflected in that contractor's past performance report when the contract is finished. We've already discussed how potent past performance reports are as a tool, and how effective even the threat of a bad past performance report can be on behavior and contract performance.

On a more personal level, you can let the contractor know how disappointed you are at what they've done or haven't done. You may say something like, "I really thought we had a good working relationship, and I honestly thought you and your company had a better handle on all this stuff than it appears you actually do. I was looking forward to working with you in a long and partnering relationship. I hope I haven't misplaced my trust. Have I?"

Finally, don't totally rule out those legal and contractual remedies. Depending on the particulars of the situation, some of them could still work. You have professionals on your staff who can give you a read on this. Go talk to your attorney to see what your options might be.

Chapter 34

The Planted
Information Tactic

The planted information tactic is a devious and unscrupulous tactic that's thankfully quite rare in government negotiations—for a good reason. The success of the planted information tactic relies on the victim's natural human tendency toward curiosity and our tendency to believe information we get in "secret" ways. It also depends, in part, on the government negotiator's own lack of scruples and sense of fairness.

Of course, most government negotiators are above reproach and can be expected to treat all sides fairly. If this is true, as you'll see, the tactic won't fly. Here's how it works.

You're in a heavy sole-source negotiation with the other side and things seem to be going well. The only real issue left to hammer out is the final price. Unfortunately, this is shaping up to be a rather big issue, with the sides fairly far apart. You, of course, have your minimum position ($1,000,000; remember, this is your walk-away price), target position ($850,000; what you really expect to end up paying), and maximum position ($830,000; what you'd be delighted to pay and still feel good about yourself) established to help you get to what you think is a fair price to pay for the item. They're holding pat at $1,430,000. Big difference. Of course, you're totally in the dark regarding their real minimum, maximum, and target positions, and they're holding their cards close.

You and your team have just finished making a counteroffer of $842,750 (still under your target, but way off what they're asking), and you're using the tactic of silence to gauge the other side's reaction and either get a bit more information from them or close the deal. One of the other side's team members (usually the bad cop or the technocrat) breaks out a pad of paper and furiously scribbles something on it, being careful to shield what he's writing with his free hand. He then passes the note to his team leader, who reads it, grunts, and puts the note down on the table near him.

Tell the truth. In the real world, you'd be dying of curiosity to see what's written on that note. It could hold the key to the whole negotiation. You notice that although the note is close to the team leader, it's at least laying right-side up and could possibly be readable if you got just a little closer. You think of something dramatic and distracting to say, and as you say it, you lean in close for effect. While you're talking you quickly glance at the note and see it says: "Boss says no less than $860K or *walk!*" Mission accomplished! Now you know their bottom line and you're going to pummel them.

Sure enough, they counter at $900,000. You, now totally prepared, counter back at the magic number you sneaked a peek at of $860,000—and it works! They begrudgingly agree. You strike a deal, conclude the negotiations at a price of $860,000, and think you're a hero. After all, the agreed-to price is close to your target and still under your minimum. What's more, you just prevented them from being backed into a corner and walking out of the negotiation. All in all, not a bad day.

Or was it? The fact is, they *wanted* you to get a sneak peek at that piece of paper. Their supposed "walk-away" price of $860,000 that you "accidentally" saw wasn't their real walk-away price at all. In fact, it was somewhere close to their target position and they're quite happy with it. In fact, they would have been willing to take closer to $830,000 if you just had pressed.

You've just been the victim of the planted information tactic. You were influenced strongly by information you got in a sneaky way, simply because you obtained it in a sneaky way. It blinded you to everything else and led you into a bad decision and a bad deal for the government.

Planted information can have such a strong effect because we tend to put more credence on information we get in clandestine ways.

We think, "It's hush-hush stuff. I shouldn't have had access to this information, but I lucked out and got it. It must be the real deal." Master negotiator Roger Dawson, in his book *Secrets of Power Negotiating* (Career Press, 2001), gives this illustration:

> Returning from a speaking engagement, I was discussing the presidential press conference with my seat mate. "I don't believe he's telling the truth," he told me. "I met a man who knew someone who works at the White House and he told me the president did know all about it all along. He's covering something up." What amazed me about this was I found myself believing what this man was telling me, rather than believing what I had earlier heard the president of the United States say at the press conference. Why? Because we tend to believe information we have obtained surreptitiously. (p. 122)

History is replete with examples of how powerful an effect planted information can have on rational decision making. During World War II, the Allies were planning the great cross-channel invasion of France to attack the Germans on the beaches at Normandy. Obviously, we didn't want the Germans to know this, so Allied Intelligence planted false information on a poor British major who had died of natural causes and set his body adrift in the English Channel where they knew the currents would carry the body to a German-held beach. The planted information was to convince the Germans that the real assault was going to hit the beaches of Calais, quite a few miles to the north of Normandy.

The Germans recovered the body, read the information, and believed it. They had tons of other intelligence information indicating that the invasion was going to hit Normandy, but they chose to believe this *one* piece of information that said otherwise. Why? Because they weren't supposed to have it. They got it surreptitiously. They concentrated their reserve forces to cover Calais, instead of Normandy. Because of this, D-Day was successful and was the beginning of the end of World War II.

History aside, we see the power of surreptitiously obtained information all around us in our day-to-day lives. Despite the massive volumes of facts and data to the contrary, just let someone publish a book or start a rumor and that's what most people clamor to believe. "Man didn't really walk on the moon. It was all a Hollywood stunt." "The Holocaust never happened." "Aliens built the pyramids." "Mickey Mouse shot JFK." "If you eat 10 Alka-Seltzer tablets and run around you'll blow up." Urban legends and conspiracy theories thrive on planted information—information that someone shouldn't have, but got in a clandestine way. But just because someone *says* it's the real story doesn't *make* it the real story.

The planted information tactic also relies on the presumption that the other side will not only see and believe, but will actually use, the planted information. Here's where we get to scruples. In your day-to-day life, have you ever gotten "inside information" that you shouldn't have gotten, but could help you out? You know you shouldn't have the information, you know it's not really fair to use the information, but the temptation to use it is there, isn't it?

Let's say, for instance, you're shopping for a washing machine. You've done your homework, and you have a pretty good handle on all the makes and models and their prices. You go into one store, walk up to their appliance department, and immediately see that it's your lucky day! One of the models you're considering is right there, but it's obvious that some sales clerk has put the wrong price tag on it. Nothing in your research confirms that the price should be so low for this model. In fact, you're pretty sure the price is for the lower end model that doesn't have all the bells and whistles (remember, you've done your homework). You immediately seek out a clerk and either plunk down the cash or pull out your credit card and say "I'll take it!" No negotiating. If you do that, they might get suspicious and recognize their mistake. No, you want to wrap up this deal quickly and profit from the store's mistake. The fact that they have incompetent sales clerks who can't price their own stuff right is *their* problem, isn't it?

We all have the urge to cash in on windfalls created by other people's mistakes. What you do in your private negotiations is, of course, up to you. When you negotiate for the government, however, taking advantage of mistakes the other side has made is something you can't do for two good reasons.

First, you represent the government. You have to be fair and reasonable to both sides. This means you can't use information that you shouldn't have gotten or that you received in a less than aboveboard way. You have to conduct the government's business with the highest integrity and be above reproach. If you receive information in a surreptitious way and it's obvious that the contractor doesn't want you to have it, using that information would be a violation of that trust. It's not the ethical thing to do. It will not only ruin your personal reputation for dealing in good faith, but will tarnish the government's reputation as well.

If word gets out that the government isn't treating contractors fairly and is attempting to take advantage of them when they can, how many companies do you think will want to continue to do business with the government? And we *need* these folks and the things they do and make!

Second, they may have wanted you to discover the information "accidentally" (the true planted information tactic). If this is true, whatever decision you come to or agreement you reach based on that information may not be in the best interests of the taxpayer.

Remembering our example, what if the clerk had intended to "accidentally" put the wrong price tag on that washing machine? It could have been a closeout model or have dimensions that make that particular model difficult to fit in a normal house. It could have scratches, dings, or mechanical problems. It could have been a refurbished or returned item. The machine could have defects the store would otherwise have had to disclose if they were asked, but you didn't ask! You saw what you wanted to see (an unfair but great deal) and you went for it. The planted information caused you to rush into the deal without negotiating. You had great pressure to close before you thoroughly researched the buy. Who really got the "great" deal?

To top it all off, when someone uses planted information on you, they've virtually taken out an insurance policy against you coming back at them later and accusing them of it—even if you catch them. If you later find that you relied on planted information to make a decision, what are you going to do? You can't go back and call them on the carpet for it, because that would be admitting that you gained surreptitious access to information you shouldn't have.

Who would look like the one with no ethics then? You're now in a lose-lose situation, and that's not a good place to be as a negotiator, especially if you represent the government.

COUNTERS TO THE PLANTED INFORMATION TACTIC

The planted information tactic is, obviously, one you can't use as a government negotiator, but that doesn't mean that it can't be used against you by unscrupulous parties. Even though it's rarely used, you at least need to know how to counter it if you encounter it. You've already equipped yourself with the most important tool to counter this tactic—you know it exists and what it is intended to do. Simply by being aware of the tactic, you have a better chance of recognizing when it's used against you and how to handle it.

Anytime you receive "windfall" information from the other side that you believe they didn't or shouldn't have disclosed to you, be suspicious of it. Resist the temptation to grab onto it and treat it as if it's the undisputed truth. After all, consider the source. Even though you received it in a surreptitious manner, it still came from the party you are dealing with, and you have conflicting interests and motives. You're setting yourself up for a fall anytime you rely solely on information the other side controls and chooses to tell you.

If you feel compelled to use it, always independently verify the accuracy of the information. Check it against other facts you know or can discover. Check it against other sources. Remember, promises of getting "something for nothing" usually result in the latter.

Finally, remember that the effectiveness of the planted information tactic relies on the other side's willingness to take advantage of information they ethically shouldn't have in the first place. It plays to people's bad side. One sure way of negating the tactic is by not having a bad side to play to. Simply refuse to use information you have obtained surreptitiously. Don't give in to the temptation.

As a representative of the government you must be fair and reasonable to both sides. If you refuse to take advantage of any information you obtain surreptitiously, you're covering all angles. If the other side truly didn't mean to slip the information, you're showing that you're ethical to deal with. If the other side intended you to get hold of it, you're making yourself immune to the effects of the planted information tactic.

Part Six

The Negotiation Event

Chapter 35

Setting the Stage

Now it's time to put it all together. You've prepared for the negotiation. You've assembled your team, assigned their roles, and briefed them. You've gathered your data, identified your priorities, and established your prenegotiation objectives. You've established your BATNA. You've done your research on the other party—both the company and the negotiators. You've assessed the relative bargaining power of the parties. You've put together your negotiation plan outlining your overall strategy and the tactics you plan to use to implement that strategy and achieve success, and you've rehearsed the plan. You've set your negotiation agenda, coordinating it with your team and the other side. You're ready, and the time to negotiate is here.

This last part of this book describes how to conduct the actual negotiation event. In this chapter, we'll look at how to set the stage for a successful negotiation session. We'll go over how to open the negotiation, how to conduct it, what to do, and what to avoid. Then we'll address the all-important topic of how to close the negotiation successfully and document the result so you have an executable and complete agreement—a true and enforceable meeting of the minds.

You'll notice that this part, on actually conducting the negotiation event, is considerably smaller than all the other parts of the book, in which we examined dealing with negotiation preparation—and that's how it should be! The key to a good negotiation is planning and preparation; that's always where the main focus of your effort should be directed. If you take the time and prepare well for the negotiation, the actual event then simply becomes an easy exercise of executing your plan. The hard work should have already been done before you walk in the door to the negotiation event.

Because you represent the government, negotiations will usually take place at your facility or a facility that you and your team control. As I noted earlier, there is a huge edge in having "home court advantage." When you are the host, however, you have the additional task of preparing for and facilitating the negotiation.

Proper preparation of the negotiating environment (the room and the area in which the negotiations will occur) can greatly influence the tone and even the outcome of the negotiation. Don't just have the other side's folks show up and plop down in the nearest room available. You want to create an environment that's conducive to business-like discussions, doesn't overlook comfort, provides relative privacy and freedom from interruptions, and generally allows the negotiation to proceed in a smooth, orderly manner. This takes planning well before the negotiation event.

Of course, the obvious reason for this is that you want the negotiation to go smoothly with no interruptions so you can achieve a well-thought-out deal in the minimum amount of time. It's also simple courtesy. You want to be a good host. It's true that first impressions are lasting impressions, and you want to lay the groundwork for a good working relationship with all the contractors you deal with. You want to create a positive atmosphere.

In contrast, if you are unprepared or sloppy in preparing the negotiating environment, it could signal to the other side that they can expect you to be unprepared and sloppy during the negotiation. This could lead them to believe that you can be taken advantage of, and that's not the best way to start any relationship, especially a contractual one. They could, for example, decide to use tactics they weren't planning to use based on their perception of your nonchalant attitude. They may think something like, "They're obviously not prepared well for this negotiation. If they don't really care that much about the negotiation, they probably won't care much about the price they're willing to pay for our stuff. Let's go for the max we can get."

Finally, proper preparation of the environment establishes your *control* of the environment. It allows you to prepare certain tactics if you've chosen to use them, and it diminishes the other side's ability to play or even introduce certain tactics against you. When the other side walks into a well-prepared negotiation environment, it's a strong nonverbal signal that you are indeed in control. It strengthens the establishment of your authority and puts you in the superior power position before the actual negotiation even starts. You want this mental advantage.

RESERVE THE ROOMS

You can't conduct a good contract negotiation at your desk, even if it's a small, two-person negotiation. The potential for distracting interruptions is too great, and you need to concentrate on getting the best value through a fair and reasonable negotiation outcome. You'll need to locate and reserve a room, hopefully in your building and near your desk, large enough to seat both teams comfortably.

Because conference rooms at most government facilities always seem to be in demand, most agencies have some process you must go through to reserve them. Think about this ahead of time and get the room reserved as early as possible. Make sure you block the reservation for more time than you think you'll need and make sure you have exclusive use of the room for that whole time. You don't want the remnants of Sally's birthday luncheon all over your important negotiation papers. Remember to reserve an additional, smaller conference room as well so one team or the other will have a secure, workable place to retreat to for private caucuses. Also schedule this room for the total time.

For negotiations that are expected to stretch beyond one day, take special care when reserving the room. Make absolutely sure you have the room for the entire time. Check and double-check the reservation. Check it again after the first day of the negotiation to make sure that no one with perceived "priority" has preempted your use of the room.

Most likely, you or the other side will not take everything with you when the negotiation session ends for the day. People may leave notes, name tags, and so forth, lying around. You may leave notes on a blackboard, whiteboard, or flip chart crucial to starting the negotiation anew the next day. You have to have some kind of plan to ensure that this stuff doesn't get disturbed, especially if your building has contracted janitorial service. The cleaning service may come in, assume the meeting's over, and completely blitz the room. Not only will you have to replace notepads, name tags, pens, and pencils, but you might lose a good part of the history of the negotiation up to that point.

Think ahead. Talk to the cleaning service contract's CO or government representative and make sure the cleaners are told to leave that room alone. Post signs on the door and around the room warning off anybody who might think of messing with the contents of the room. Do this even if you have a key and can lock the room (cleaning service contractors have keys too). Of course, be sure not to leave anything that's procurement-sensitive in the room under any circumstances.

CLEAR SCHEDULES

Well in advance of the negotiation event, make sure your schedule has nothing on it that could require disrupting the negotiation. A pop-in and pop-out negotiator appears confused, disorganized, and uninterested. You will lose much negotiation power to the other side (unless, of course, it's part of a tactic). If you try to juggle several balls at the same time that you're negotiating, you'll constantly have to deal with interruptions and you won't be able to concentrate on the important issues at hand.

Make sure that your boss, your staff, and your coworkers know you're hands-off during this period. No "Gotta take this call." No "Gotta sign this now." No "Gotta see the boss about this or that." Make up your mind that the negotiation is the center of your known universe until it is successfully concluded. Make sure that anybody else who could possibly interrupt you knows it too.

It's equally important to make sure that all the members of your team do the same. Each and every member of your negotiation team must understand that they're devoted to this task and this task alone until it's done. No "Gotta see Johnnie's baseball game." No "Gotta go to this other meeting." No "Boss says I gotta go check e-mail." Personally ensure that their schedules are cleared for the entire anticipated time of the negotiation. Take the extra step to call their bosses and confirm that their schedules are clear. Stress how important it is for so-and-so to be solely devoted to the negotiation and not to be interrupted or pulled out for any reason whatsoever.

There's nothing more distracting or power draining than for someone to stick their head in the room in the middle of a negotiation and pull out one of your team members. I'm convinced that it would be better not to have that person participate at all than to partially participate or to bail on you before the deal is done. You need these folks. They're important members of your team, and they need to concentrate and be as focused as you are. If their bosses don't support you on this, elevate the matter to your own boss. It's that important, and I tell you this from bitter personal experience.

CHECK AVAILABILITY OF EXTENDED NEGOTIATION TEAM

Remember that the folks you take with you into the actual negotiation event are usually just part of your entire negotiation team. They can sometimes even be just the tip of the iceberg. You probably have a boss or a review committee that won't be attending the negotiation, but may have to approve the results or condone certain tactics as the negotiation progresses. You may even set up these people as your ambiguous authority if you've chosen to use that tactic. You may also have legal counsel standing by for emergencies, program managers and program technical folks who may have to be consulted or kept in the loop, additional contract specialists to run down information, price analysts, cost analysts, and any number of others. Make sure that these individuals will be in place and accessible during the negotiation.

You don't want the negotiation to hit a snag and come to a standstill because someone who has a needed piece of data, advice, or approval authority isn't available. Unfortunately, many negotiators learn this lesson the hard way. You need approval to raise your BATNA, but the boss is at a dental appointment and the finance folks are at a going-away luncheon. You need to verify some data the contractor has presented you with, but the only person who can validate the data is out on sick leave. You need to brief the program manager on a significant, but promising, deviation from standard methodology, but the program manager is sailing to the Bahamas this week with her family. In all these cases, you can't go forward with the negotiation. You're forced to stall, maybe even postpone, and you lose credibility and power in the negotiation.

You can't fault the boss, the finance folks, the program folks, or your legal staff. Life happens. You must take a good share of the blame, because it was your job to ensure that these people were lined up and ready to assist should they be needed. Now, they don't have to be on as tight a leash as your actual negotiation team, but they do have to be available. Make sure they are or that they have backups named who can step in for them.

Don't get upset if someone you're relying on has a true emergency and isn't available; it happens from time to time and can't be helped. You can't control the whole world. However, with proper planning, you can reduce the likelihood of an absence bringing your negotiation to a standstill.

SET UP THE ROOM

After you've reserved the room, cleared your own and your team's schedules, and verified the availability of your supporting cast, you can now concentrate on setting up the negotiation room for an effective, professional event. Make sure to allow plenty of time before the other side is expected to arrive to set things up; better yet, set up the room the day before so you can concentrate on those last-minute negotiating details that always seem to crop up right before the other side arrives.

As far as amenities and courtesies go, refer back to page 80 for a useful list of items to assemble. You may even come up with your own negotiation preparation checklist, or use one your agency or office has standardized. If your office doesn't have a preparation checklist and you do lots of negotiations, this might be your chance to shine and create one for your office to use.

If you have elected to use the climate control tactic, now is the time to set the thermostat so the room will be a little too hot or a little too cold. Be sure to remind your own team members of this, so they can dress accordingly.

Survey the room and arrange your team's seating for maximum effect. If possible, make sure your team is seated facing the door. That way, they can better see and control who goes in and out, and who may be trying to interrupt the negotiation. It puts you more in control of the entire room.

We have already talked about the importance of assigning roles for your negotiating team members. What we haven't talked about yet is how to seat them at the table to best use their roles, either singularly or in concert with other roles, to affect the negotiation. If you remember from Chapter 3, the ideal negotiation team consists of three to five members playing the roles of team leader, good cop, bad cop, technocrat, and sweeper. Ideally, you'll have just one person playing each role, and I'll explain how to place these folks strategically around the table. In my opinion, an ideal seating arrangement for your team should look something like this:

Sweeper   Good Cop   Team Leader   Technocrat   Bad Cop

Negotiation Table

The team leader should always be seated at the center of the table, in the middle of his or her team. This reinforces his authority and position, and lets him better control the activities of the team and interact with all members of the other side more easily.

The technocrat should sit next to the team leader on either the right or left side. Remember, this is the facts-and-figures person. He is an excellent complement, backup, and reinforcement to the team leader, and should be at his elbow to lend statistical and data support. Being next to the team leader also allows the technocrat to restrain a team leader—in an easy, subtle manner—who may be getting out of the negotiation range supported by the facts and figures.

If the technocrat's role is used as a tactic—spewing forth confusing facts, figures, and data—his or her placement next to the team leader has an extra benefit. After the technocrat has propounded sufficiently, the team leader is in an excellent physical position to put out a restraining hand, stop the technocrat in mid spew, and bring the negotiation back around to the "big" issues. This, of course, is part of the tactic. By intervening, the team leader garners support from the other side, setting up the team leader's next proposal or counter to have a better chance of being accepted by the other side.

The bad cop is placed next to the technocrat at the end of the negotiation table, preferably the end that is closest to the door. Because the bad cop's role often complements the role of the technocrat, this puts them in an ideal position to play off each other. It also separates the bad cop physically from the team leader, allowing the team leader to maintain better the perception of fairness and impartiality in the other side's eyes. Being at the far end of the table allows the bad cop to have an excuse to bellow a little, or at least talk louder when he is playing his role. Being next to the door allows the bad cop to storm out of the room more easily if he is using the walkout tactic, without tripping over cords, chairs, briefcases, or other team members.

A smooth, brusque storm-out is always more impressive than a clumsy one. If a planned storm-out is foiled by impediments, it can easily turn into a comedic episode instead of an effective negotiation tactic.

The good cop should be seated next to the team leader on the opposite side of the technocrat. This placement, close to the center of the table, allows the other side to focus on them as they play their role and endear themselves to the other side with their charming ways. At the team leader's elbow, the good cop can also be an affable "yes-person" to the team leader, wholeheartedly and pleasantly agreeing with important points the team leader makes. The good cop's pleasant nature and willingness to agree with the other side's team members can also reinforce the team leader's role as a strong and resolute force.

A restraining arm put on an overly agreeable (but planned to be that way) good cop by the team leader every now and then reminds the other side they won't have the world given to them. They will have to deal with the more forceful and restrained team leader.

Of course, one of the good cop's main roles is to play foil to the bad cop when the good cop/bad cop tactic is used. You may think that it's best to sit the good cop and bad cop next to each other. I have found, however, that it's best to separate them. In our placement so far, we have both the team leader and the technocrat seated between the good cop and the bad cop. When the good cop/bad cop tactic starts, this allows the technocrat to add to the drama by glumly staring at his or her data and papers in an irritated way. The team leader, meanwhile, pushes back in his chair and follows the conversation with his head—back and forth, back and forth—as the players play their roles. What the team leader and technocrat are doing is helping convince the other side of the authenticity of the tactic by their reactions to it.

Remember, you want the other side to hate the bad cop and love the good cop. Having a couple of people between the good cop and bad cop can help subconsciously reinforce what you want the other side to believe—that these two people have very different ideas. Not only are they mentally apart, but they are also physically apart.

The bad cop is at the end of the table, farther away from most of the other side's team members, and is seen as an outsider to them because of it. The good cop is fairly centrally located, close to most of the other side's team members, and is better perceived as on their side or "one of them" because of it. It makes it easier for the other side to like the good cop and want the bad cop to go away, which is exactly what happens as soon as the bad cop performs the walkout tactic. Boom. Your good cop is now set up perfectly.

The sweeper is at the far end of the table next to the good cop. As you have learned, this is to allow the sweeper to observe better everything that's going on in the room, and it especially enables her to pick up on hidden gestures or unusual actions by the other side. She has a "sweeping" panoramic view of the negotiation table.

If the sweeper is going to be used to perform the sweep tactic, this placement physically separates her from any negative association of being next to the technocrat or the bad cop, so she can better maintain her aura of pleasantness, aloofness, and impartiality. Being next to, but outside of, the good cop helps the sweep tactic too.

Remember, you want the other side to forget the sweeper is even in the room for the tactic to be effective. Because the good cop is affable, likable, and talkative, it draws the other side's attention away from the sweeper and toward the good cop. While the good cop is talking, leaning across the table, and drawing in the other side, the sweeper remains quiet and smilingly aloof. This better enables the other side to ignore (unconsciously) the sweeper, setting them up perfectly for the sweep tactic.

If you go to all the trouble to assign roles and intend to seat the players strategically, it's a good idea to make name tags and put them where you want your team members to sit, so those places won't be taken by folks from the other side. If you know the identity of all the other side's team members, and you should have asked for this information when you sent out the draft agenda, make name tags for them too. Before the other team arrives, you can assign their seats simply by setting out the name tags. This allows you to break up what you know to be strong seating arrangements the other side may wish to use and reduces the chance they will be able to play their own strategic seating game.

For instance, if you know who the other side's bad cop is likely to be, seat that person as far from the door as possible, and seat their good cop next to them. You may also want to try to separate their technocrat from their team leader. You should, however, always be courteous and seat their team leader at the center across from you (the team leader for the government side).

PREPLAN LUNCH AND BREAKS

You probably have already set up the times for lunch and planned breaks in your written agenda. A little planning beforehand will ensure that these periods go smoothly without obstructing the progress of the negotiation and without endangering your negotiation objectives. Although it may seem trivial, a lack of planning exactly how and where you conduct these breaks could, at a minimum, disrupt the flow of the negotiation. Worst case, it could jeopardize a successful negotiation outcome for your team.

It's the most normal impulse in the world to think that, out of courtesy, you should go out to lunch with the other side. I don't recommend it. First, you may need that time to review facts or pull thoughts together to be better prepared to continue the negotiation after lunch is over. This time is golden, because you'll probably be hit with unanticipated information or circumstances you haven't anticipated or prepared for. Use this time wisely.

Second, having lunch with the other side doesn't give you a break from the negotiation. Despite lip service to the contrary, it's hard not to continue to talk the issues if the other side's players are sitting next to you at the lunch table. Your mind doesn't get a well-needed break. And in that more relaxed atmosphere, there's more danger that one of your team members could become too relaxed and divulge information or state a position you didn't want presented or you were waiting to bring up at a more strategic time. You have less control over your team. It could also allow the other side to corral one or two of your team members in an attempt to divide and conquer.

I made the mistake one time of allowing one of my team members to ride in the car with the other side to a restaurant so they wouldn't get lost on the way. During the ride, my team member was pummeled with questions and requests for additional information. He was also asked if he *really*, personally believed our position was fair. The other side, in classic divide-and-conquer style, attempted to make him more sympathetic to their side, while extracting critical information about our positions. All this was done in the "friendly" guise of a ride to the restaurant. After all, we were taking a break from the negotiation, right? Yeah, right!

Bottom line: Make plans to keep your team together during lunch and breaks. Plan for privacy. Have your own "retreat room" already set up for breaks and have your lunch venue planned in advance. You can provide the other side with a list of recommended restaurants, together with directions, when you send out your draft agenda. Let them take care of themselves; they probably want to use that time privately anyway.

This approach eliminates the possibility of anyone on your team becoming a divide-and-conquer victim. It also keeps your team together and focused on the negotiation. Having preplanned team lunches also prevents your team members from scurrying back to their own offices to check e-mail, do other work, and get their minds pulled off the negotiation.

Chapter 36

Opening the Negotiation

So, you've planned it, prepared for it, and now the big day has arrived. Your team members and members from the other side have filed in and taken their places in your well-prepared negotiation room. Although we know the negotiation really started long ago, when you sent out your first draft agenda, the hour is here to start the negotiation event. There's small talk and chit-chat, but soon all eyes start wandering to you, waiting for you to start the proceedings. How do you start? What do you do? First impressions are lasting impressions, so a strong opening is crucial to setting the tone for the entire negotiation.

Here's a suggested checklist for you to use to make sure you get that strong opening:

1. Introduce yourself and your team.

2. Have the other side introduce themselves.

3. Establish your authority.

4. Verify the other side's authority.

5. Make an opening statement.

6. Allow the other side to make their opening statement.

7. Transition to your first tactic.

8. Throughout the previous seven steps, *listen!*

MAKE INTRODUCTIONS

Every negotiation should start off by everybody knowing who everybody else is. If you are the government team leader, you should start the negotiation by thanking the other side for coming and by introducing yourself first. Be timely about this; you don't want to give the other side's team leader an opportunity to take control of the negotiations before they start by initiating the meeting. You want to be firmly in control. It's *your* negotiation.

You then introduce the members of your team by name and position. Do this even if you think the other side already knows them. Don't have your team members introduce themselves; you do it for them. They should pleasantly nod and smile when they are introduced. After all your team members are introduced, let the other side's team leader do the same for their team.

Although the introductions themselves are a mere formality, it's your first chance to assert control over the negotiation, demonstrate your authority, and show your ability to lead and control. Don't wobble, waffle, or defer to other folks. Get the message out that you are the boss.

ESTABLISH YOUR AUTHORITY

After the introductions are completed, establish your authority as the government team leader. You have already established your authority with your own team beforehand while you were planning for the negotiation. Now it's time to extend establishing your authority to the other side.

Simply let the other side know you are the team leader and are solely responsible for the conduct and flow of the negotiation. You will be calling breaks, setting lunchtimes, calling quit times, and so forth. Everything discussed during the session must go through and be approved by you. By doing this, you're setting up yourself and your team for success.

Put the other side on notice that they will have to deal with you on everything eventually. This lessens the chance they will be tempted to try to divide and conquer or to take control of the flow of negotiations. It's especially crucial if you have a team member who outranks you or is a higher grade than you. You want the other side to know that, despite grade or rank differences, you're the boss of your own team. Stating this to the other side with that person in the room deepens its effect and is very important to do. Now the other side knows they can't go "over your head" to another member of your own team.

When you establish your authority, what you *don't* do can be as important as what you *do*. Remember, you don't want to open the negotiation by making a draconian proclamation such as, "I'm the contracting officer! I'm the only one who has sole authority to obligate the government and work out the final terms of this contract!" Establishing authority like that is condescending, confrontational, and won't go well for setting up trust and respect for a successful negotiation. It also aces you out of the possibility of later using the ambiguous authority tactic.

Remain assured and in control. Let the other side know you are in control of the negotiation process and your team, without telling them you are in total control of the ultimate result. Preserve your backdoor ambiguous authority retreat route.

VERIFY THE OTHER SIDE'S AUTHORITY

After your authority is established, it's time to make one last check on the actual authority of the other side's team leader to obligate their company without outside approvals or reviews. You should already have done this during your draft agenda process, but always verify it right before you start negotiating. Remember, if you go into a negotiation with more authority than the other side, you may just be wasting your time.

Don't ever start negotiating and revealing your positions until you verify the authority of the other side to commit. You want to make sure you're dealing with only those folks who are at the table, not other folks who are not at the table. If you don't, the other side will pull the ambiguous authority tactic on you.

The best way to do this is to be straightforward. Just ask. If you have properly planned, you should already have this commitment, because you asked for it when you sent out your draft agenda. At that time, you should have forced the other side to bring someone to the table with the ultimate authority to commit their company. Just verify this to make sure nothing has changed. It could go something like this, "Ms. Hester, before we start, I just want to make sure you have authority to commit your company to any agreement we may reach. I know in your response to our draft agenda you said you have no boss, board of directors, or review committee you have to defer to. Is that still the case?"

If the answer to that question is no, seriously consider suspending the negotiations until they can provide someone who is able to commit their company. This should be very embarrassing to the other side if you previously got their promise, through their response to the draft agenda, to send someone with the required authority. You have a defensible position to suspend, and the other side will lose power when the negotiations resume.

MAKE AN OPENING STATEMENT

After you're sure you're dealing with the right folks, you now turn matters to the issues at hand. Your opening statement should be a *Reader's Digest* summary of why everyone is there. It should be very positive and delivered in a way that lets the other side know, right off the bat, that you assume everybody's in complete agreement with the general problem to be solved and will reach an amicable agreement on how to solve it. In fact, your opening statement could be in the form of a question, like, "Folks, can we all agree we're here to find a better way to provide logistics support for our troops overseas?" (Wait for nods; that's something everyone should be willing to agree to.) "And can we all agree we need to find the fairest, most equitable solution to this that represents best value for all involved?" (Wait for more nods.)

You don't want them to answer these questions (they're rhetorical), but you have framed the entire exercise in a way that everyone can easily agree to. The answers to these first two questions could also be your first two "yeses" in what you hope will be a long string of "yeses." Your opening statement unites both parties in a common cause and points them toward a common goal. It fosters trust and reinforces the idea that you are all, ultimately, on the same side.

Never go into particulars or positions in your opening statement; focus on the ends, not the means. You may want to elaborate a little bit on the problem, give some additional background, or state general objectives, but keep it brief and don't go into depth. The intent of your opening statement is to get everyone focused on a common goal, which will reduce hostility, allow for the free flow of communication and ideas, and not lock the other side into entrenched positions.

ALLOW THE OTHER SIDE TO MAKE AN OPENING STATEMENT

After your opening statement, give the other side's team leader an opportunity to make their own opening statement. Other than just simply being courteous, this serves several purposes. First, you get verbal buy-in from the other side about the ultimate goal of the negotiation. The other side will rarely disagree with the ideas and goals you have presented in your opening statement because you couched them in such general terms. Accordingly, their opening statement is usually a confirmation of the objectives and goals you have laid out.

Once committed, the other side will have a hard time retreating from their commitment to want an equitable, fair, and reasonable outcome along the general terms you have proposed. During deadlocks that may occur later, you can always remind them of their commitment.

Next, as we've seen before, it gives you your first agreement (other than maybe agreeing on the draft agenda). Remember, there's something magic about saying the word *yes*, and if the other side says it in response to your opening statement, they will have a harder time saying no as the negotiation progresses. You "draft" them into your team to solve a mutual problem and they usually will confirm this with their opening statement.

Lastly, the other side's opening statement could give you important clues and key information about their plans, strategies, tactics, and goals for the negotiation. It could give you a peek into what you can expect from them. Sometimes the other side will forgo an opening statement or simply agree with yours. But on other occasions, they may elaborate, which is what you want.

If they agree with your opening statement in general, but voice some reservations about your ambitious delivery dates, for instance, you now have additional key information about what's important to the other side. This allows you to adjust your strategy and tactics accordingly. This is the most crucial point of the opening—to be "all ears."

TRANSITION TO YOUR FIRST TACTIC

After the other side has made their opening statement, it's now time for the game to begin in earnest. Here's where you start executing your negotiation plan by transitioning to your first planned tactic. There's no set way to go here; it will depend on the situation and what you have devised in your negotiation plan. Remember, you already have their proposal and you've had time to evaluate it. They will be expecting you to start by giving them some feedback or reaction to what they have already given you. Nevertheless, you can transition to the negotiation by stating no position, stating your minimum (best case) position, stating your target position, or attacking their proposed position.

I am a big fan of starting off by stating no position. Now, that doesn't mean you should sit on your thumbs and say nothing. The other side is waiting for your response to their proposal, and you rarely get lucky and have them elaborate without prodding them. You may start with something like, "We've read your proposal and we think we understand it. Have you had any further thoughts on what you've sent us?" or "Has your thinking changed on anything?" or "Has anything new come up we should know about before we start?"

Questions like these immediately put the other side on the defensive and tend to pull them into elaborating on their proposal, giving you additional information without offering any from your side in return. You don't tell them you think their proposal is good or bad; you just ask them about it in general. On a few occasions I have been able to get concessions from the other side right off the bat without giving up a single thing, and the negotiation just started!

You could also start off by revealing your minimum (best case) position and gauging the other side's reaction to it. If you have determined that your side has a lot of relative power in the negotiation, this is another effective way to start. If you perceive your relative power to be somewhat weaker than the other side's, you may want to start off by revealing your target position, which could lead to a quicker agreement, but it robs you of some negotiation headroom.

The last way to transition to the negotiation from your introduction is to start addressing, point by point, weaknesses or other issues you are concerned about in their proposal. This is personally my least favorite method, and I only even consider using it if I perceive my side to be in a huge relative power advantage position. It immediately engenders an "us versus them" mentality, throwing the other side into a defensive crouch and unraveling much of the goodwill you created in your opening statement.

Eventually, some of these hard issues will have to be addressed, but I never like hitting the other side with them in the face from the get-go. I fear, however, that this is how most government negotiations start.

If you elect to use this approach, I recommend that you ease into it instead of jumping into it. Let them know the general concerns you have about their proposal, but let them suggest the particular ways to make it better. Don't tell them what you think it should be. You may say, for instance, "Your proposal looks like you have a good handle on the problem, and it seems you generally have a well thought out way of solving it, but we're a bit concerned about the price. Why is it so high? What's driving these figures?"

See what you've done? You've forced them to give you additional information without revealing anything about *your* position on price. You haven't told them *why* you think their price is too high; you've asked them to explain that to you!

LISTEN

The very start of the negotiation is the most crucial time to pick up useful information about the other side's real agenda and positions. They're most unguarded at this point, especially if you have done a good job setting the stage with an effective opening statement. Keep attuned to everything they say, how they say it, mannerisms, body language, reactions to your statements, and their responses.

This is the first time you may be able to figure out who, for instance, their bad cop is going to be or what tactic they have elected to start off with or what's truly most important to them. It is imperative that you and your team members *listen!*

Chapter 37

Conducting the Negotiation

After you have opened the negotiation and transitioned to your first tactic, conducting the negotiation from this point on should be a simple matter of following your negotiation plan. Don't cling to your plan rigidly, however. Things will change during the negotiation as information is swapped between sides. Your plan has to be flexible enough to bend to incorporate these inevitable changes.

Since how you conduct the negotiation will depend on what you are negotiating, how you planned it, what happens during the event, and the personalities of the individuals involved, there is no set process for how it should be done. Instead, I've compiled a list of negotiation do's and don'ts you can use as a guide. Feel free to use these and feel free to add your own.

DO'S

- Know your authority as a negotiator and that of your counterpart.

- Have respect for the other side's position and viewpoints.

- Keep the overall objectives of the negotiation clearly in mind.

- Be fair and reasonable to both parties.

- Obtain and maintain the initiative.

- Establish an ambiguous authority.

- Get the other side to commit first. It enables bracketing.

- Prepare a memorandum of what happened after each negotiation session.

- Prepare interim summaries as agreements are reached on individual issues immediately after agreement.

- Remember you're not in the negotiation alone. Use your team of experts to help you prepare and conduct the negotiations.

- Be unpredictable. Mix up your strategies and tactics so you don't use the same ones all the time.

- Be patient. Often, 80 percent of concessions are made during the last 20 percent of the negotiation.

- Tailor your negotiation for each offeror in the competitive range. Evaluate their offer against the solicitation, not other offeror's proposals.

- Realize that FAR Part 15 does not require you to reach agreement on every element of cost. Stick to the major issues and the cost drivers.

- Know the difference between "cost" and "price" (price = cost + profit or fee).

- Use a contract type that allocates risk fairly. Remember, contract type is usually negotiable.

- Understand how to interpret body language.

- Carefully guard your travel schedule, or keep your return date open-ended.

- Always ask open-ended questions. Questions phrased so they can be answered with a yes or no give you limited information.

- Practice active listening. Use summary phrases such as "Did I hear you correctly in saying …." or "From what I'm hearing you tell me, your point is …."

- Even though you have someone to take official minutes, let the other side see you taking notes.

- Redirect personal attacks on you as attacks on the problem.

- Pause after asking a question; don't be a motor mouth.

- Ask for more than you expect to get; it gives you negotiating room.

- The less you know about the other side, the more negotiating room should be built into your initial position.

- Flinch at a proposal. React with visible shock and surprise. A concession often follows a flinch.

- Position the other side to feel good about the negotiation by making a small concession at the end.

- Consider "no" as simply the other side's going-in position.

- Position your most difficult issues last. The more time you can get the other side to invest, the more likely you can get concessions as negotiations drag on.

- Control the pace of the negotiation.

- Never give up big chunks of negotiating room up front.

- Never give anything away without getting something in return.

- Make sure when you give on your "give" points, it brings you closer to agreement on your "must" points. Control the order of issues to make this happen.

- Feel free to call a caucus anytime you are confused, lose control of your team, or need to reevaluate.

- Use the tactics outlined in this book, if it's fair for you to use them.

- Watch out for the tactics outlined in this book and be prepared to counter them.

- Feel free to use and be on the lookout for any other tactics not covered in this book; there are hundreds of tactics!

DON'TS

- Never reveal or discuss your position, strategy, or tactics to anyone outside those who absolutely need to know.

- Don't make concessions without getting something in return. Ask for one right away.

- Don't try to become well liked or popular with the other side during negotiations.

- Never allow more than one person on your team to talk at one time on a given issue. Maintain control of the negotiation.

- Don't allow your team to be separated, even during breaks or lunch.

- Never let the other side see disagreements among your team members (unless it's planned).

- Never bluff unless you are willing to have your bluff called.

- Never sign an agreement you don't consider fair and reasonable.

- Never negotiate unprepared.

- Never engage in conduct that:

  – Favors one offeror over another

  – Reveals an offeror's technical solution to another offeror

  – Reveals an offeror's price without their permission

  – Reveals sources of past performance data

  – Knowingly furnishes source selection information in violation of the Procurement Integrity Act.

- Never indicate to offerors that they will win the award.

- Don't make up false statements or cite fictitious regulations.

- Don't allow contractor "buy-in."

- Don't allow an offeror's low initial price to overshadow life cycle cost considerations.

- Avoid entanglement in personal issues. Don't take the negotiations personally.

- Don't react to emotional outbursts. Let the other party blow off steam. Use the "feel, felt, found" formula.

- Don't go in with your best offer up front. It leaves no room for the other side to feel they have successfully negotiated and won.

- Never say yes to the first offer or counteroffer.

- Never offer to split the difference. Encourage the other side to offer to do it. You don't have to split down the middle. You can use their willingness to get closer to your objectives. You can split more than once.

- Don't make your last concession a big one. It could create hostility.

- Avoid making equal-size concessions. It will encourage the other side to keep pushing.

- Don't let the other side write the contract, write the memorandum of agreement, or take the official minutes.

- Don't be afraid to admit you don't know and to ask questions.

- Don't narrow the negotiation down to one issue. If you do, you now have to have a clear winner and a clear loser.

- Don't assume the other side wants what you want.

These are just some of the things you need to consider as you proceed with the negotiation. Again, feel free to add or modify this list as suits your personality and the situation. As you go through the negotiation, you want to continue to build up or reinforce trust, and stress a mutual purpose.

You know your minimum, target, and maximum positions for each issue. You know that the other side has their own. At some point between the two side's minimums and maximums, hopefully there is that zone of potential agreement. Your job is to discover that zone by finding out as much about the other side's position as you can, while divulging as little about your own position as you can.

Start with the end in mind, and keep your focus there throughout the negotiation. In this way, you'll keep both teams focused on the big picture and won't get bogged down arguing over minute points.

Chapter 38

Closing the Negotiation

How you close the negotiation is just as important as how you start the negotiation. Assuming that you haven't come to an unbreakable deadlock and have had to break off the negotiation, all eyes will eventually turn to you as the negotiation winds down and you get closer to an agreement. Because you are the leader of the government team, it's your responsibility to lead both sides toward closure, and to signal when it's time to end the negotiation and document the results.

You've got to be a good closer. If you're not, the negotiation could wander interminably. The longer it does, the more opportunity there is for additional problems to crop up, situations to change, and conflicts to arise over small issues. You need to put the pup to bed when the time's right.

How do you know when the time is right? Most of the time, in government negotiations, it's obvious. You've marched through all the issues and have come to agreement on them. Time to close. Other times, it's not so obvious.

Because you are usually the buyer, not the seller, you have control over when the close occurs and how it will happen. Here, we will look at a few of the most common methods of closing, how to prepare the ground to execute the close, how to make sure everyone is truly in agreement, and how to make everyone feel like a winner.

PREPARING THE GROUND FOR CLOSING

Before launching into the methods of closing, it's important to discuss how to increase your odds that the close will be timed right and be effective. Preparing for the close signals to the other side that you're ready to close, and it puts them in a more receptive position to accept your close on the terms you have both agreed to so far.

When you're ready to close, instruct your team privately that you will be doing all the talking from that point on. When you take over all communication for your team, it's a clear signal to the other side that you're moving to close. It focuses all their attention on you without the possibility of getting sidetracked or dragged down bunny trails that may lead away from closing.

Start drawing together, in big-picture terms, all the agreements you have come to on all the issues discussed so far. By this time, you should have already grouped smaller issues into packages that are easy to understand. Ask the other side if they agree with your summary; you want to make sure everyone understands the entire scope of the agreement exactly as you understand it.

You want the other side to commit to your view of how things stand. If you don't, loose ends or disagreements may unravel everything you've done. Start talking about end-game terms such as method and frequency of payment, delivery terms, and warranties. As you do this, let your body language also signal you're ready to close. Have your papers assembled and in a neat stack. Have your team do the same. Let your tone of voice indicate decisiveness and finality.

METHODS OF CLOSING

These are a few common ways a government negotiator can choose to close. Most of the principles are borrowed from a long history of training for our commercial sales force on how to close deals, modified for the unique situation of a government negotiator.

The Total Agreement Close

This is, in my opinion, the most common and best way to close. It's simply summarizing and agreeing in total to all the individual issues you have discussed and agreed to so far. Throughout the give and take of the negotiation, both sides have made concessions that have been agreeable to all. You may have wanted more on this issue, they may have wanted more on that issue, but you all can at least agree on the total package, even if it includes some warts.

Emphasize the benefits to both sides of accepting the agreement as a whole. Assure the other side that agreeing on the total package won't set precedents for future negotiations on individual areas they might not be too happy about. Use this close when you have been able to reach agreement on all the important issues and most or all of the lesser issues.

The Ambiguous Authority Close

Use this close if you still have an unresolved issue or issues that you do not want to or have no more room to move on, but closing the negotiation now is in the best interest of the government. First, summarize all the points of agreement as in the total agreement close, then inform the other side of your final position on the contentious issue and tell them you have no authority to move more, blaming your lack of flexibility on your ambiguous authority. Of course, you would have had to set up an ambiguous authority beforehand to use this close.

The ambiguous authority close would sound something like, "I've made the best argument I could, but the review committee has given me no authority to make any other offer" or "Sorry, folks, but this has to be my final offer. My supervisor absolutely refuses to make any more funds available over what I have right now" or "I tried my best to present your argument to the director, but she's adamant that if we can't agree to the terms and prices on the table now, she'll look for another alternative to satisfying our need."

This close is intended to force the other side to accept your position as it stands or risk getting nothing. The danger, of course, is that the other side might just choose to accept nothing rather than go through with the deal. You should have already protected yourself against that possibility by establishing your BATNA.

The Power Close

This close assumes you are in the power position and the other side needs the deal more than you do. It could be viewed by some as intimidation, and usually weakens your important ongoing relationship with the other side. For these reasons, I believe government negotiators should avoid using the power close unless absolutely necessary.

The power close is essentially the ambiguous authority close without the ambiguous authority. You present your final offer—take it or leave it. You're the government representative and you have determined no other deal will be fair and reasonable. You can elect to justify your position (lack of bucks, cheaper alternatives, and so on) or you can simply lay it on the table without justification. You basically challenge the other side to fish or cut bait. Because the other side may choose to cut bait and bail out on the negotiation instead of fish with you, you'd better make absolutely sure you can live with your BATNA before you try this one.

The Either/or Close

With this closing method you give the other side a choice between two acceptable alternatives. Either alternative must be acceptable to both sides.

This close is best used when you have reached agreement on everything but one major issue and you have some tradeoff flexibility on that issue. An either/or close would sound something like, "Well, we're down to this: Either you agree to cut your price down to $50,000 if you can't meet our desired delivery date requirement or we'll pay you your total asking price of $75,000 if you meet it. The choice is up to you."

The alternatives don't have to be equally acceptable, but you have to anticipate that both will at least be acceptable to the other side. Also, you've got to be willing to live with either choice yourself, because you've passed decision authority over picking between them to the other side.

The Silent Close

The silent close is used commonly by salespeople all over the world. You perform it the exact same way you perform the tactic of silence. You simply present the other side with your final offer and be quiet. Be absolutely silent. Who knows? The other side just may say yes. If they don't, your silence will soon get deafening, forcing them either to give in and close or to throw in an additional concession to close.

The Split-the-Difference Close

This is a common way many negotiations, government and otherwise, end up being concluded. It's used when both sides have agreed on everything else but that all-important issue—price. You're down here and they're up there, and that difference is the only thing holding agreement back.

At this point, many, many government negotiators make the mistake of offering to split the difference 50/50 to reach an agreement, but that's not the split the difference close! Go back and read about the bracketing tactic (Chapter 20). You should *never* offer to split the difference. The split-the-difference tactic encourages the *other side* to split the difference.

You'll have to gauge for yourself which one of these six methods of closing is right for your particular situation, and each negotiation situation is different. You may have other closing methods that work well for you; if you do, use them. These closing methods can sometimes be used together for better effect, either sequentially or in some sort of combination.

ENSURING TOTAL AGREEMENT

Whatever method of closing you use, you must make sure that both sides fully understand the terms and conditions they are agreeing on, because they will control the party's mutual relationship, performance, and expectations after they are cemented. You want to make sure all parties agree to the same thing.

At this point, you should not only confirm agreement on the total package, but make sure that all sides see the details the same way too. Take a look at the terminology you're using. Define the terms clearly and ensure agreement on your definitions. Remember, ambiguities are construed against the drafter of the language, and this is your last chance to eliminate them.

Look at the details. What exactly does "ASAP" mean? What do you mean by "within two weeks"? Two weeks from what? What exactly do you mean by requesting the contractor to "cooperate fully with the program office"? What do you mean by "fully"? What's "cooperation"? If differences in interpretation or misunderstandings arise during this review, make sure they are clamped down and agreed to, not left open-ended.

Lay out the terms in writing and have the other side look over them and agree to them. Have them sign the agreement and give them a copy. This doesn't have to be your official documentation of what went on in the negotiation (we'll talk about how to do that later), but it should be clear and complete enough to make sure the other side fully understands and agrees to the entire deal. If you have been keeping good notes and doing interim summaries as the negotiation progressed, this should be very easy to do. The majority of the work has already been done.

Don't take the easy way out and simply choose to ignore differences you know exist in the spirit of getting the big deal done. Phrases like, "We can work that out later" or "We can settle on the details later" should not be in your vocabulary when you move to close. This is a common mistake that can have serious consequences later.

Even the creators of our Constitution made this mistake and it eventually cost more than 620,000 American lives. Progress on the Constitution was gummed up by some bothersome issues all the state delegates couldn't agree on. They elected to press on anyway and deal with the problems later.

After the Constitution was completed and ratified, they got together again to iron out the bugs, which eventually gave us our first 10 amendments to the Constitution (known collectively as the Bill of Rights), but one issue remained open—a state's right to secede from the Union. Because the Continental Congress couldn't come to agreement on the issue, they simply chose to ignore it. When the Constitution was adopted, it was silent on the issue. It was also ignored during the framing of the Bill of Rights. It was just too hot an issue and the country needed to press on with framing itself. But the issue never went away.

"Four score and seven years" later, the issue that had been consciously ignored had to be decided by the bloodiest war in our nation's entire history—the Civil War. More Americans died during that war than in all the other wars we have ever fought *combined*.

Finally, you can never close a negotiation knowing there's a mistake in the other side's understanding of the agreement, reasoning, expectations, facts, or figures. As a government negotiator, you must be fair and reasonable to all sides.

If you know the other side has an erroneous understanding of the scope of their commitments, or a math error that makes their price unreasonably low, you must disclose this fact to them. If you don't, you're not only being unfair, but you may be found by a court or board to have "negotiated in bad faith." If this happens, the other side may be relieved from performing the contract. The contract may be voided and now you get nothing at all. What would that do to your customer's program time lines and funding? What impact would this have on the mission of your organization?

In contract law, a contract is not a contract and can't be enforced unless there has been a true "meeting of the minds" between the parties. This can't occur if you know the other side is thinking things are one way when you're committing them to something else.

MAKING EVERYONE FEEL LIKE A WINNER

Your job as a government negotiator is not to beat down the other side and "win" the negotiation. Your job is to negotiate a fair and reasonable agreement for both sides (and the taxpayer) that satisfies your mission requirements. There should never be a "winner" or a "loser" after a negotiation. Even if you have "maxed out" all your negotiation objectives, you should never feel smug or superior; both sides need to win. This preserves the working relationship of the parties during contract performance and for any future negotiations that might occur.

It also ensures that the resultant deal, be it a contract or a modification, will be carried out cheerfully and produce the results it's intended to. The ultimate goal of an acquisition is not contract *award*, but contract *performance*.

Whatever deal is eventually agreed to will now have to be carried out by the parties. If you have made the other side feel like a loser in the negotiation, their performance of the agreement could reflect it. If they're grudgingly performing because they contractually have to, what effect do you think this might have on the quality of their performance, their commitment to customer satisfaction, or their willingness to accommodate future changes? What kind of effective working relationship have you set up, and how is this relationship going to affect you and your customers in the future?

Even if you're royally successful in your negotiation, here are a couple of things you can do to make sure the other side feels like a winner too. First, many expert negotiators suggest that you save a little concession to give away unilaterally at the end of the negotiation. It doesn't have to be a big concession, or anything that's important to your team; it's the thought that counts. Even if the concession is seen as unimportant to the other side, it at least gives them the satisfaction of having the last victory in the negotiation. Try to make it something that will be of value to them, but something that doesn't mean too much to you.

Review your remaining "give" points for candidates. Make sure to give it away at the very end of the negotiation so the other side will know they aren't expected to reciprocate. Doing this allows the other side to save face, make a positive showing to their bosses, and generally feel better about the deal they have agreed to. The cost of a small concession given in this way can return huge dividends in contract performance.

Finally, make sure to congratulate the other side for a job well done. It doesn't matter how well they actually performed during the negotiation; congratulate them. Praise them for their professionalism and their negotiation skills. Tell them you learned something from them. They probably spent long hours preparing for the event just like you did, so let them know their time investment was productive.

Everyone likes to have their self-esteem boosted and their value as an employee and an individual confirmed. Allow them to go away not only feeling good about the deal, but feeling good about you and good about themselves. WIN–WIN is not always the best strategy to choose, but it should always be the desired outcome.

Chapter 39

Documenting the Negotiation

Well, you're finally here. You've planned for the negotiation, carried it out successfully, and come to a final agreement that all sides can live with. Congratulations! But you're not quite done yet. As the old saying goes, nothing is done in government work until all the paperwork is done. The next, and final, job of the negotiation process is to document the results.

You've probably been harped on your whole career about the importance of properly documenting your work actions, and at no time is this more crucial than it is now. Both sides will not perform as agreed to in the negotiation, but as documented in the agreement instrument. You will not administer the agreement by what you intended it to be, but by what it says. If later there are disagreements, disputes, or protests over your actions, what you intended will not matter much. What you documented will rule. That's how the courts and boards determine your intent.

You should already be pretty well prepared for your task of documenting the negotiation. If you kept good minutes, did your written interim summaries, and did a good job of summarizing the final results of the negotiation immediately after it concluded, your job will be a whole lot easier. In addition, the results will be much more accurate, enforceable, and defensible.

You should have already folded your interim summaries into your final negotiation summary, and you should already have reached agreement on your final negotiation summary with the other side. In a competitive negotiation, you should have already done this for each offeror you negotiated with. These pieces can now be welded together to paint a picture of the entire negotiation. In a sole-source negotiation, or if you are negotiating a modification or some other sole-source action, this final negotiation summary can become the primary source for your documentation actions.

THE PNM OR PRICE JUSTIFICATION

One of the things a government CO must determine, before going into any agreement that will obligate federal funds (contract, contract modification, etc.) is that the agreement is being entered into at a fair and reasonable price. In most cases this determination has to be backed up by some kind of written justification. For contract award decisions, this justification is usually called a *price negotiation memorandum*, or PNM for short. This is the record of your negotiations and how you have determined the final outcome to be fair and reasonable. If you are documenting a sole-source negotiation or a modification, it may be called something else, such as a price justification or justification of fair and reasonable price. Check your agency's guidance.

Remember, your final negotiation summary is not your PNM or price justification. The final negotiation summary is a record of what went on during negotiations with a particular contractor and can be given to that contractor at the conclusion of the negotiation. Your PNM or price justification documentation contains *all* the information you considered to make your award decision or to determine the final price to be fair and reasonable. It will contain much more information than the final negotiation summary. Some of this information may still be procurement-sensitive or source selection information, so your PNM is never shared with the other side.

Different agencies vary widely on content, format, and dollar thresholds for written PNMs and justifications, so you'll have to check your agency's own particular guidance on how, what, and when to write. Usually this guidance can be found in your agency's supplement to FAR Part 15.

Take great care when you prepare your PNM or justification. This is usually the most important document that courts and boards will use in the event of a protest or a claim. Make sure it tells the story of how you arrived at a fair and reasonable price clearly and logically. Welcome any required reviews your agency may have set up for these documents; you want as many eyes on it as possible so it can be as complete and accurate as possible. Remember also to treat it as procurement-sensitive information. Disclose it to only those in the government who have a valid need to know.

RELEASE OF CLAIMS

If you have negotiated a modification to an existing contract, you may have another step you must, or can, elect to take along the documentation trail. You may be required to obtain a release of claims from the contractor. Even if you are not required to, you may elect to obtain a release of claims if you determine that doing so is in the government's best interest.

A release of claims is not required for contract award or for most contract modifications. It's only required for bilateral modifications that definitize negotiated settlements resulting from change orders issued against noncommercial contracts (see FAR Part 43.2). However, check your agency policy on when they require a release of claims. They may want you to do it for other types of modifications in addition to what's required by the FAR.

Even if you're not required to obtain a release of claims by the FAR or by your agency's regulations, it's still sometimes a good idea, and that's your call as a CO. The release of claims language is designed to lock down the agreement so the contractor can't come back later and ask for additional adjustments as a result of the change. It gives you extra security that the deal you struck for the modification is the deal they will live with, and the compensation offered is all they will ask for.

Here's what the standard release of claims language looks like:

> Contractor's Statement of Release. In consideration of the modification(s) agreed to herein as complete equitable adjust-

ments for the contractor's [describe] "proposal(s) for adjustment," the contractor hereby releases the government from any and all liability under this contract for further equitable adjustments attributable to such facts or circumstances giving rise to the "proposal(s) for adjustment" (except for) …."

Yeah, I know—legalistic and jargonistic. But sometimes it can protect you against having a negotiation you thought was put to bed wake up and bite you. It lessens the chance the contractor will come at you later for additional adjustments, because the contractor has already agreed not to.

I know of one CO who required all his contractors to execute a release of claims for each and every modification to each and every contract he was responsible for. I think that's overkill, but the FAR doesn't prevent it. My advice is to use the release language sparingly, and only when you feel a little uneasy about the negotiation result and the future intentions of the contractor.

If you use release language, don't be surprised if the contractor comes back and asks you to sign release language of your own. This is common and results in a mutual release of claims. You may want to get some sort of legal review of the language before you sign it.

OBTAINING REQUIRED REVIEWS AND APPROVALS

After you have prepared your documentation of the results of the negotiation, you *still* may not be quite done. Your agency may require some reviews and approvals before you can move to formalize the actual agreement.

The only advice I can give you here is to check your agency's requirements, because each agency has different ones. Most agencies will, at the very least, require some sort of legal review for actions over a certain dollar threshold. Don't look at these reviews as impediments or an encroachment on your authority; many COs have been saved from making terrible mistakes by these reviews!

DOCUMENTING POST-AWARD ACTIONS AND PROVIDING POST-AWARD NOTIFICATIONS

You're almost there, but not quite. If you have awarded a competitive contract, the unsuccessful offerors in the competitive range have the right to request a post-award debriefing. These debriefings are designed to let those offerors know why they weren't selected and how they can do better in the future. They are also great at defusing the possibility of a protest. FAR Part 15 covers when and how to do them, and we won't get into that here. Just be aware that minutes must be taken of the debriefings, and these minutes must become part of your overall negotiation record.

Be careful during these debriefings. Although not considered negotiations (the negotiations are already done for that action), some contractors use the debriefings to start their intelligence-gathering activities for future negotiations. Remember, any time you sit down with a contractor, for any reason, you could end up negotiating and not even realize it.

Finally, you may have some post-award notifications to send out. Although not a part of the negotiation process per se, the result of your labor is not complete until these are done. You have to, of course, let the winning contractor know they've won. You have to let the losers know they lost. You may have to notify the Small Business Administration or the Department of Labor about the award. Check the FAR and your agency regulations about these post-award notifications.

PREPARING THE CONTRACT, AWARD, OR AGREEMENT DOCUMENT

You're now ready to create the document that will stand in lasting tribute, for good or bad, to your negotiation efforts. Usually this is the contract award document, but not always. Remember, you have many reasons and opportunities to negotiate. It could be a contract or a contract modification. It could be something else, like how to handle a warranty problem, or it could be a blanket purchase agreement, basic ordering agreement, or basic agreement. It could be an agreed-to small business subcontracting plan, or a delivery order or task order against an existing contract. It could be settling final indirect cost rates or agreeing to a forward rate pricing agreement. It could be settling a dispute or protest, or informally agreeing on how to handle contract performance issues. It could be a memorandum of understanding with another federal agency, or even an agreement reached with your own program office.

Each of these documents will have their own particular preparation requirements. You'll have to check the FAR, and especially your own agency's policies, for guidance on the particulars, which can vary not just by agreement or document type, but sometimes by dollar value. Some agencies may require an additional round of approvals after the agreement document has been prepared.

Whatever document you produce or procedures you follow, your goal is the same: to create a legally enforceable document that will govern both sides' conduct and accurately represent the mutual intent of the parties. You establish the scope and boundaries of an ongoing and hopefully mutually satisfying relationship. This, in turn, should deliver to the nation the goods and services it needs in a way that brings best value to your customer, the contractor, and the taxpayer.

That's your job. Isn't it good to have such an important one?

Chapter 40

In Conclusion

Way back at the start of this book I made the statement that the practice of negotiation is an art. That's my personal opinion, and some smart folks disagree with me (imagine that). Some experts say it is more proper to call the practice of negotiation a *skill*, not an *art*. They argue that the ability to practice an art is innate (something you are either born with or not) whereas the ability to practice a skill can be taught, learned, and improved by practice, even if you are not born with a gift.

For example, Michelangelo was an artist, not a skilled painter. He didn't slap the Sistine Chapel masterpiece together after long hours of practice on paint-by-numbers sets; he was born with a gift. Likewise, Napoleon successfully practiced the *art* of war; he didn't win by using battlefield *skills*. He was just a "natural."

I do believe that some people are born with a natural talent for negotiating and need very little instruction on strategies and tactics. They seem to know instinctively what to do and when to do it during a negotiation. Maybe you're one of these people. However, I believe the effectiveness of practicing any *art* can be improved by acquiring *skills*.

This applies to the art of negotiation. Anyone, regardless of whether they were born with a natural talent to negotiate, can improve by acquiring negotiation skills through reading, training, observation, and experience. These skills must be honed by practice, and new skills must constantly be acquired to improve results. Thus, there's hope for those of us who weren't born with a natural talent to negotiate.

In this book I presented some skills that you can add to your arsenal to improve your negotiation results. You may have already known some of them. You may know better ways of applying some of them. Some of them may just flat-out not work for you. But if even just one was new to you or proves useful to you in the future, you've gotten worth out of this book that could pay immeasurable benefits later. You've also given me immense satisfaction in knowing I did my job in writing it.

My challenge to you is to improve constantly. Continually look for ways to improve, increase, and hone your negotiation skills. Read every book you can. Observe every session you can. Find a mentor who's a good, seasoned negotiator. Learn from your mistakes—and, believe me, you'll make some. Better yet, learn from the mistakes of others. Use your everyday negotiation experiences to gain insight into becoming a better government negotiator. Most of all, have fun when you negotiate. If you do, chances are you will do it well.

Appendix A

Recommended Reading

Here's a list of excellent and timeless books I believe will be particularly helpful in furthering your study of negotiations. Every serious negotiator should have these books in their library. Happy reading!

Cohen, Herb. *You Can Negotiate Anything* (New York: Bantam Books, 1982).

Blanchard, Kenneth, and Spencer Johnson. *The One-Minute Manager* (New York: William Morrow, 1982).

Dawson, Roger. *Secrets of Power Negotiating* (Franklin Lakes, NJ: Career Press, 2001).

Fisher, Roger, and William Ury. *Getting to Yes* (New York: Penguin Books, 1991).

Hindle, Tim. *Negotiating Skills* (New York: DK Publishing, 1998).

Shapiro, Ronald M., and Mark A. Jankowski. *The Power of Nice* (New York: Wiley & Sons, 2001).

Appendix B

Sources of Data

Here's a useful list of places to go on the Internet to obtain additional information you'll need to prepare for negotiations. The list is not all-inclusive by a long shot, but it's a good place to start.

Central Contractor Registration (CCR): www.ccr.gov
Information on businesses wanting to do or doing business with Uncle Sam; easily searchable database; good for source identification and company profiling.

The Consumer Price Index (CPI): www.bls.gov/cpi/
Index of common consumer goods and services put out by the U.S. Bureau of Labor Statistics (BLS); heavy on retail prices.

Dun and Bradstreet: www.dnb.com
Provides detailed company information, for a fee.

Excluded Parties Listing System (EPLS): www.epls.gov
List of companies you can't do business with, so don't waste your time with them!

Federal Supply Schedules: http://fss.gsa.gov
Great for finding government pricing on common supplies/services.

GOOGLE: www.google.com
Internet search engine (one of many, but a good one). Just type in the name of what you are looking for and be amazed at the results. This is a great site to locate websites of professional organizations dealing with what you are buying.

GSA Advantage!: www.gsaadvantage.gov
Electronic online shopping for thousands of supplies/services; features key word search (key words, part numbers, national stock numbers, company names); a must for market research.

GSA Schedules e-Library: www.gsaelibrary.gsa.gov
Searchable GSA schedule and governmentwide agency contract (GWAC) database.

Past Performance Information Retrieval System (PPIRS): www.ppirs.gov
Provides information on how contractors have performed on government contracts in the past; great source of info to help plan your negotiation; password login required.

Producer Price Index (PPI): www.bls.gov/ppi/
Another BLS-created index; concentrates on wholesale prices and is more appropriate for government use, because the government normally buys in bulk.

Small Business Administration (SBA) Homepage—Government Contracting: www.sba.gov/GC/
Validates contractor business size, 8(a), HUBZONE, SDVOSB, and SDB status.

Thomas Register of American Manufacturers: www.thomasregister.com
Helpful in identifying sources for products, prices, and company profiles.

Wage Determinations OnLine: www.wdol.gov/
Find out prevailing area wages before you negotiate!

Index